joshuanism
a path beyond christianity

michael vito tosto

Copyright 2013 by MSI Press, LLC

All rights reserved. No part of this book may be reproduced or utilized in any form or by any means, electronic or mechanical, including photocopying, recording, or by any information storage and retrieval system, without permission in writing from the publisher.

For information, contact:

MSI Press
1760-F Airline Highway, 203
Hollister, CA 95023
Orders@MSIPress.com
Telephone/Fax: 831-886-2486

Library of Congress Control Number 2013945228

ISBN 978-1-933455-70-9

Cover design by Michael Vito Tosto & Carl Leaver

"A rose by any other name would smell as sweet."

—William Shakespeare

Acknowledgements

I can think of only two people to whom I am indebted:

First and foremost, my lovely wife. Valerie, without your love, support, and gentle heart, none of this would ever have happened. Like a drop of water on the tongue of a parched man languishing in the desert, you came along at just the right time. Thank you for saving me.

And second, Betty, for possessing the courage to take a chance on *Joshuanism*.

Contents

PRELUDE: A Provocative Conversation ix
PART ONE: post/Christianity 17
    Expressions 21
    post/Christian 23
    The Crisis Crossroads 26
    The post/Christian God 30
    Changing Perceptions 34
    New Perceptions 40
PART TWO: Joshuanism 45
    Jesus Christ 46
    Joshua of Nazareth 49
    Looking For Joshua 53
    Joshuans 58
    Joshuanism: A Path beyond Christianity 60
    Christianity and Joshuanism 64
    Opposition to Joshuanism 66
    The Joshuan Pages 72
PART THREE: Joshuan Theology and Belief 75
    Joshuan Thought 75
    Joshuan Theology 77
    The Dismantling 80
    Absolute Deliverance 84
    The Invited and the Respondent 88
    Scriptural Relegation 93
    Diversified Uniformity 101
    Mosaic Theology 105
    Zen Joshuanism 108

The Fusion.	113
The Joshuan Creed	124
PART FOUR: Joshuan Community	129
The Extraction	130
Tables	131
Joshuan Leadership	136
Joshuan Forums	138
The Three Cornerstones.	140
PART FIVE: The Practice of Joshuanism.	147
The Unfolding	148
The Five Elements	152
The Joshuan Way	168
Joshuan Love.	176
The Mind.	180
The Body	183
The Soul.	184
Regarding the Joshuan.	186
The Daily Life of the Joshuan.	196
Becoming a Joshuan (Choosing Joshuanism)	199
EPILOGUE: The Joshuan Revolution	203
Closing Remarks	213
APPENDIX.	215

Unless otherwise noted, all excerpts from the New Testament are from the unpublished translation known as The Joshuan Pages (TJP)

PRELUDE: A Provocative Conversation

It is somewhat absurd the way this all began. Three of us were standing in an ice skating rink, arguing about goatees. It was a Sunday afternoon in late January, sunny but chilly. Earlier that morning, I had led worship at church, as I always did. Afterward, the pastor told me that some families from the church were going ice-skating that afternoon. He was a friend of mine, and he therefore knew that ice skating resides near the top of the list of things I hate. Nevertheless, he wanted me to come, so I went.

When I showed up, I found the pastor and his wife sitting on the sidelines, lacing their skates. As I approached, I noticed they were discussing the pastor's appearance. His wife, significantly younger than he, thought he looked too old. He was only in his forties, but she felt he needed a makeover, that he dressed and groomed himself in a manner that was blatantly outdated. To be honest, I could see her point. Not that anyone needs to look stylish, mind you. But, well, you just needed to see Pastor Luke to know he did need some help when it came to even a remote grasp of fashion. The guy could preach, to be sure. He was brilliant from the pulpit, oh yes. But he just looked like a guy who wore a giant, invisible, neon sign that said, "I have no clue."

I sat down next to them with no intentions whatsoever of skating. For one thing, I am not good at it, and for another, I do not enjoy it. I was only there because I wanted to be where my friends were and because Pastor Luke wanted me there. I pulled out my pipe to pack it with tobacco but then noticed the "no smoking" sign hanging on the wall to my left. I stowed my pipe back into my pocket and decided to throw my two cents into the conversation.

"You should grow a goatee, Luke," I said.

His wife loved the idea. "Yes!" She agreed. "Yes, you should, Luke. You would look really good with a goatee. I think that's a great idea."

Luke considered this idea in the lovably quirky way he considers ideas, and then said, "I don't know. I am not really a goatee guy."

His wife, who was now ready to hit the ice, stood up and said, "I am going to make sure you grow a goatee." With that, she turned, flew onto the rink, and skated away.

At that moment, another guy from our church sidled up to our conversation. He was my age, but we were nothing alike. I did not dislike the guy, but I did not exactly like him, either. More than once, he had openly opposed both the pastor's leadership and my own as the worship leader. He professed to be a Christian, but honestly, I never saw a single shred of evidence to support his claim. I am not saying I am only a friend to believers. Nothing could be further from the truth, and I know we are supposed to love our enemies. But this guy... he made it so hard.

Anyway, he had overheard everything.

Luke was ready to skate now, and he stood up to shake this guy's hand.

Then this guy, who apparently had not come to skate either, said, "A goatee is a bad idea. A very bad idea."

"Why is that?" Luke asked.

"A pastor should not have facial hair," the guy answered.

I was incredulous at this response. I could not believe it. So, I countered, "What difference does the pastor's facial hair make?"

"It is simply not pastoral," he answered. "And it's disrespectful to God."

"Why?" I probed.

"I wouldn't expect you to understand," he said. Then to Luke he added, "Neither I nor my family would attend any church where the pastor has a goatee." Then he turned and walked away.

Not that it really mattered, but Pastor Luke never grew a goatee.

Later that night, long after I should have been asleep, I zipped my hoodie, laced my Chucks, and went for a nocturnal meander through my neighborhood. A light snow was falling, but I did not mind in the least. I walked in the direction of an abandoned schoolhouse from the 1920s, located a few blocks from my apartment, a place I frequented often on restless nights. My typical *modus operandi* was to sit at the top of the massive stone steps, smoke my pipe, and ponder this or that. That night I wanted to ponder the bizarre goatee conversation. Since I now had the freedom to smoke my pipe, I lit it up, puffed away, and recalled the episode from earlier that day in the skating rink. The incident itself was of little importance, just one of the many, tiny oddities that those who lead churches often experience. But the more I thought about it, the more I became agitated. Not agitated at the guy who hated pastors with facial hair, but agitated because the incident demonstrated on a small scale just how heavily burdened the work of God is by the painfully crippling minutiae of that which does not even matter! That a man would refuse to attend a church because of the pastor's facial hair incensed me with powerful indignation toward all the thousands of microscopic, insignificant details that people use to limit the freedom of others and the expression of God's work.

I wondered how many leaders across the country—and indeed the world—were burdened by such nonsense. Then I started wondering how many believers, leaders and lay alike, were burdened in their personal lives and personal journeys with God by stuff that does not matter. Things like petty squabbles over nothing at all, legalistic backbiting about the definition of an inconsequential word, limitations on personal expression (like facial hair), dress codes (as though God cares about what clothes we wear to church), individual preferences, the style of worship music, who is going to change the light bulb in the men's bathroom. I began to see Christianity not as the dynamic, inspired, revolutionary, and irresistible movement I thought it was supposed to be but rather a diffused institution, a disarmed, crumbling establishment that was circumventing its own effectiveness and relevancy with self-inflicted wounds.

I wished that somehow we could be freed of all this triviality that weighs us down. But how?

That was in 2003. A few years later, I was visiting a friend in Wyoming. Joe was a Christian musician and one of the few guys I admired. He lived on a sprawling piece of beautiful ground with breathtaking mountains crowding every direction the eye could look. There was an enormous tree on his property that offered ample shade on a hot summer day. So, one afternoon when my friend was busy, I took a lawn chair and a book to that tree and proceeded to read lazily in the shade, hemmed in on all sides by staggering rocky peaks. I was very relaxed as I devoured my book, which happened to be *A Generous Orthodoxy* by Brian McLaren (whose writing I was into in those days). After about an hour, Joe walked out of his house and strolled over to me.

"Who are you reading?" He asked.

"Brian McLaren," I replied.

A look of disdain spread across Joe's otherwise friendly face. He silently regarded the book in my hands for a moment, seemingly searching for the best way to say whatever it was he was about to say. I was sure he knew who Brian McLaren was. Joe might have been a musician, but he was also educated and well read. At length, he finally found what he wanted to say. "You shouldn't be reading that," he announced gravely.

"Why not?" I asked.

"McLaren's dangerous."

"Dangerous?"

"Oh, yes. Very."

"How so?"

He sat down in the grass next to me and was silent again, a faraway look on his face. Finally, he said, "Brian McLaren advocates things that God would never want."

"Like what?"

"Well, he thinks it's okay to blur the lines between the different Christian denominations."

"Blur the lines?"

"You know, that they should mingle. That each can bring something good to the table. That a person can draw the good things from different denominations and roll them into one experience."

I was completely bewildered at this side of my friend I had never seen before. "I think that's a wonderful idea," I said coolly.

"What's so wonderful about it?" Joe challenged.

I thought about it for a moment. "Well," I began, "Doesn't Paul say there is only one faith, one church, one body? Aren't we all on the same team?"

"No," he said flatly. "We're not."

"What do you mean?"

"I mean that I am a Baptist. As such, I believe that Baptists have the right idea. Christians who aren't Baptists may be Christians, but they don't please God."

"They don't please God? Why not?"

"Because they're not Baptists. Look, Mike, I know you mean well, but there are things you just don't understand. We who are right must protect what we know to be right and stand against those we know to be wrong even if they claim the same Jesus as we do."

I do not recall for certain, but I am sure my jaw hit the ground. I do know that I threw up my arms and bellowed, *"What?"*

"And furthermore, it's our job to show those who are wrong just how wrong they are. Your friend, Mr. McLaren, would have us rubbing elbows with them instead of standing against them. Such talk is dangerous. We must keep our separations."

I think it was that last sentence he said to me that forever sealed my fate. *We must keep our separations.* I probably did not realize it at the time, but that was the beginning of my journey toward everything that has come to fruition in the writing of this book. I know Joe was just one man, but he was the voice of so many others. Sure, there are plenty of people out there who long to reunite the divided Christians, but there are just as many people out there who want to "keep our separations."

That story was just one instance out of so many that compelled me to begin wondering whether or not a person could accomplish what Jesus said were the two greatest commandments (love God, and love your neighbor) without ever having to walk through the crumbling, dysfunctional realm that is Christianity. That was a question I began to explore with increasing intensity as the years went on.

Eventually, an idea began to form within me. I shunned it at first. In fact, I avoided it as if it were a disease. Why? Well, the idea felt altogether presumptuous and self-aggrandizing (as if I were worthy enough to "change" Christianity or offer something "beyond" Christianity). The idea also felt slightly rebellious, as if the very thought of undoing some of what has been done and starting over would somehow

Joshuanism

incur God's wrath. After all, we are taught in Christianity that all things Christian are sacred, right?

Then one day I asked myself this question: just what exactly in Christianity is sacred? I came up with this list:

1. God is sacred, including all three parts of the Trinity;
2. We humans are sacred because we are made in the image of God;
3. God's Word (the Bible) is sacred;
4. Our faith is sacred because without it we could never come to God;
5. Our creeds are sacred because they form the substance of what we believe and why we believe it;
6. Our worship is sacred regardless of how we do it;
7. Our bonds of love are sacred if they're authentic; and
8. Our hope is sacred.

After I had made this list, a new question occurred to me: something may be sacred, but does being sacred mean that same thing is not or cannot be subject to change? Does *sacred* mean *unalterable*? The question was too heavy for the moment. I put it on my mental shelf and decided to revisit it at some later date.

Then I decided to make a list of that which was possibly not sacred in Christianity (and therefore open to interpretation, alteration, modification, or, dare I say, obliteration). I came up with this:

1. Our institutions are not sacred;
2. Our preferences are not sacred;
3. The operation of our particular denomination is not sacred;
4. Our cultural identities within the local church, the denomination, and the religion as a whole are not sacred;
5. Our Christian terminology is not sacred;
6. Our human fingerprint upon God's revelation of himself is not sacred;
7. Our personal interpretations of the Bible are not sacred; and
8. Our traditions are not sacred.

Once I had made these two lists, I began to sense that maybe I should stop avoiding the idea that was starting to form in my mind. Maybe it was not so presumptuous after all. Maybe it was not really all that rebellious. Maybe it was my job to express this idea and let others do with it what they wanted.

Michael Vito Tosto

So, I finally sat down and fleshed it all out on paper. This book is the finished product.

Let me now tell you a few things about this book. At its heart, this book details a completely new path to God through his Son, what some might call an *alternative* to Christianity. I want you to know that now, before you begin. In this book, I propose a radical, revolutionary hybrid of what was once merely a religion but what could now be something much more dynamic. I introduce some new ideas. I reshape some old ideas. I offer new expressions and a fresh perspective. I ask some interesting questions and suggest some startling answers. I put certain long-held assumptions on trial, and I throw the spotlight onto many of our timeworn traditions. In some cases, I take a wrecking ball to the erected establishment. Why?

Consider this: if a man inherited a house in a state of extreme disrepair, dilapidated beyond salvage, would he still go about attempting to renovate the pre-existing structure? Or would he tear the whole thing down and rebuild something new in its place? Think about that as you read this book.

Inevitably, there will be those who think I am creating a completely new "denomination" of Christianity here. That certainly is neither my intention nor my hope. Another arm of a crumbling institution is the last thing we need. My heart in this is only that our faith and our love and our unfolding dramas with God will find *new* and *organic expression* and *new evolution* within a completely fresh and distinct *path beyond* Christianity.

Therefore, I invite you to enter into a provocative conversation with me. That is all this is, by the way. A conversation. I have something to say, and I am going to say it. Then I will wait and see how you respond.

Michael Vito Tosto
December, 2012

Michael Vito Tosto

PART ONE: post/Christianity

Imagine you had a time machine. Imagine also that you had one purpose in mind for this time machine: to ask human beings living at different intervals in history a series of prepared questions. The goal? A detailed analysis of how humanity's worldview has evolved over the centuries.

Consider Wiktionary.com's definition of the term *worldview*:

> [*Worldview*] – One's *personal view* of the world and how one *interprets* it / the totality of one's beliefs about *reality* / a general *philosophy* or view of *life*.

With this definition in mind, suppose your first stop in history was the year 5,000 BC somewhere in Mesopotamia. (We must also assume that you would somehow be able to communicate linguistically with the peoples you would encounter). After you went through your list of questions and noted the answers, perhaps your conclusions for the worldview of that time period might be something like this:

> *These people have an extremely primitive worldview. Their entire lives are based on survival. Their relation to the planet they live on is governed by fear of the unknown and a lack of scientific explanations for geologic phenomena. Thus, they see their world through the worship of a varying array of differing deities, whom they have created to explain these unknowns.*

I have a degree in history, so I feel safe in submitting that this is a somewhat accurate assessment of what the worldview in 5,000 BC was like, at least in that part of the world.

Suppose your next stop in time was the year 800 ad, in present day France. You spoke with some people of that time and place and compiled an updated worldview. Perhaps it would read something like this:

> *These people live their entire lives through their belief in and adherence to the Christian religion. They see life in terms of heaven and hell, good and evil, sin and holiness. Feudalism dominates their way of life, so they*

tend to see the world through a relationship between the lords and the peasants. They live in a state of frequent war and thus tend to view the world as a brutal place. They have very little scientific knowledge and therefore have almost no understanding of the cosmos or their place in it. They believe the Earth is flat and that it resides at the center of the Universe.

Suppose your next stop was Rome or London sometime in the 1600s. Galileo has viewed the planets through a telescope. Isaac Newton will soon discover gravity. John Locke is alive and doing his thing. The Renaissance has already changed thought and knowledge. Humanism has burst upon the scene. Copernicus has proposed heliocentricity. The Enlightenment is about to dawn. What would the worldview be like now? Would it not be drastically different from the worldview of 800 ad? Perhaps *drastically different* is an understatement. Maybe *completely unrecognizable* is more apropos.

Imagine you moved on to speak to some humans in 1950, five years after Hiroshima and Nagasaki. How would their worldview differ from the one in the 1600s? One glaring difference is that it would include a possibility that humans could destroy the planet they live on. In addition, consider these weighty new developments: Einstein has split the atom and introduced to the world the theory of relativity, antibiotics are changing the way diseases are fought, and innovations like the telephone, radio, television, radar, and sonar have revolutionized how humans communicate. Consider, also, that since the dawn of humanity's time on the Earth, horses, wind, water, or raw manpower took people everywhere they went. By 1950, however, humans are buzzing around in planes, trains, and automobiles (and very soon they will be in space). One might say their worldview shrank as travelling about the globe became faster and easier.

Then think about this: no astronomer living in the year 1700, peering at the moon through an old telescope, would possibly have believed humans would one day walk on its surface. He may have fantasized about it; that is not entirely inconceivable. However, he would never have believed it to be anything other than a fantasy. Similarly, no Pony Express rider carting mail across the country on the back of a horse in 1860 could have ever fathomed a day when a person could sit in the luxury of their home, or in the back seat of a car, or at the top of a skyscraper, and, having pressed a few buttons on a handheld device, send a message digitally and instantly to someone on the other side of the planet. Was the word *digital* even in the vocabulary in 1860?

The point here, which is quite obvious on its own, is that as time passes, humans evolve. And as humans evolve, their worldviews evolve with them.

I am writing this in the year 2012. As I sit here and write, I am contemplating how much the world has changed in the last ten years. How much *we* have changed.

Joshuanism

What is our worldview today? Is it the same as it was even five years ago? Will it be different next year? Could the people living a hundred years ago have even fathomed the worldview of today? Can we even fathom the worldview of ten years from now? The people who study this kind of thing tell us that from this point on, as each year passes, humanity's evolution scientifically, medically, technologically, socially, culturally, and even spiritually will gain tremendous speed and grow exponentially beyond what we might even be able to handle mentally. In other words, we are evolving too fast even to comprehend it.

As I have been thinking about these things, I have also been thinking about Christianity. I believe in the Son of God, so I do not think about Christianity from the outside looking in. I think about it as a veteran member of it, one who cares greatly about its past, present, and future. I know that Christianity is not immune to change. I know that as humans have changed over the centuries, Christianity has changed, too. And when it changed, it usually changed as a result of 1) a shift in the worldviews of the humans living at the time; and 2) men and women who saw that it needed to change and who, through God's work in their lives, brought about that change successfully. I also know from studying history that when Christianity changed, it almost always happened amidst great turmoil and struggle from within.

With all of these things in mind, suppose we went back to our time machine and undertook a new endeavor. This time, limiting our travels to the last 2,000 years, we would only visit Christians, and we would do so with one goal in mind: piecing together a map of how the Christian worldview has changed.

The Christians we spoke to in the decades after Jesus lived would have firsthand knowledge of the events. As a result, they would probably be confident of what they believed in beyond anything we can imagine because they actually *saw* what we have only heard about. They have a *movement* on their hands, and it's growing. Their worldview is filtered through a lens of possible and probable martyrdom. Their physical lives mean little to them, and they boldly adhere to the message they preach, a tactic that for many of them results in their violent deaths. Most of them believe Jesus is going to return much sooner than he ends up returning (since, as of this date, he still has not), so their worldview is based on an assumption that the world will not be around much longer.

The Christians we spoke to in the 400s would be quite distinct from the ones we spoke to in the decades after Jesus lived. These Christians aren't really a part of a *movement* anymore. They are part of an *established institution*, the *official religion* of the Roman Empire (which is unfortunate, because the point of a movement is that it *moves*, which means it's *alive*—institutions, on the other hand, are *stationary*; that is why they are called institutions). A Pope now rules the Christian realm like a king would rule a kingdom. There are numerous rituals in place, many of which reflect a strong pagan-Roman influence. Deification of the Virgin Mary, a theme which seems to figure nowhere in the writings of the *New Testament,* is becoming prevalent. Only the clergy have access to the written scriptures. The regular lay Christian cannot sit in the privacy of his home and read them for himself. These Christians see the world through the lens of hierarchy, each level of Christianity having its authority; coming first from God, moving through the Pope, through the Bishops, through the priests, and eventually reaching the layperson. The everyday Christian has little to say about how things are done within this religion. Their superiors do most of the thinking for them. Hell features prominently in their worldview, the prospect of which serves as a scare tactic to preserve the structure of the hierarchy and the power of those in charge.

The Christians we spoke to in the late 1340s would have all kinds of problems on their hands. The Black Death is decimating the population. No one has any idea about microscopic organisms called *bacteria*. All anyone knows is that people are dying by the tens of thousands every day and no one has any idea why. These Christians see their world as having been turned upside down. They do not understand anything anymore. Their long held belief that if they did good God would protect them seems to have been quashed. They feel God has abandoned them. They begin to question his existence and the validity of the religion passed down to them. Nothing makes sense. Even the priests seem unable to pray this disease away. Prayer, in fact, seems to be completely useless. The ensuing deep-seated and widespread doubt and disillusionment that seizes multitudes of Christians eventually finds rebellious expression as Europeans begin seeking other explanations for the mysteries of life and the Universe. This gives way to the Renaissance and Humanism, both of which eventually lead to the Enlightenment, which, in turn, eventually leads to the Industrial Age, which, in its turn, eventually leads to the Age of Information (which is where we are today, in the year 2012).

Here is an interesting question: what would we encounter if we spoke to the Christians living in 1950s America, a time period not so far removed from us? Many of the Christians who were alive then are still alive now. Yet, would we entirely recognize the expressions of Christianity and the Christian worldview if we went back and spent a week in 1956? For one thing, we would definitely see segregated churches. For another thing, we probably would not see any electric guitars, drum sets, or projectors littering church sanctuaries. There would undoubtedly be an organist, possibly a pianist, and rows of pews stocked with hymnals. To these people, God probably resembles a bearded Charlton Heston. You wear your Sunday best to church because God loves suits and ties. The denominations hunker down and tend to their own personal kingdoms, rubbing elbows with each other as little as possible or not at all. And perhaps most important, this is a Christian worldview characterized by traditions, Americanism, ethical values, and a specific, rigid code of moral conduct.

Now to bring it even closer to home, say we spent a week in 1995. Here Christianity seems synonymous with being a Republican, at least in most circles. In fact, to the Christian worldview in the 1990s, God himself is most likely a Republican. The quality of church worship music is beginning to replace the quality of preaching and teaching. In other words, people now search for the "right" church based not on who is teaching what but by how good the band is. Christians see the world as being categorized into "us" and "them," or "the lost" and "the saved" (a mindset that is not exactly new but in the recent years seems to have become more of a definitive factor in the Christian worldview).

Here is another interesting thought: suppose we reversed the process and instead of visiting Christians from various time periods, we pulled a Bill & Ted and used our time machine to pluck Christians from the first century, the 300s, the 1350s, the 1600s, and, say, 1845, and transported them all to the present. What would they think? How would they react? If you dressed them in some baggy jeans and Coldplay T-shirts and sent them to a Gen-X styled worship service, or to a Sunday school class to discuss the challenges of day-to-day Christian living, or to a screening of Mel Gibson's *The Passion*, would they have any connection to or recognition of the faith they practice in their own time period?

The point here is that Christians living at different stages of history saw the world differently and *expressed their faith differently* as a result. To put it bluntly: Christianity changes. Anyone who thinks otherwise is mistaken. Moreover, anyone who resists change within Christianity by arguing that Christianity does not and should not change is deluding himself. Christianity changes all the time. *All the time.* Just as humanity is constantly evolving, so, too, is Christianity constantly evolving. Why? Because Christianity is made up of humans! God may be its soul, but *we* are its substance.

So, then, consider this time period that we are living in. This is the greatest age of radical change humanity has ever known. This is the most rapid stage of cultural, social, and scientific evolution the world has ever seen. Ever! It's like when you stare out the window of a speeding train. The world outside flies by in flashes of barely recognizable images; it's just a blur. That's how it is. We are here, and the world around is just flying by in a blur. That's how fast humanity is changing. That's how fast we are evolving. And it's only going to get faster and faster and faster.

In view of all this, I ask the question: in the midst of this tremendous change, this terrific evolutionary upheaval, where is Christianity going?

Personally, I believe God is moving his believers into new *expressions*.

Expressions

Let's talk a little bit about *what* Christianity is. Christianity is described by different people as being many different things, depending upon with whom you talk.

If you were to ask the people *within* Christianity what it is, they would probably say it is a form of spirituality, a relationship between God and humanity through the person of Jesus Christ. They may say Christianity is the Gospel, the good news. They might also say it's a group, a body, an international assembly of believers.

If you were to ask those *outside of* Christianity, they might say it is a world religion, just one of the many offered. If their experiences with it have been negative, they might talk about the woes of organized religion or describe it as some sort of club of what to them might seem like hypocritical, judgmental people who talk about being "saved."

There are all kinds of ways to talk about what Christianity is, but one thing it's rarely described as being is *a dialogue*. I have come to look at Christianity this way, and it has revolutionized my thinking.

What do I mean by a dialogue? Quite simply that Christianity is an ongoing, manifold *conversation*. When I read the *Bible*, God is communicating with me. When I pray, I am communicating with him. When I go to church or to a small group or spend any time anywhere with any Christians, perhaps we converse about our faith, or open up about our struggles, or share our questions. Perhaps we ponder the answers out loud and share what God is doing in our lives. In other words, we *talk*. We *communicate*. We *connect*. We *bring* what we have to the table. Therefore, Christianity is an open dialogue between God and us, us and God. It's also an open dialogue between me and you, you and me. And Christianity is an open dialogue between us (believers) and the world (nonbelievers). That is what I mean by manifold. It's *multifaceted*

When I think of *why* Christianity is alive, I, of course, think about God, Jesus, and the whole story of the *New Testament*. When I think of *in whom* Christianity is alive, I think about us. The hearts of the believers. The Church. But when I think about *where* Christianity is alive, I think of two places. Obviously, the first place is our beliefs, our creeds, our faith in God and our adherence to the "stuff" we profess. The second place, however, might not be so obvious, at least not to some. When I think of *where* Christianity is alive, I do not think only about *what* we believe, but *how we communicate* it. Because I look at Christianity as being, among other things, a dialogue, I therefore believe Christianity lives in our *expressions*.

Christianity is filled with expressions: answered prayers, a sense of comfort, the peace that surpasses understanding—all of these are God's *expression* of his love to us. His sending of his Son, the work of Jesus at the cross, the resurrection, forgiveness—all of these are God's *expression* of his love to us. Our worship, our devotion, our prayers, our sacrifices, our offerings, our obedience—all of these are our *expressions* of our love to God. A helping hand, a word of encouragement, an open door, a gift of financial assistance, a listening ear, a ready shoulder—all of these are our *expressions* of love to each other.

There are other types of expressions within Christianity, too. Our traditions are expressions. Our liturgies are expressions. Our divergent styles of worship music are expressions. Our charities are expressions. The architecture of our church buildings and the décor we choose for them are expressions. Each particular denomination's differing way of going about things is its particular expressions (i.e., this is how *we* do church, this is how *we* think, this is what *we* believe, this is *our* approach to theology, and so forth.). Our language as Christians; the terminologies and jargon we use; the names we have for the elements of our practices, customs, rituals, and observances; the *conversations* we have; the *ideas* we speak and nurture with one another; the *applications* of our beliefs; the unique ways we as individual believers and as groups of believers manifest our Christian ideals and behaviors—these are all forms of expression. I maintain that it is in our expressions that Christianity lives, not just in our beliefs.

Want proof? Think about this: what good is faith that is not expressed? What good is a belief in God that goes unvoiced? Where is the power in the Word of God if no one reads it or speaks it? What good would going to church be if nothing happened there? Who among the unbelievers would discover what Jesus did and who Jesus was if no one relates that information? How authentic is a praise that never leaves our lips? What good is a worship song that no one sings? What is the point of having a heart to aid your friend in his suffering if you never communicate your availability to him and he never communicates his suffering to you? How can you get an answer if you do not ask the question? Does a creed have any meaning if no one recites it? If you have the desire to pray but never end up actually *expressing* the prayer, either verbally or silently, did your intention benefit you? Did it benefit God? Did it benefit anyone at all?

So merely to *believe* is not enough. Merely to *intend* is not enough. Merely to have a thought or idea is not enough. It is the *expression* of these things that validates them. As the apostle James says, faith without deeds is dead. What is a deed if not an expression of faith? Just as wind makes the leaves blow, so also does authentic faith validate itself by finding expression. James could just as easily have said *faith without expression* is dead. As I said before, when I ponder the direction Christianity should take in this time of radical evolution and change, I keep coming back to a hope and a dream for new expressions.

Let me share with you the first in a long line of possible new expressions.

post/Christian

This term is going to throw many people off. It might shock them, confuse them, or even offend them. On the other hand, perhaps it will arouse their curiosity. Stimulate them. Open a new avenue of thought and possibility within their hearts and minds. Either way, this is only the beginning of what is going to be a juggernaut of new, radical, revolutionary ideas. So if you are truly along for the ride, strap yourself in and let's get started.

The first thing we need to get out of the way is this: *post/Christian* does not mean *anti*-Christian or *un*-Christian. It just means something *more than* Christian, or more accurately, something *coming after what is* Christian...something *beyond* what is Christian.

> [*post/Christian*] – 1) a term meaning that which was/is Christian, but existing in a *furthere*d state, or an *altere*d state; 2) the manifestation of Christianity after having undergone a transformation; 3) the embodiment of a hybrid Christianity, which retains the main beliefs of Christianity, but which also proposes new *expressions* of those beliefs, suggests *new* beliefs, and asks new questions; 4) the *product* of a state of change within Christianity, or a term describing the process of that which is still in an *unfinished* state of change; and 5) a term referring to a new *time period*, similar to the word "postmodern," meaning that a new age is upon humanity, the *post/Christian* age, an age when believers are no longer a part of Christianity, but of *post/Christian*ity, or an age when believers are no longer that which was/is Christian, but are now characterized by that which would be considered *post/Christian*.

Confused? Think about it this way: after the Protestant Reformation, it would have been entirely plausible and understandable if the advocates of the Reformation chose not to call themselves Protestants, but post/Catholics. What would such a name have meant? It would have meant that they were identifying themselves as something that was no longer Catholic. It was *related* to Catholicism in that it sprang from Catholicism, but it was no longer entirely Catholic. It was new. It was different. It retained some of that which spawned it, but it also embodied new and reformed...what? Expressions.

Had they called themselves post/Catholics instead of Protestants, would it have meant they had ceased believing in Jesus? Would it have meant they longer belonged to God? Would it have meant they suddenly rejected all the creeds that had originally shaped their beliefs? Would it have meant they were renouncing their faith? No. All it would have meant is that they were now letting the world know that they were something that was *coming after* Catholicism; something that had progressed *beyond* what Catholicism was; something that directly addressed, challenged, and sought to rectify the problems and concerns within the status quo; something that, in the midst of change, was moving from one way of expressing Christianity into another way; something that had a new identity; something that took the substance of what existed and *reformed* it to make it, in their estimation, better.

Joshuanism

That is all I mean by the term *post/Christian* or *post/Christianity*. It is the idea that as humanity evolves throughout the 21st century, so, too, does the expression of Christianity, or perhaps I ought to say so, too, *should* the expression of Christianity. It means that we are in another period of reformation. It means not that *what* we believe changes but that who *we are becoming* as a result of those beliefs in the 21st century *is* open to change. It means that just as the Christians who lived in 1350 might not recognize the Christians of 1950, so, too, are we becoming something that the Christians of 1950 might not recognize. It means that we are evolving. We are graduating. We are pushing forward into a new, fresh, advanced state of existence as believers. We are finding new ways to practice, apply, view, and *express* our love, our faith, our salvation, our understanding of God, and our experiences with him. It means we begin doing things not in a way that violates our beliefs but in a way that makes them relevant for our time and reflects the direction humanity is taking. It means that we begin reimagining how to go about not just *doing* church but *being* The Church. It means that we enter into new conversations, ask new questions, seek new answers, thrust farther into what is possible with this grace we have been given. It means we drop the baggage of the past, if it is indeed baggage, and pursue a new future unfettered and unburdened. It means we are bringing the message of God and Jesus and love and salvation to the unbelievers in fresh, relevant, reconceived ways. It means that new and old are mixed together to create a hybrid, a morph, a fresh manifestation. It means we become something that is no longer quite Christian but rather something *more*, something *different*, something *else,* something *beyond.* That is the meaning of *post/Christian*ity.

Consider this: the believers who went on the violent Crusades in the name of Jesus thought that was acceptable. The believers who lived their entire lives never reading the scriptures for themselves, deferring to the purview of the priests, thought that was acceptable. The believers who owned slaves in the Americas thought that was acceptable. The believers who burned "heretics" at the stake thought that was acceptable. The believers who upheld their segregated churches thought that was acceptable. But none of those things are acceptable anymore because we have evolved beyond them. Is it really so shocking that we should question who we are as believers *now* to see if there are things we think are normal and acceptable, but that, as we progress, we might find we are mistaken about?

That is the essence of *post/Christian*ity, or what I call *post/Christian* thought: to constantly subject our worldview and theological opinions to scrutiny in the face of our ongoing development as a species.

The Crisis Crossroads

We have already established that Christianity does change and that it has changed. Moreover, we have established that, throughout history, it has usually changed amid struggle. Often, in the history of Christianity, the status quo has been brought to a junction, or a fork in the road, where it can either develop alongside the shifting advancements in humanity's social, cultural, and educational evolution at any given time (thus remaining relevant, applicable, and accessible to the people it seeks to reach), or it can die. And if you think Christianity cannot die, consider that time and time again in the *New Testament*, the apostles and church leaders continually admonish us to keep the faith, to stay strong, to stay alert, to hold to the hope we have, to be ready to give an appropriate answer to the questions we are asked, to keep the community of believers pure, to resist temptation, to avoid all kinds of evil. Do you think these cautions are given solely for the safety and sanctity of the *individual*? Or are they pertinent warnings to *the Church at large?* You might say to yourself, "God would never let Christianity die." Are you really so sure? Doesn't the *New Testament* say there will be terrible times in the last days? Doesn't it say that many will fall away? Didn't Jesus himself wonder out loud in *Luke* 18 whether or not he would find faith on Earth when he returns? Furthermore, consider that God, for whatever unfathomable reason, has chosen to do his work not entirely directly but indirectly through *us*, through *the believers*, through *humanity*. Can humans mess all of this up? Do you even have to ask? Have you looked at the human race lately?

So, this junction I mentioned, this fork in the road, refers to a point in time and in the evolution of all humans and the believers among them when Christianity needs to reinvent itself to stay relevant and alive. This does not mean we reinvent the *message* of Christianity, the *beliefs* of Christianity, or even the *values* of Christianity, but it does mean that we can and should reinvent how we present that message, how we practice those beliefs, how we hold to those values. I call this junction the *crisis crossroads*.

There have been many in the last two millennia. Christianity is filled with people who chose correctly at the crucial moments, when the crisis crossroads came upon them in their day. They were agents of change. Radical change. Positive change. Let's discuss just a few:

1. **The Apostle Paul.** Until he came along, the other apostles were mostly bringing the message of Jesus only to the Jews. Paul changed all that and preached that the message was for *everyone*, not just for Jews, but also for Gentiles (non-Jews). This had implications not just for a single race of people but also for the entire planet. That's powerful change.

2. **The Emperor Constantine.** Now, granted, he was not exactly the most devoted of Christians. Many legends surround him, especially the ones dealing with how he saw "visions" that led to his conversion. In reality, though, the more plausible story is that Constantine saw a threat in Christianity's unstoppable growth and therefore employed the age-old wisdom that says, "If you can't beat them, join them." By embracing, endorsing, and officiating Christianity as the Empire's religion, Constantine essentially stabilized his kingdom. In other words, his motives were mostly political. However, he did preside over the Council of Nicaea in 325, and we do have to give him credit for being aware of the times: he saw the need for an official creed that stated unequivocally the immovable beliefs that made up Christianity. Thus, the Nicene Creed was born, a creed that, along with the Apostles' Creed, forms the foundation of all Christian thought and belief to this day.

3. **Augustine of Hippo.** Many have heard of this individual, usually by the name of *Saint* Augustine. Few know, though, that he is considered to be one of the fathers of Western Christianity. What this means, basically, is that most of the conventions in Christian theology either directly originated with him or were derived later from his work. Doctrines like *original sin* and the *fall of man*, which later went on to form the theological basis for *why* Christianity even had to *exist* in the first place, find their greatest expression of development in the work of Augustine. At a time when the Roman Empire was beginning to crumble and the West teetered on the brink of the coming Dark Ages, Augustine's theological innovations secured the survival of Christian thought.

4. **Johannes Gutenberg.** By inventing the printing press, this individual (who was a believer) paved the way for making the Word of God a household item, taking it out of the exclusive privy of the priests and offering it (eventually) to anyone who wanted to read it. Consider the staggering implications of this astounding moment of change in history. If you own a *Bible*, pick it up and feel it in your hands. It is there because of Johannes Gutenberg.

5. **Martin Luther.** You know about this individual. You know what he did. If ever there was a believer who challenged the complacency, irrelevancy, and duplicity of the status quo of his time, it was Luther. He revived the idea that all of this is supposed to be about grace and faith. He challenged the authority of the Pope and Catholicism. He ve-

hemently fought against the moral corruption and decadent lifestyles of the clergy. He preached that the *Bible*, not the Pope, was the only source of divinely revealed knowledge. In so doing, he brought a new, positive consciousness to the community of believers, and the Church has never been the same since. We could go on...

These are just a few. There have been many more: Justinian, Thomas Aquinas, John Calvin, John Wesley, William Wilberforce, G.K. Chesterton. Each saw what was happening in their time and brought something new to the table. Each one was as an agent of change. The heart of *post/Christian*ity is to do the very same thing today.

Not everyone will agree with me. Some will look around at their comfortable expressions of Christianity within their comfortable churches and say to themselves, "Nothing needs to change. We're not at one of these crisis crossroads." The irony, of course, is that as soon as anyone makes this statement, or even thinks it, they are confirming all the more that the crisis crossroad *is* upon them—is *definitely* upon them—because any time comfort creeps into a movement, it ceases to be a movement. Why? Because as I said before, movements, by definition, require *moving*. They require *motion*. Comfort, on the other hand, is the breeding ground of things that are *not* in motion, things at rest, things in a state of apathy and indifference. And we know that objects in motion tend to stay in motion. Objects at rest tend to stay at rest.

The hope of *post/Christian*ity is to get things moving again, to remove that which is institutional and rediscover that which is in motion. We want a movement on our hands, not an institution. Why? Movements *spread*. Movements are like a wildfire. Movements change the world. Institutions do not spread. That is the very definition of an institution, that something is *instituted*, or *set in place*.

A movement is supposed to be *irresistible*. Otherwise, it wouldn't move very far. What is irresistible about an institution?

Have you ever asked yourself this question: what is the good news? Christians talk about the Gospel, or the good news, all the time. But just what exactly *is* this good news? Correct me if I am wrong, but I thought this good news was supposed to be something in this vein: that as deeply and desperately and violently that we humans crave real life, so, too, does God crave to give it to us and that this life is possible because God himself entered our world by being born as a human. Further, I thought the good news was 1) that this human, Jesus, lived a perfect life that showed us the way toward upright living and was offered up on the cross as the punishment for our sins and the procurement of our redemption; 2) that this Jesus, having died on that cross, performed the most astounding feat ever achieved by a human being when he rose from the dead; and 3) that anyone and everyone who hears the message and believes can share in this life, this freedom, this restoration, this health, this connection to something wonderful. I thought the good news was that humans could now *know* God! This news is supposed to be *irresistible.* This news is supposed to be sweeping across humanity, ushering ferocious change on this planet. This news is supposed to be propelling the hearts of all humans toward God.

So why isn't it? Why are churches shrinking? Why are people walking away from the Christian religion in droves? Why is atheism spreading its seductive fingers across the surface of the human race? Can we really blame science, as so many do when faced with the apparent decay in Christian relevancy? Personally, I do not think science is to blame because I also believe that if the hearts of humans were disposed toward and connected to God, they would see the wonders of science as telling the same story of that same God. So, what is it then? Why are Christians portrayed in the media as being impossibly beyond reach, steeped in utter irrelevancy, and clinging to lifestyles that no sane person would ever choose? Why do all the other possible false avenues and false options offered to humans for the comfort of their souls, such as sex, drugs, and power, sometimes look a million times better than the message of this good news?

Could it be that the expressions of Christianity no longer do the job? Could it be that Christians have become so enveloped in their worn out way of doing things and saying things that the world just doesn't look or listen anymore? When nonbelievers spy on the doings of God's people and see them bickering over words, dividing over non-issues, clinging to expressions that fail to woo and lack any connection to the changing world, why should they see anything there that would turn their hearts toward the God who loves them?

Be honest now. If *you* were a nonbeliever who stood outside the window looking in, would you see anything that falls anywhere near the realm of the *irresistible?*

The aim of *post/Christian*ity is bring the irresistibility back. To revive the power of the message. To find new expressions so that the good news, which really *is* good news, will begin to *look* and *sound* like good news again.

So, to recap, let's consider these questions:

- Does God change? No.
- Does Jesus change? No.
- Does grace change? No.
- We spent some time talking about worldviews. Did the worldviews of Christians change over time? Yes!
- In all that time, did the *message* of Christianity change? No.
- Can the way we *express* that message change? Yes! Can the delivery of that message change? Yes!

- Can the way we go about *doing* our faith, *walking* our walk, *talking* our talk, and *affecting* our world change? Yes!
- Does *"post/Christian"* mean we do not believe in Jesus? No!

Therefore, *post/Christian* thought is merely an attitude that says, "I can be *committed* to the message of Jesus, but at the same time, I can also be *open* to the evolving of its expression."

We need to be open to this kind of evolution if we want to stay relevant and dynamic in our changing world. We are not *of* the world, no. But we are *among* the world, and we have a responsibility to *affect* the world. Therefore, we must evolve with it, or perhaps it would be more accurate to say, we must evolve *alongside of it*. We must. Because, my friends, we are at the crisis crossroads, perhaps the most important one we have faced yet.

The post/Christian God

A profound moment in my journey to seek and know God took place in an art gallery. I was in Seattle, visiting a friend of mine. I had some free time, and John had some free time, so I decided to fly out and kick it in the Emerald City for a few days. This was during the height of my Christian experience when I was still green behind the ears and miles away from questioning any of the marvelous things I believed. In fact, I was working at a church at the time, directing the music and worship ministry. The trip west was a welcome diversion.

John and I were strolling through the gallery, surveying the local talent, when a curious painting caught my attention. John went over to ask the docent something, and I stood in front of the unusual painting, studying it deeply. The painting, you see, was titled *God*. But the painting itself was quite simple. The artist only used two colors: a purple sphere on a black background. That was it. And the artist called it *God*. I found this quite mystifying. So, I stood there perplexed until John retuned. He sidled up to me and looked at my face. Then he looked at the painting. Then he looked back at my face again.

"What's the problem?" He asked.

"No problem. I just don't get it."

"What don't you get?"

"A purple ball on a black field? What does that have to do with God?"

"Are you sure the artist intends that this is a painting *of* God?"

"Well, it's called *God*."

"Yes, I know. But maybe the artist is communicating something *about* God, rather than trying to portray what God looks like."

"Maybe."

"Think about it," John said. "I am going to the bathroom."

So, there I stood for what seemed like hours but what was probably only a few minutes. I kept staring at the painting, trying to decipher some hidden message. *Black field. Purple ball. God.* Was there possibly some kind of significance in the colors? Did black mean something? Did purple? Was the sphere important? I just did not get it.

I finally wandered away and sat down in a corner, waiting for John. *Black field. Purple ball. God.* I just kept mulling it over.

Then, it came to me. Whether or not my conclusion was what the artist intended or not, I'll never know. Nevertheless, the conclusion satisfied me and delivered to me a completely new attitude about God.

What was my conclusion? This: by merely painting a purple ball on a black background and calling the painting *God*, the artist was making a statement about our *perceptions* of God. By creating an image that had no prior association with God, the artist communicated that God is probably nothing like we imagine him to be, that he is most likely so far beyond our concepts of him that nothing we know about him could ever come close to actually hitting the true target. I was fascinated by this insight. By simply painting a purple ball on a black field, the artist reminded me that humans are made in God's image, not the other way around. But here I am, a human, always trying to fit God into my own image. The more I thought about that, the more I began to wonder what, if anything, I was believing about God that was completely erroneous. I was sure there had to be something. I am, after all, a human being. If to err is human, then to be human is to err.

After a few weeks of chewing on that thought, I actually found something. It turns out there *was* something I was believing about God that was completely erroneous. It had to do with my biological father. Now, I am sure I am not the first human to experience what I am about to describe or the first human to figure it out. But the epiphany in my own life was staggering, for more reasons than one. So what was this erroneous belief? Well, you see, my father, who was not a bad man, was not exactly the best father. Oh, he provided for my material needs but nothing beyond that. In the almost three decades I knew him (he died when I was 28), I cannot remember a single instance when the man ever said he loved me, that he was proud of me, that he was there for me, or that he valued the person I was becoming. Neither did he ever hug me, touch me, or any other way show me the least bit of warmth. Nothing sensitive, emotional, or affectionate ever came from that man, or if it did, it never came in my direction.

It was not until that obscure painting in Seattle got me thinking about my perceptions of God that I realized how I had transferred my association with my dad over to God. Because my dad made it quite clear that I was a huge disappointment to him, it was only natural for me to assume God must have felt the same way. As a result, I formed these perceptions: God is hard to please; God is easily disappointed;

God is not affectionate; God is cold, distant, and insensitive. Now, I would never have cognitively communicated these things to myself or anyone else. On a conscious level, I didn't even know that I thought this way. But I did. And because I did, my interactions with God were corrupted and infected by an erroneous perception. Why erroneous? Because God is *not* hard to please. God is *not* easily disappointed. God *is* affectionate. God *is* warm and close by and full of love. The funny thing is that I would have acknowledged those things verbally. But in my heart, something else was going on. In my heart, I believed contrarily to what my verbiage declared. The scary thing is how long I went before realizing it.

This discovery led to other discoveries, and before long, I was constantly evaluating what I believed about God. This tendency stayed with me and developed over the years until finally it became second nature to me to continually question my perceptions. As I did, it seemed like God kept changing. Of course, he *wasn't* changing. It only seemed like he was. I was the one who was changing. Little by little, as my eyes opened more and more, I had to keep shedding old, erroneous concepts of God and embrace new ones. I can look back now and plainly see the unfolding of these changes, thanks to my journals. Ah, yes…my journals. I have made many mistakes in my life. Many, many mistakes. Terrible ones. However, one of the good decisions I made long ago was to begin documenting my journey with God. I have kept detailed records of my pilgrimage for the benefit of my own review and reflection. I am glad I did this because as I look back today and review and reflect I can see clearly the evolution of my perceptions about God. What I believe about God has changed. I must therefore assume it will keep changing. I hope that this change is actually leading somewhere. I hope each stage of change in perception is bringing me closer and closer to the accurate image. I suspect this is the case.

In view of these matters, we must observe that just as Christianity is associated with the Christian God, so, too, is *post/Christian*ity associated with the *post/Christian* God. Now, are we talking about two different Gods? No, there is still only one God. But we *are* talking about two different attitudes toward that one God, or two different *perspectives.*

Before we go any further, let's first review some elementary information about God. Perhaps the most elementary aspect of God is this: he does not change. The person, the entity, the being, the soul, the heart, the mind, and the spirit of who God is (the Judeo-Christian God, the *triune* God, the *only* God) never changes. We know this, of course, and no believer with a sound understanding of Biblical theology would ever challenge this bedrock belief. Why? First of all, we *choose* to believe that. That's called faith. But aside from that, we also know logically that if God *did* change, that if he were *subject* to change, he would thus prove himself unstable, rendering himself something that is *not* God. For to be God is to embody all the things that being a God requires. One of those things is *constant.* Another one of those things is *consistent*. To be subject to change (i.e., mutation, modification, adjustment, unsteadiness, and the like) not only nullifies the possibility of being constant but is also therefore the exact definition of inconsistent.

Now this all sounds like double-talk. Nevertheless, it serves to establish a basic fact about the God we profess to believe in: he…does…not…*change*. Nothing about God changes. The *substance* of who God is never changes (by "substance" we mean the elements of his being, or his nature, whatever those may be). The *personality* of God never changes (by which we mean his disposition, his attitude, his character, and so on). The *attributes* of God never change (he is forever *love*, he is forever *light*, he is forever *good*, etc.). The *will* of God never changes (that is, he never changes his mind, he is not subject to whims or mood swings, he doesn't reverse that which he has set in motion, he doesn't say one thing and do another, he doesn't suddenly abandon the plan midstream). The *pace* of God never changes (he will never cease to do things in his time, he never rushes nor retards his speed, he carries on the same manner at all times). The *work* of God never changes (he will never suddenly decide he is no longer interested in the salvation of his creation). And the *existence* of God never changes (God will never cease to be). Nietzsche was wrong. If God is dead, he was never God to begin with. God is God precisely because he cannot die.

Not only is all of this so, but we must also acknowledge that which is painfully obvious but perhaps easily forgotten: we cannot add anything to God, nor can we subtract anything from him. We cannot *alter* God in any way. We cannot affect the continuation of his existence (we cannot kill God or give him life), the nature of his being (we cannot make him something he is not), the qualities of his character (we cannot make God sin), or the boundlessness of his knowledge (we cannot teach God something he does not know). Why not? He is God. We are not. He is the *Creator*; we are the created. He is not made in our image, but rather we are made in his.

So, in view of this, the idea of a *post/Christian* God cannot really mean anything all that scandalous since we are openly acknowledging beforehand that God does not change either on his own or at our bidding (now, we *can* touch God's heart, we *can* elicit his response to our prayers, we *can* affect his interactions with us based on whether or not we believe in him since without faith one cannot *please* God, or so the *Bible* says—but we cannot alter his nature). No one disputes the constancy of who God is. Therefore, just as *post/Christian* does not mean *anti*-Christian, so the idea of a *post/Christian* God does not mean *anti*-God, or *un*-God, or something *other than* God, or a *new version of* God. Nor does it mean anything rebellious, sacrilegious, blasphemous, disrespectful, atheistic, or even satanic. We are not attempting to add anything to who God is, take away anything from who God is, or propose any kind of alteration in our core beliefs of who God is.

The term *post/Christian God* is merely a continuation of the same train of thought we had when we discussed *post/Christian*ity. Now, Christianity *does* change.

We have established that. But God does not. Since he does not, then the term *post/Christian God* must be a reflection, similar to *post/Christian*ity, of that which does change. *We* change, and just as our expressions of Christianity follow suit as humanity evolves, so, too, do our *perceptions* of God follow suit. Or at least, they should.

> [*post/Christian God*] – 1) a term referring to a deliberate effort by believers to begin thinking of God in new or different ways; 2) the idea that it might be okay to begin asking new questions about God, re-evaluating previously held notions about God, and re-examining our theologies to determine whether or not our perception of God must change *as we do*; 3) an attitude of *openness* toward our thoughts about God; 4) a willingness to entertain the *possibility* that we might not and probably don't have all the information on God, nor could we, when we're brutally honest, since that which is infinite cannot be fully, thoroughly, or finitely ascertained; and 5) a term referring to a commitment to seek God, a commitment to discovery, a commitment to the belief that if we seek we will find, and a commitment to a mindset that admits there is definitely still *more to learn*.

We cannot alter God, obviously. What we *are* altering, then, what we *are* adding to or subtracting from, is *our perception* of God. Therefore, the term *post/Christian God* actually has more to do with *us* than with God. After all, the created cannot change the Creator, and the created cannot invent a new Creator. Nevertheless, the created *can* endeavor to look at God anew, pushing past any archaic or erroneous perceptions, continuing to seek the truth.

Changing Perceptions

Let us consider this question: what do you believe about God? This is a key question because believing *in* God is only half the battle here (the easier half, to be honest). It's what you believe *about* God that counts. So, be honest with yourself. What *do* you believe? Do you really believe he is good? Do you really believe he is just? Do you really believe he cares about the minutiae of your daily life? Do you really believe he has your well-being in mind? Do you really believe he can do the things he says he will do? Do you really believe he *wants* to do the things he says he will do? Do you really believe he is loving? That he *is* love? That not only is he love but also that he loves *you* specifically? That he is forgiving? That he forgives *you*—especially you—for the terrible things *you* have done?

Or perhaps you tell yourself and your fellows that you believe these things, but if someone were to shine the light within the deepest, darkest, dankest recesses of your heart of hearts, maybe you would find out that you do not. Maybe your lips say you trust him, but your heart says otherwise. Maybe your head pretends to believe in something that your soul rejects in reality. Because, you see, your faith in God's *existence* actually does very little. Plenty of people believe in God and continue to live dead lives. Why? Because it's your faith in *what* God is *like* and *who* God *is* that has any real bearing on that which brings life or changes life. It's what you believe *about* God that has any meaning. In other words, our *perceptions* of God are everything.

Now, I do not wish to repeat myself, but by way of a recap: we have already established that humanity changes. Of course, humanity changes. After all, we are not still living in caves, right? We have also already established that since its inception, Christianity has changed, and will continue to change and evolve as humanity changes and evolves. If this is so, then the most relevant question we can ask is also the first question we *must* ask, and the question is this: do our perceptions of God change as well?

The answer is yes! Shall we prove it? Let's monitor the changes in humanity's perception in God, beginning with three pre-Christian examples:

1. Prehistoric humans believed God was responsible for earthquakes and thunderstorms and any kind of disruption to their world that they could not explain. But *we* now know that was just the Earth doing its geological thing. We have access to scientific knowledge they did not. Therefore, while we would view their perceptions of God as painfully primitive, they would view their perceptions as normal because to them and their time these perceptions *were* normal.

2. Some ancient civilizations, like the ones in pre-Columbian America, believed God was a bloodthirsty God, that he desired the sacrifice of virgins. But *we* now know, through God's revelation of himself, that God does not desire violence as an act of worship, that all the violence (if you want to look at it that way) needed to satisfy God took place when Jesus died on the cross. However, to the peoples of that time, their perceptions were normal.

3. Many ancients believed that God, or gods, resided in statues of stone called idols. They believed the likeness of the idol captured the essence of God, or the god in question, and that placing these idols about one's abode, praying to these idols, and sacrificing to these idols would prompt the corresponding God or gods to interact favorably with the humans who worshipped them. But *we* now know that there is only *one* God and that he does not reside in the hand-fashioned objects of stone. We know he resides everywhere at once.

Why did these perceptions change? Because people changed. They grew, and as they grew, they *outgrew* erroneous perceptions about God (and not only about God, but about the world, the Universe, reality, etc.). Whenever humanity reaches a new stage in its development, perceptions of who God is and what God is like always end up developing alongside, bringing the perceptions of God in step with knowledge humans have attained at that time. This means that as the human race evolves culturally, socially, scientifically, technologically, cosmologically, and even spiritually. So, too, does humanity's perception of God evolve to match those advancements. Why shouldn't this be the case? It makes perfect sense.

What about the *Christian* perception of God? Has the Christian view of God changed in the last 2,000 years? Consider these three examples:

1. The Gnostic Christians of the second century did not even believe God created the Earth. They believed an intermediary entity called Demiurge did. They also believed in dualism, that the forces of evil in the world were equal in power and divinity to God. Mainstream Christianity has rejected these ideas, preferring to adhere to the *New Testament*'s version of God as the Creator of the Universe (including the Earth) and as the Supreme Being in that Universe, with the forces of evil not only unequal in power (lesser) but also conquered and subdued by the work of Jesus.

2. The medieval Christians believed God was an old bearded man in the sky, much like Zeus, angry and irritable, ready to pounce on the first sign of wrongdoing, but *we* now know that was just a concept their medieval minds had created based on their own cultural evolution and wherewithal and the erroneous version of God imparted to them through the teachings of the priests and the passing down of old conceptions and customs. The medieval Christians also believed that God was honored by the proceedings of the Inquisition, that punishment and purification through torture or even hideous execution brought not only glory but also a smile to God. This is frightening notion when you think about it. It's one thing to burn someone at the stake, as bad as that is, but it's quite another thing altogether to imagine that this delights God.

3. The Christians of the Crusades, the Christians of African slavery, and the Christians of segregation and racial persecution all saw God as being *on their side* or *of their same opinion*. Their perception of God was filtered not through what God had revealed about himself but rather through what they wanted to see. They called on the name of the same Jesus you call on and attached his name to their position, their agenda, and their view. *We* know their perception of God was mistaken, but these men and women operated under the banner of the same Chris-

tianity you operate under. The passage of time showed the Crusades to be largely political and based on greed. The passage of time showed slavery to be ungodly and appalling. The passage of time showed segregation to be unjust and archaic. The passage of time showed racial hatred to be contrary to the *Bible*'s command that we should love each other. Nevertheless, at the time these things were being done, the humans doing them believed God was right there with them, grinning, with thumbs up. But we grew. We evolved. And these perceptions (though they still live on in some parts of the world) crumbled.

There are more examples we could review together. Many, many more. What can we conclude from this? Even Christians, who are famous for assuming their ideas about God are as constant as God himself, are not immune to shifts in perception. Some humans are Christians, but all Christians are human. And no human, believer or unbeliever, is immune to a changing world and the alteration in perceptions that change always brings.

Here's a thought: if you were to pluck out of history the medieval men or women we just discussed and ask them what they believed *about* God, what they believed about *who* God is, and what they believed about what God *is like*, their answers would undoubtedly seem outdated to us, but to them they would be perfectly understandable, perfectly balanced, perfectly expressed, and perfectly contemporary. Why? Because the medieval man could not have imagined or fathomed the changes humanity would undergo in the next 700 years. Wherever they were in their evolution, their perception of God was filtered through that position. You see, our perceptions of God at any given point in history are a product of 1) his revelation of himself to us; *and* 2) the evolution of our capacities for understanding him or his revelations at that time.

Whatever they thought 700 years ago, that is where *they* were. So the question, then, is this: where are *we?* Do *we* know *all* we need to know? Will people 700 years from now look back on us and view some of the things we thought about God as being bizarre? Will they reflect on our perceptions and say to themselves, "Those people believed crazy things," just as we say when we reflect on what the ancients thought about God? This is an interesting question because it implies that we, us, now, in this great age of information and knowledge, might still be believing things about God that are just as false as some of the things humans believed hundreds of years ago.

Let's think about that for a moment. Just what is the state of our current perceptions of God? The question is vital because the truth of the matter is this: even now, knowing all we know, not all believers alive today view God the same way.

Suppose you assembled a hundred believers in one room, representing the many different denominations and expressions of contemporary Christianity. If you could search the innermost hearts of each person, would you see identical perceptions of God dwelling within them? Better yet, suppose you assembled a hundred believers all from one particular group like, say, the Presbyterians. To make it even more interesting, let's say these one hundred Presbyterians are all pastors and ministers, trained in Christian theology, steeped in Presbyterian thought. Would you still see identical perceptions of God dwelling deep within them? Or would each person's perception, although completely bathed in and filtered through the *same* scriptures, the *same* church teaching, and the *same* denominational doctrines, be unique to each person?

We all know the answer even if not all among us will admit it: we each see God a little differently. Why is this? After all, God is who he is whether we see him or not and regardless of how we see him. He exists as he is apart from our perceptions, right?[1] So, why, then do humans from all walks of life with access to the same *Bible* containing the same revelations tend to perceive God differently?

Let's look at it this way: when you say or hear or see the word *God*, what images are brought to mind? What stigmas? What baggage? What associations? What false notions? What polluted opinions? What subtle errors? These, too, are important questions because everyone sees God not fully through God's own revelation of himself but also through his own filters. What you—you specifically—believe about who God is and what God is like could quite possibly be affected and filtered or even tainted through whom you saw your parents as, what you were taught as a child, what your experiences on this planet have been like, what nation you grew up in, if you were loved or abused, and any number of other cultural and environmental factors.

This is why we could have a hundred Presbyterians, or Catholics, or Baptists, or whatever group you want to insert in there, and still have a hundred different perceptions of who God is. The voiced facts may not change. If asked, they will probably give the standard answers about what they are *supposed* to believe about God. However, a deep probe of the hearts of each person would undoubtedly reveal a veritable tapestry of differing perceptions.

It is a firm fact: God does not change, but *how we see* him *does*. It just does. God knows this. He understands it. He expects it. I suspect also that he waits for humanity to evolve so he can show us more of himself, more of who he really is.

Therefore, what we have here is an interesting dichotomy. On the one hand, we have God, who does not change and who has revealed himself to humanity. The revelation itself is immovable (though unfinished). On the other hand, we have humans,

---

1 I call this Perception Separation, which we will get to in a moment.

who do change, and who may or may not be interpreting that revelation of God differently. Our perceptions of the revelation are therefore not immovable.

In a dichotomy like this, should God conform to that which humans believe about him, or should humans aspire to deepen their knowledge of what God is really like? I suspect you know the correct answer.

Now, you might be wondering what I meant when I said that God's revelation is unfinished. You may even have bristled when you read that. Let me explain how it actually makes perfect sense that God's revelation to humanity is unfinished by sharing with you a term I conceived to communicate this very notion.

> [*Perpetually Incomplete Revelation*] – the idea that since God is infinite, he can *never* be finitely known; therefore, his revelation of himself to humanity is, by definition, unfinished.

In other words, God's revelation of himself to us can never be *complete*. Even if we accept that God has chosen to say no more, to reveal nothing further of himself to humanity (and *post/Christian* thought does *not* accept this), the window of sight we have regarding God is woefully incomplete. It has to be because, as I have said twice in this section already, that which is infinite cannot be finitely ascertained. It would not make any sense if we assumed that God has no more of himself to show to humanity. If that were the case, God would have to be as finite as we are. If God is infinite, then he has no end, and that which has no end could never be fully observed or comprehended. Therefore, God could never be fully revealed to humanity because the fullness of God has no end, and if God can never be fully revealed to humanity, then his revelation is incomplete and will always remain so.

The good news here, however, is that the idea of a Perpetually Incomplete Revelation suggests that humans can see *more* of him, know *more* of him, and receive furthered revelations of him as they evolve in their capacities to do so—but even then, there will still always be more to learn, more to grasp, more to discover; perpetually unto infinity.

Even if you are uncomfortable with the idea that God's revelation is *unfinished*, even if you choose to go on viewing his revelation as *complete*, surely you can still acknowledge that you yourself have not yet thoroughly exhausted the fullness of that revelation. Surely, you can admit that even if you lived to be 120 years old, you could still never reach a place in your theological or spiritual consciousness where you know everything there is to know about God. The revelation is incomplete no matter which way you look at it: either the revelation is itself fundamentally incomplete, or it is incomplete in your own life and will forever remain incomplete in your own life. Regardless of which approach you choose, the result is the same. God's revelation is everlastingly incomplete and forever unfinished. It has to be. Why? Because if you knew everything there is to know about God then you yourself would be God.

Are you God?

Then you still have more to learn, as do I.

New Perceptions

Imagine you were able to stand in God's presence and see him as he is. Imagine also that he offered you a chance to ask any question and as many questions as you wanted. Now, imagine that one of the questions you asked was this: "God, is there more of you to know, more of you to see, and more of you to understand than I currently have access to?" Do you honestly think God would say no?

Or to reverse it, imagine your question to him was this: "God, do I know everything about you that I need to know? Are my perceptions of you completely correct?" Do you honestly think God would say yes?

The answer should be obvious. You are finite. God is infinite. You have an end. God has no end. You have a limit to what you can understand. God is the very definition of limitlessness. You exist in time and space. God exists in eternity. To assume, therefore, that a human being could ever have the final word on what God is: the soul of absurdity. We might as well entertain the fantastic notion that a cat can fully understand the human anatomy or that a snail can tackle trigonometry.

The real problem here is human arrogance. Humans may no longer believe that the Earth is at the center of the cosmos, but we still think *we* are. We are convinced that if extraterrestrials visit our planet, they come seeking us. We view the Earth as existing for our benefit rather than the other way around. It pleases us to take stock of all we have built and achieved and pat ourselves on the back for being masters of the Universe. And when it comes to God, we love to quantify him with cleverly worded, logically attractive theological explanations and then congratulate ourselves for being intelligent enough to map out the fullness of an endless God. This is such a shame because perhaps the second biggest mistake humanity ever made concerning God (the first being our decision to embrace sin) occurred the moment we deceived ourselves by thinking we could express the infinite with a finite equation.

To seek the *post/Christian* God, then, is to do so without this arrogance. To seek the *post/Christian* God is to come to him with a clean slate, an empty canvas upon which he can paint whatever *he* likes instead of us painting whatever *we* like. To pursue the *post/Christian* God is to assess these matters, question our perceptions, and view God afresh. That's it. That is all it means. The term *post/Christian God* is simply a *conversational tool*, designed not to change a God who does not change and cannot be changed but to change *us* (our minds and our attitudes). Perhaps now you see that the term *post/Christian God* is not sacrilegious at all.

Besides, is this not the essence of theology?
Theo = God
ology = the study of

A *post/Christian* perspective of God is just a form a theology, a form of studying God, a progressive approach designed to spur *us* toward new, unencumbered perceptions. And we *need* new perceptions.

Why do we need new perceptions? Because of the existence of what I call Perception Separation.

> [*Perception Separation*] – an awareness that God exists above and
> beyond our perceptions of him, or *separate* from our experiences with
> him.

God's revelation of himself to us, though perpetually incomplete, is nevertheless *perfect* (nothing imperfect issues from God); but human reaction, interpretation, and application of that revelation is and must be as imperfect as the humans themselves are. Therefore, the idea of Perception Separation states that God exists above our belief systems about him, even the Christian ones; that God is not limited to acting and performing in a manner that concurs with what *we* perceive or know about him, or what *we* expect from him. God cannot violate himself, no; but he *can* violate what we know about him because it's possible for what we know to be incorrect.

This means that not only should we have the *desire* to pursue new, evolved perceptions that reflect an ever-increasing accuracy regarding God's true nature, but we also have an *obligation* to do so. Perception Separation implies that the gap between who God really is and how we see him is not a fixed gap. It can be shortened. We can close the distance, little by little (though never to completion), and if we have the ability to do that, we also have the responsibility to make sure we do it. It is therefore our *duty* to seek the truest, most accurate picture of him we can possibly attain at our given stage of evolution. *That* is why we need new perceptions. The development of the human race is counting on it.

Another reason we need new perceptions is that we must assume that God *wants* us to gain more knowledge of him. If God wants something, it must be something worth having for both him and us. According to this logic, we need new perceptions because God himself would have us know more of him when we are ready to do so. I call this Requisite Desire.

> [*Requisite Desire*] – the idea that to be God is to *want* to be known.

In other words, God, by definition, must be a being filled with infinite *wisdom*, *goodness*, and *love*. Consequently, wisdom that does not ache to be imparted is a useless wisdom. Goodness that does not seek to be shared and felt by another is a useless goodness. Moreover, love that does not vehemently crave expression is not true love at all. To be God, then, is to nurture a requisite desire (or, a desire which cannot

not be present) to be known. His revelation may be perpetually incomplete, but we must assume that God wants to move us forward toward a greater grasp of that revelation, or a furthered understanding of it, or, dare I say, a *new stage* in the revelation.

Therefore, we must also assume that this is why God created humans with the same requisite desire within them—that we would have a longing within us to know God that corresponds to the longing within God to be known. If to be God is to want to be known, then to be human is to want to know God.

If you still wonder whether humanity needs new perceptions of God, put this book down, and look out your window. Turn on the television, and watch the news. Look at our species. Observe the world and what it's doing. Take stock of what is happening all around us. Humanity *is* changing. The world *is* changing. Christianity *is* changing. Believers *are* changing. Who we were in the 1950s was nothing like who we were in the 850s or the 1550s. Who we are becoming *now* is nothing like what we were in the 1950s. What we can *do* now is like nothing before. We can now look across the great gulf of space and see stars and clouds of gas on the other side of the Universe. The men and women who study these wonders can tell us all kinds of things about what elements make up these stars, how much they weigh, the speed at which they are moving, and so on. Is it really such a radical idea that we as believers should want to update our perception of the God who made these wonders? Is it really so hard to understand that just as scientists can, with each new discovery, reinvent what we know about the Universe, we as believers need to see ever more clearly the God we believe is responsible for all of this? Don't you want to grasp God better? Don't you want to see more of him, know more of him, and understand more of him? If your capacity as a human evolved to allow for *more* of God, wouldn't you want more?

I would. And I do. That is why I have been asking the following questions and pondering the possible answers:

1. Though God does not change, does he *alter* the *way he interacts* with humans at any given time to correspond with their level of development? In other words, does God show a little more and a little more and a little more as humanity evolves enough to see more and know more?

2. Does God *wait* to reveal anything? Does he hold back to allow us to catch up to him?

3. Does God allow the revelation of himself to be understood differently by humans living in different times? In other words, is God's revelation of himself so infinite and manifold that it can be seen differently and interpreted differently at progressing stages of human development without losing its truth and purity? The revelation is immovable,

but is it as infinite as the God who authored it? Can we see the same revelation in different ways at different times?

4. Is it even fathomable that God may have more to say and more to reveal than has yet been said or revealed?
5. Has God been waiting for us to ask these questions?

As I think about these things, I know that there are those who would respond to some of these questions with a reprimand, especially question #4. They will say, "Shame on you! God has already said all he needs to say in the *Bible*."

My response is this: how can you, a mere human, ever know with complete totality what God will do or what God wants to do? Who are you to put limits on God? Who are you to speak for God? Who are you to decide for God? Who are you to presume to fully know the mind of God? I would be very careful about declaring with authority matters that belong to God.

Now, having said that, let me say this: I do believe in God's revelation to us. It's just that I wonder if God has more to say. Not only that, but I am also simply wondering if it is okay to wonder.

This I pray: *God, just hearing the word* God *brings all kinds of images and thoughts and perceptions to mind. I ask that you would rid my mind of the ones that do not truly reflect the real you. I continue to seek the truth, and I continue to seek you. I will never stop craving to know you in the deepest, truest way possible. So be it.*

Here is a worthy endeavor: re-read the *New Testament* with these aims in mind:

1. What does God say about himself?
2. What do I really believe about God?
3. Are my truest beliefs and perceptions about God really reflected in the *New Testament* or were they derived elsewhere?
4. What, if anything, have I been believing about God that is outdated, completely erroneous (filtered through my own interpretations), or inadequate?

Take notes. Journal your discoveries. Ponder these matters. As you do all of this, ask God to open your eyes, to speak to you, to change your mind about him, if indeed it needs to be changed. Tell him you want to know who he really is. There is only one God, of course, and as we have noted many times already, this one and only God does not change. But perhaps *you* need to change. Perhaps your mind does. You will never know if you never evaluate what you believe. You will never have an answer if you never ask. It is surprising what God will reveal to those who have a genuine heart to know the truth and who ask with faith. I have seen it in my own life.

Michael Vito Tosto

I have seen God change even though he does not change. In truth, I was the one who was changing. I have grown. I have pushed through to new levels of discovery and understanding. I have struggled and wrestled and grappled with God over a period of almost three decades (I asked my first theological question when I was 7 years old), constantly pressing the issue of who God really is and what he is really like. I have widened my scope of theological consciousness, always asking questions, always seeking answers, always retracing my steps, always pondering how far I have traveled and what I have learned along the way. In some ways, the evolution of my perceptions corresponded with each new stage of gradual maturity in my walk with God. In other ways, they were the products of spectacular breakthroughs and life-changing epiphanies that came out of nowhere and thrust me almost violently into a whole new world. In any case, I had to be willing to allow this change to happen. I had to be willing to let go of comforting notions of God if it turned out those notions were erroneous. I had to be willing to grab on to those new perceptions that perhaps didn't go down as comfortably as the ones I was relinquishing. I guess what I am talking about are growing pains. Sometimes it hurts to evolve. Sometimes we do not want to give up the things we believe about God. But remember this: God is who he is regardless of what you believe about him. Whatever he is, he has been that way for eons before you were born and will go on that way for eons after you die, even unto eternity. God knows much more about God than you do. If he brings you to a new revelation, I would listen. I would follow. I would let go of that which you are clinging to and take hold of that which he is offering. Why not? Why bother believing in God if you do not want to know him as he truly is?

That is what *post/Christian* thought is all about. It's not evil. It's not satanic. It's not rebellious. It's not sacrilegious or blasphemous. It's just a term, a tool for us to use. It's just a mindset that endeavors to push further into the mysteries of God than we have yet. Is this really so shocking? It doesn't have to be.

PART TWO: Joshuanism

I was sitting in my cubicle, pretending to be busy about my work (this was back in the day when I had a real job, when writing books for a living was just a pipe dream). What I was really doing, though, was surfing the Internet, checking out a new guitar I wanted to buy. As I was reading about it, I heard the ding of the interoffice email alert, so I minimized the web browser and opened up the new message that had been instantly sent to every person in the building. It was an email about a former coworker, a girl who had recently quit. In fact, she had come around the office to say goodbye just a few days before. The reason she quit had been big news. She was a singer and had landed some big record deal, the chance of a lifetime. She was moving to Nashville to start a new life and begin her dream job. Now, here I was in my cubicle, reading a tragic email just a few days after she had left. Apparently, she never made it to Nashville. The email was informing all her former coworkers that she had been in a car accident en route to her new destination. She had not died, but her legs had been severed from her body.

As I read the email, stunned by its news, I heard Theresa in the next cubicle. She had evidently clicked on the email at the same time I did. She gasped and said, "Oh, Jesus!"

Now, I knew Theresa. I knew her well. I was very aware that she was not a believer, that not only did she consciously reject Jesus, but that she frequently ridiculed those who did believe. So, as I sat there, my thoughts wandered away from the girl with the severed legs and settled on Theresa. I began to wonder why this woman, who did not have Jesus in her, who did not have any regard for him whatsoever, had called out his name in a moment of tragedy.

That was almost ten years ago. Just a few days ago, I was walking down the sidewalk toward my apartment when a man getting out of his car a few feet away accidently shut the door on his fingers. He let out a sharp cry of pain and then, with what seemed like a lifetime worth of anger and disappointment exploding outward from the depths of his being, he hissed these words we have all heard a million times: "Jesus *(expletive)* Christ!"

Michael Vito Tosto

Jesus Christ

What exactly is it with this name, anyway? It's everywhere. Have you ever really stopped to notice that? *Jesus*. How many millions of people, at this very moment, all over the world, are praying in that name? How many millions of people, at this very moment, all over the world, are cursing that name, or cursing *with* that name? How many times in a day is the name of Jesus printed on a sign, on a T-shirt, on a bracelet, on a billboard, on a bumper sticker, or on a pamphlet? How many people are doing their good deeds today in the name of Jesus? How many people are doing their evil, vile deeds today in the name of Jesus (mistakenly thinking that he supports whatever sick cause they have)? How many people are politicizing the name of Jesus today? How many people, at this very moment, are laughing at that name and at those who believe in it?

Are the names of other religious and spiritual leaders treated this way? I see the names of the Buddha and Krishna from time to time. I occasionally see something about Moses in culture. Because of the Islamic tendency to threaten any use of his name or his image, we almost never see or hear anything about Mohammad. When we do, the instance is usually surrounded by controversy. As a result, the name Mohammad is perhaps the closest in comparison to the storms that surround the name of Jesus. Nonetheless, the name of Jesus stands alone as being the most famous, the most infamous, the most controversial, the most incendiary, the most confrontational, the most cursed, the most hated, the most loved, the most challenging, and the most historically significant name that has ever been known, uttered, written, and invoked in the history of all humanity. There has never been a *name* like it.

It's fitting, too, when you think about it. There has never been another *person* to have claimed (and been able to back it up) that he was God incarnate. While the other religious, spiritual, and philosophical leaders, such as the Buddha or Confucius, lived and died doing all they could with the best of intentions to try to *find* the way, *preach* the way, and *show* the way, Jesus was the only person to ever say that he *was* the way. We can point to no other time in history when God invaded humanity by becoming *one of them*. Only one person has ever made that claim. Only one has ever been able to validate that claim with miracles—miracles witnessed by multitudes and well documented by the apostles. Only one has ever died a death that belonged not to him but to every other single human being that has ever lived or will ever live. Although he is not the only human to experience a resurrection (the *New Testament* tells us that Jesus raised Lazarus from the dead and that, at the time of the crucifixion, many dead people came back to life), Jesus was the only human to experience the new, resurrected body. Only one human has ever claimed to be the linking pathway between God and the humans separated from him. Is it not strange,

Joshuanism

then, that this same, exclusive, extraordinary human is also the owner of the most noteworthy name in all history?

Well, maybe it's not so strange after all. It rather makes sense. Jesus, his name, and his message have all changed the world—in good ways and bad ways.

The last two millennia have been filled with all kinds of tremendous good done in the name of Jesus. Consider these examples:

1. A message of love and forgiveness has been preached in all locations where the name of Jesus is carried by those who bring it with true faithfulness and authenticity.

2. Hospitals have been created, orphanages established, charities erected, ministries founded, and churches built in the name of Jesus. Through these various organizations, millions of lives have been positively changed over the centuries.

3. Broken homes, broken families, and broken people have found healing, redemption, forgiveness, restoration, and radical transformation through the name of Jesus.

4. Every day millions of prayers are offered up to God from the lips of the faithful in the name of Jesus: prayers for peace, prayers for the safety of others, prayers for the will of God to be done on Earth, prayers for the comfort of those who hurt, prayers for the salvation of the unbelievers. If we maintain God listens to prayers and answers them when he sees fit to do so (which believers do maintain), then this massive, prayerful activity can only be viewed as a tremendous accomplishment for the purposes of goodwill and love.

But sadly, there has also been much, much evil done in the name of Jesus. Such as:

1. The bloody Crusades were fought in the name of Jesus, and thousands were slaughtered on his behalf. In fact, it was considered a well-known truth that the more "infidels" a Christian knight killed, the greater his reward in heaven would be.

2. The Inquisition (a religious tool of torture, terror, and control which operated under the name of Jesus) was implemented by "believing Christians," who opened and closed the proceedings of the Inquisition with prayers in the name of Jesus. No one can even put a figure on how many were killed as a result of this great evil.

3. The Aztecs and the Incas were violently wiped out by Christian warriors whose political and empirical endeavors to gain lands in the New

World were "justified" under the false banner of bringing the message of Jesus to the heathens. Think about that. Entire nations obliterated in the name of the one who actually came to save them. Genocide in the name of Jesus! It is unfathomable.

4. Throughout Christian history, Jews have been made the scapegoats of all kinds of social, political, or religious upheaval. Christians (who often forget that their Savior was a Jew and that he commanded them to love even their enemies) have amassed quite a record, spanning several centuries, of persecuting and brutalizing the Jews.

5. In our own time, many use the name of Jesus to attack that which they cannot understand, that which they fear, or that with which they disagree. Examples? A teenage daughter becomes pregnant and is thrown out of the house because her parents cannot bear the shame brought to their "believing" household. Perhaps she gets an abortion and her parents, who forget that love and forgiveness cover a multitude of sin (including their own), cut her off in the name of Jesus. Families are torn apart. Churches split over disagreements, and each opposing faction believes Jesus is on their side. A gay man is murdered by those who believe Jesus has told them to do so. When asked about it, they tell the world this, and the media spreads the message. The result is that people attach the name of Jesus not to love but to hate. People use the name of Jesus to divide the world into the "saved" and the "lost," using his name like a tool of judgment—a judgment that Jesus himself said belongs to God alone.

These are just a few cases. The point is that while no one should be ashamed of the Son of God, we should all be quite saddened by how his name is used in the world, how his message has been distorted and destroyed. We should all be quite aware that while the name of Jesus has been an agent of soothing mercy and peaceful kindness to some, for others it has been an agent of terror, hatred, and destruction.

Therefore, just as we discussed the need to begin reassessing what we know and believe about God, so, too, should we be begin to reassess how we see Jesus. Perhaps it's time to enter into new conversations about our Savior. Perhaps it's time to ask new questions. What can we learn about our Savior if we start looking at him from a new perspective? Not a perspective that violates or denies who is presented as God's Son in the *New Testament*, but merely a perspective that stimulates *us* toward greater change, not *him* (since he doesn't change).

Is such a new perspective even possible? I believe that the answer is yes.

Joshua of Nazareth

Here is an interesting exercise. I am going to give you a word. As soon as you read it, become a spectator of your own thoughts. Watch what images come to mind. Observe the many memories and associations that are immediately rushed to the front of your inner world. Ready?

Sex.

It probably didn't take long for you to conjure up from within your psyche a wealth of memories, stigmas, images, nuances, innuendos, and either good or bad connotations. Why did I choose this word? Because it's a *loaded* word. A charged word. A word that is so powerful in the English language that it can barely escape someone's lips or be seen with the eyes as the three letters, s, e, and x, without these attendant trappings instantly following suit. For some people, the word brings pleasant associations: memories of love and ecstasy perhaps, or possibly images that are gratifying to the mind. For other people, the word brings shame and guilt. Perhaps they suffered rape or some other kind of abuse. Perhaps they struggle with sexual sins. We could spend a whole book exploring the world of implications that flood the mind at exposure to this single word. There is no way to ever reach a place mentally where the word *sex* fails to have this kind of power. You will never hear or read the word *sex* and be able to separate it from the instant baggage that the word brings to your mind. Never. Some words are like that.

Now, I am going to give you another word. Do the same thing you did before. Be a spectator of your own thoughts. Watch and listen for what instantly comes to mind. Ready?

Nek.

Now, unless you are some erudite academic, you probably didn't even recognize that word. I feel safe in assuming that most of my readers did not. Because you did not recognize it, because you read the word and heard it within your own mind but had no definition to immediately attach to it, the kind of baggage that came with the word *sex* most likely did not come with the word *nek*. You might have been tempted to equate it with the English word *neck*, but because your mind recognized the spelling as being different, it knew instantly that it was not the same word. If there was no definition the mind could attach to the word, the word was left void of any images or associations. Thus, it was emptied of all the implications that came with the word *sex*.

What does *nek* mean? It's the ancient Egyptian word for *sex*. In fact, the word *nek* is still used in Egypt today.

So, what we have here are two words that point to the same action, two words that share one definition, two words that imply one action: sexual intercourse. If for some bizarre reason we decided to begin using *nek* in the English language, a

49

change in terminology would do absolutely nothing to alter the action the word points to, right? Intercourse would still involve everything it does now, regardless of whether we called it *sex* or *nek*. Intercourse itself would not change. Intercourse *cannot* change. It will always be the insertion of one organism's genitalia into another's (forgive the crudeness here, but we must make this point). If we started calling intercourse *nek*, what *would* change? Our perceptions! The baggage! We would suddenly have a word on our hands that means the same thing as the word *sex* but comes to us without any of the history associated with the word *sex*. The new word is therefore virginal, at least for a while (because if you give humanity enough time, all things virginal will eventually be sullied).

Now, does the word *nek* do for the minds of those who speak Egyptian the same thing the word *sex* does for those who speak English? Definitely. But it's English we are interested in for this discussion. If this book is ever translated into Egyptian, the scenario would be inverted. However, for us English speakers, the point should now be thoroughly driven home. While one word is a charged word to us, the other word is empty. Even now, after you have been told what *nek* means, the word is still empty. You now know rationally that the word means sexual intercourse, but the three-letter word itself is still powerless in your mind. You have no history to associate with it. It's fresh, unblemished, and free of all the things that weigh the word *sex* down.

You know what else is a charged word? *Jesus.*

As soon as you hear it, your mind is inundated with clutter. An immediate image is formed. Instant connotations surface. It's to the point now where these images and connotations are involuntary. The word *Jesus* triggers them before you even have a chance to stop them. You cannot escape them any more than you can escape the instant implications that come with the word *sex*. Whether you know it or not, some of these images and connotations are faulty. Some are damaging. Some are so far from the truth of who Jesus really was that they have you thinking and believing things that in no way help you. In fact, they damage you. They keep you from even suspecting that something might be wrong. You could have an entirely erroneous image of the Son of God and never even know it because your mind brings that image to attention so quickly you automatically assume it is a true, accurate image.

But what if that image wasn't true? If it wasn't, would you want to know about it? I can't speak for you, but I certainly would want to know about it. Is there something like *nek*, something we can use to free our minds of those images the name *Jesus* brings in the same way *nek* frees our minds of all that the word *sex* brings?

There is. It seems that few people these days ever stop to remember that Jesus Christ's real name during his time on Earth was Joshua, which in ancient Hebrew was *Yĕhōšuă'* (יְהוֹשֻׁעַ). It was only after both his message and the story of him that the apostles spread outward from Judea and Galilee in the decades after he lived that the Greek version of Joshua's name began to replace the Hebrew name in widespread usage. Hence, Joshua ended up being known as Jesus, which is derived from the Latin name, *Iesus*, itself a version of the Greek name, *Iēsoûs* (Ἰησοῦς), which, in turn, is a version of the Hebrew name, *Yĕhōšuă'* (Joshua).

Joshua = Jesus, in Greek

Jesus = Joshua, in Hebrew

The point here? Well, when you want to get your mental or emotional arms around something, don't you, organically, go to the root? Don't you trace the thing back to its beginning and look at it from that perspective? Don't you try to strip away what you have added to it (through years of false associations and the faulty nature of human filtering) and try to see it unblemished by the hands of time? Don't you want to know as much as you can about its original context?

I do. I think it's imperative. If Jesus was who he said he was, if he is who he says he is, and if I want to know him like I say I do, then wouldn't it be the most logical thing in the world that I should try to see him, to view him, to know him, to understand him, to seek him, and to discover him in the most genuine way possible? After all, is it really so unmanageable to believe that many people are believing in a "false Jesus" who has been shaped and fashioned after their own image, through their own preferences, in their own perceptions—a *version* of him that either obscures much of his true nature or fails to reflect in any way anything resembling what Jesus was and is and will forever be? Personally, knowing what I know about humans and our tendencies to view God as having been made in our image rather than viewing us as having been made in his, I think it's very possible.

This is why I have been making a concerted effort to begin looking at my Savior (the same one you call on) by his other, more organic name. Not his Greek name, but his Hebrew name. I look at him as Joshua. I pray to him as Joshua. I speak of him as Joshua. I worship him as Joshua. I think about him as Joshua.

Joshua of Nazareth. Joshua the Messiah. Joshua the carpenter, son of Mary and Joseph, from Galilee. Joshua, the Hebrew who lived in the first century, who spoke Aramaic, who was a subject of Roman rule. Joshua, who happened to be the Son of God, God in the flesh, God incarnate, the sinless one, the anointed one, the Son of Man, the God/man and man/God. Joshua, whose great story would conclude with his death on a cross and an empty tomb.

Joshua. The same person you call on as Jesus Christ.

Now, by doing this I am not changing the *message* of Jesus. I am not invalidating his ministry, his work at the cross, his miraculous return from the dead, or any of the wonders that all of these things purchased for us (such as forgiveness, sanctification, justification, redemption, reconciliation, and anything else you can think of). I am not *lessening* him, *augmenting* him, *altering* him, or in some sly way *rejecting* him. I still believe God entered the world in the person of his Son in the first century. I still believe that Son lived a perfect life. I still believe that same Son died on the cross. I still believe that same Son rose from the dead. I still believe that same Son ascended to heaven and sits at the right hand of God. I still believe that same Son is the way, the truth, and the life, and that no man comes to Father without first going through the Son by faith through grace. I still believe that same Son will return to Earth to judge the living and the dead. I still believe all the things I'm supposed to believe *about* that Son, and I still believe *in* that Son.

I just do it all through his Hebrew name, not his Greek name. Is this really such a big deal? When you talk to God, do you always call him *God?* Don't you also sometimes call him Lord, or Father, or even Yahweh? Just because you address him in different ways does not mean you are addressing multiple gods. You are still addressing the one God you believe in. It is the exact same thing to address God's Son as Joshua instead of Jesus. Two names, one Savior. There is nothing blasphemous or irreverent in this endeavor. It's merely a tool to open the mind and the heart to something new.

Am I *ashamed* of the name "Jesus," you might ask? I am not ashamed of the *owner* of the name. I am not ashamed of the *power* of the name. I am not ashamed of the *message* behind the name. I am not ashamed of anything, really. I just see the health and the awesome potential for new expressions and perceptions that looking at God's Son in a *fresh way* implies. I see the benefit in viewing the Son of God in an *organic* way, stripped of all the stigmas and all the baggage the name "Jesus" carries with it. (I am saying the *name* carries stigmas, not the *owner* of the name.)

Therefore, by shifting my perception of the Son of God away from Jesus Christ and toward Joshua, I accomplish these things:

1. I eliminate needless, harmful, encumbering, and distracting associations that both the world and my own mind conjure up at the thought of the name *Jesus*. This allows me to see my Savior with a fresh perspective and present his message to the world free of baggage.

2. I open my mind to new perceptions about my Savior, things that perhaps I would have remained blinded to had I continued carrying the stigmas that accompany the name *Jesus*.

3. I can see an organic version of my Savior—perhaps even the most accurate version I have yet seen—because the old filters attached to the name *Jesus* are now removed.

4. I find new expressions of devotion to my Savior, revitalizing my energy and excitement toward worshipping him because I am closer to seeing him as he really is (because anytime anything is freed from the encumbrances that surround it, a clearer vision is available).

Now, perhaps many people will not see the benefit in these things. Perhaps some people may think I am playing too loosely with the "Name above all names."

However, isn't the *power* of the name really found in the *owner* of the name? For instance, I saw a Major League baseball player from Latin America on TV recently. His first name was Jesus, pronounced in the Latin fashion (which, to me, sounds like a sneeze). Is that guy imbued with some special power—a power I lack—because his name is Jesus? Of course not. Without the Savior, the name is just a word. In the Latin world, thousands of men are named Jesus. And think about this: how many millions of men in the world are named Christian? For that matter, how many millions of men in the world are named Joshua? Are these people special in a manner that you and I are not? No. Therefore, the "Name above all names" only has meaning when it's the *Son of God* in question. And as we have already noted, the Son of God's name was Joshua before it was Jesus.

Looking For Joshua

If you are a Christian, then I assume you pray *to* the Son of God or *through* the Son of God on a daily basis. If you are really passionate about your faith, perhaps you pray in this manner many times a day or all day. One would also assume that you live your life as the Son of God taught you to do and in a manner befitting someone who professes to have life-changing, saving faith in him. If you are a Christian, you probably read your *Bible* somewhat regularly; perhaps you even study it thoroughly. You probably go to church and are happy to do so. Maybe you are involved in your church, serving when and where you can, participating in its activities, functions, outreaches, etc. If you are a Christian, you most likely travel in Christian circles, having mostly Christian friends, doing mostly Christian things. You probably listen to Christian music, read Christian books, and avoid forms of entertainment that would elicit temptation. You probably seize opportunities to preach to friends or family members who *aren't* Christians, hoping to win them over to the message of God. Perhaps you do this with gentleness and patience. Perhaps you do it with a browbeating zeal (let us hope not).

So let me ask you two questions, in view of all this:

> **Question #1:** in all this Christian activity (doing all these things, saying all these things, behaving in this manner), how often do you ever stop to ask yourself exactly what you are doing, why you are doing it, and what you really, truly believe? Do you do it because it's what you were brought up to do? Do you do it because you are afraid to do otherwise? Do you do it because you have done it for so long that you know no other way of living? Or do you do it because you deeply, truly, passionately, vehemently, desperately, profoundly believe unwaveringly, steadily, firmly, and determinedly in the Son of God?

And if you do...

Question #2: what exactly is it that you believe *about* the Son of God?

The question sounds deceptively simple, doesn't it? But it's not.

"I am a Christian!" You might say. "What do you mean 'what do I believe about the Son of God?' I know all the answers. I know all the right stuff. I have read the material. I've heard the stories. I've been around this stuff for a long time."

Well, has it ever occurred to you that "being around this stuff for a long time" can become a problem? Has it ever occurred to you that living the Christian life can easily become just another *way of life*, something that we do, or have been doing for so long, that it's just a monotonous, rote function of everyday living that is as natural for us as *not being* a Christian is for others? In other words, can you become so entrenched in your Christianity that you forget the deepest, truest aspects about your original reasons for taking up this journey with God? Can you be so immersed in Jesus that you actually end up hazing him over? Can you become so Jesus-focused that you no longer see him from the perspective of *who he really is* but rather from a perspective of *what you have brought* to the image? Seriously, think about it. What happens if you stare at a dot on the wall? Eventually it blurs out and you no longer see it. Are you entirely sure this cannot happen to you when it comes to what you believe about Jesus? Moreover, can you be entirely sure you have never once allowed something erroneous, something distortive, or something...*human*...to cloud your vision of him?

I have been considering these matters in my own life. As I have begun looking at the Son of God afresh, thinking of him as Joshua, I have been asking myself the same question I just asked you (question #2): what exactly is it that *I* believe about the Son of God?

In an effort to answer this question honestly, I decided to go back and see just exactly what the *New Testament* has to say about the Son of God. However, in doing so, I did not look for Jesus. I looked for Joshua. This is what I found:

1. Joshua was in no way concerned with whether or not humans had their act together. First of all, he knew that no one did or ever really does, anyway. Second, he seemed to go out of his way to demonstrate that morality and behavior were not at the top of his list of priorities. He did this by completely upsetting the social order. He seemed to prefer the company of the worst people around, morally speaking. The unscrupulous, unethical, unpolished dregs of society (hookers, thieves, shysters, the infamous tax collectors, even murderers) all seemed to make him feel more at home than the impeccable "churchgoers" of his day. Sure, he admonished everyone to leave their lives of sin, but he never waited for this happen before choosing to immerse himself in anyone's company. This arouses a provocative question: if Joshua were

walking about on Earth today, would you find him in the churches? Would you find him in *your* church? Or would he be out there rubbing elbows with the people to whom you as a Christian would never condescend to speak? Think about that. Here you are, doing all the right things, speaking in the right ways, going to *Bible* studies, getting your behavior in order, and yet, that toothless, homeless bum on the corner, the one who you know will buy booze the instant you give him any money; well, the Son of God would probably prefer to hang out with him rather than with you or me. After all, it's not the healthy who need a doctor but the sick.

2. Joshua never once, at any point in time, said he came to initiate a new World Religion. He never gives any indication that he has come to erect a new institution, establish a new philosophy, or construct some imposing building with a steeple, sound stage, and coffee bar. He never shows the slightest interest in having anything to do with that which was *organized*. He makes no impassioned speeches about the virtues of breaking away from Judaism and forming a splinter group that will eventually become known as Christianity. In fact, there is almost nothing *religious* about Joshua at all. Personal? Yes. Conversational? Yes. Soulful? Yes. Dynamic? Yes. Controversial? Yes. Radical? Yes. Spiritual? Yes. Sinless? You bet. But religious? No. I see nothing *religious* about his work, his words, his life, his lifestyle, his manner, his aims, his interactions, his death, or his resurrected body.

3. Because of the constant attention we fix upon the *divine* aspects of Joshua (that he was God *incarnate*, the *Son of God*, the second person of the Trinity, and so on), we tend to forget that he was very much *human*—just as human, in fact, as he was divine. A thorough reading of the *New Testament* accentuates that which we seem to have lost or forgotten. Joshua *was* fully human. He felt what we feel. He ached in the way we ache. He experienced temptation, anxiety, uncertainty, frustration, indignation, weakness, loneliness, even sorrow. He got hungry. He got thirsty. He got tired. He had moments, it seemed, where his own life was overwhelming him. He cried. He laughed. He was more like us than we can possibly fathom. Whereas "Jesus" seems to be the leader of a religion, austerely "God-like" and reverently regarded as something *other* than what *we* are, we discover in Joshua a link to the conditions that we experience everyday on this planet. Our Savior was the Son of God, yes. Nevertheless, in Joshua we remember the fullness not just of his divinity but also his *authentic humanity*.

4. Joshua appears completely uninterested whatsoever in *image*. He shows zero concern for who looks good, who looks right, who looks the part, or who appears to have everything in order. Yet, how many of us would allow our churches to be led by those who do not have the right image? Whereas we look to the appearance of the individual (and we therefore think that our Savior does, too), the real Joshua looked *past* the image and found the *heart*.

5. Unlike the religious leaders of his day, or any day for the matter, Joshua never allowed himself to be caught up in the petty disputes of humanity. He never took sides. He never championed this cause or that agenda. He never showed a preference for one group's interpretations over another group's. He never allowed the distractions of human disagreements over money, theology, policy, semantics, legalities, or personal choices to disrupt the flow of his work. In each case, whenever confronted with all the many reasons humans squabble, Joshua always brought the conversation back to that which really mattered in the end: the heart and the mind.

6. Joshua seemed to go out of his way to show disdain for the accepted spiritual boundaries. In other words, he disobeyed that which, according to the religion of his contemporaries, he was supposed to obey. One of the Ten Commandments of Judaism specifically requires children to "honor their mother and father." Joshua completely disregarded that when he slipped away from his parents and absconded to the temple as a child. Another commandment requires one to "remember the Sabbath and keep it holy," yet Joshua shows little concern for this one as well. He was always telling his disciples to do this or do that on the Sabbath. He himself healed people on the Sabbath. Joshua also spoke blasphemy, equating himself with God (although he had a right to do so, unbeknownst to his accusers). In all of these things, Joshua turned upside down the idea that any of this was ever supposed to be about the *keeping of rules*.

7. In contrast to everyone else in his day (those who took religion quite seriously and ordered their entire lives around the practice of their religion, taking great care in implementing the particulars of their religion and getting their "lives in order" by the daily application of their scriptural teachings), Joshua basically marginalized all that pious hubbub and narrowed the whole thing down to one priority: love. At one point in the story, Joshua is confronted with a question about what is the most important aspect to living a holy life, the most im-

portant aspect to pleasing God, the most important aspect in gaining salvation though spiritual endeavors. In this crucial moment, which would be recorded and therefore distributed down through the ages as a perpetual message to any and all those who would ask the same question, Joshua has a chance to insert any answer he wants. Does he begin preaching about the merits of moral living? No. Does he give an itemized list of scriptural instructions, ones that, if followed, will deliver this salvation? No. Does he talk about getting involved in the local synagogue? No. Does he say, "Clean up your act (i.e., spruce up your language, stop smoking, stop drinking, read the scriptures more, pray harder, pray longer, give up that vice, cut your hair, dress better, get with the program, write checks to your local Pharisee, etc.)?" No. The spotlight is on whatever it is that's about to come out of his mouth, and history will remember (then somehow forget) how he answers this question. So what does he say? See for yourself in *Matthew* 22. "Want to do everything you need to please God?" He says (paraphrase), "then do this: be loving. Be *about* love. Have love. Give love. Nurture love. Prize love. Acquire love as a noun and do love as a verb. Love *who*? God. Who *else*? Your neighbor and your enemies. That is everyone. That's EVERYONE!" Joshua was about love. Love. Love. Love.

How many of these things reflect what you know and believe about your Savior? Does the version of God's Son you believe in, talk about, think about, and worship remind you at all of this Joshua we have been discussing? If the Son of God returned to Earth today, would we recognize him? Would we look for "Christian" traits within him and find none? Finding none, would we reject him for failing to reflect the image of who our Savior is based on what *we* have decided that image is *supposed to be?* The Pharisees, teachers, and religious leaders of the first century (the regular "churchgoers") rejected Joshua for failing to resemble what they assumed the Messiah should look like. In other words, they rejected him because he did not look like *them*, he did not do what *they* did, he did not talk like *they* talked, he did not pray like *they* prayed, he did not keep the company *they* kept, he did not adhere to the codes *they* adhered to, and he did not care about the priorities *they* cared about. Joshua was *different* from them. Joshua was *discomforting* to them. Joshua was *revolutionary*. Joshua was socially and culturally *disturbing*. Joshua had a way of upsetting the status quo (something people in power *always* hate). Joshua had a way of exposing the hidden truths of men's hearts; the ones duplicitous people hope will stay hidden. He was always bringing the conversation back to the very thing humanity needed to hear, the very things the religious leaders wanted kept quiet; things like love, acceptance, freedom, hope, the heart, human transformation, and evolution. Not evolution from a fish to a monkey to a man but evolution from death to life. Evolution from pointlessness to purpose. Evolution from *trying to do good* to just *being good without having to try*. Evolution away from living in a manner that displease God's heart and toward existing in a manner that gladdens God's heart.

The people of Joshua's day rejected him to the point of killing him. They simply could not accept the reality of who he really was. So what about you? What about me? Are we going to go on deciding for God what his Son is supposed to be like? Or are we going to go back to the beginning, look at him afresh, see him as he is actually presented, and get on board with a new vision (which is really just a *restored* vision)?

Here is a worthy exercise. If you want to discover Joshua for yourself, re-read *Matthew, Mark, Luke,* and *John* with these questions in mind:

1. What does Joshua actually say about himself?
2. When asked, what does Joshua say he came to do?
3. What traits do you notice about the way Joshua interacts with humans?
4. What priorities does Joshua have?
5. How does Joshua respond to the different walks of life he encounters?
6. Does Joshua have the same aims you have? Does he have the same aims your church leaders have?
7. Does he truly reflect the version of Jesus you have known for so long?
8. When asked, what does Joshua say is important?
9. How does Joshua react to the theological experts of his day?

As you do all this, actually try looking at him as Joshua. You might be surprised how your faith can be revitalized by this fascinating exercise.

Thus, from this point on, the name "Jesus" will no longer be used except in contrast to our new expressions. From now on, when we talk about the Son of God, the Savior, the deliverer of the human race, the Messiah, we will refer to him as Joshua.

This means *we* get a new name, too.

Joshuans

I promised you a plethora of new expressions in this book, and I intend to deliver. Here is a revolutionary one for you. If anyone hears what I am saying, agrees with me, is encouraged by this effort to find new expressions, new perceptions, and new frontiers for our faith, and thus joins me in propelling all of this toward something that truly is *post/Christian*, then we, together, you and I, are no longer "Christians" by name. We hold to many of the same beliefs, have the same faith, and worship the same Savior, but we are no longer Christians. We are *Joshuans*. Just as a Christian is someone who believes in Jesus, so, too, is a Joshuan someone who believes in Joshua.

> [*Joshuan*] – 1) a human who, by faith, has met God, now lives *in God*, and now has God living *in them*; 2) someone who has left their old life and old self, has been transformed, is *being* transformed, and is putting on a new self; 3) a person who resembles a Christian in many ways but in other ways is a completely new conception; 4) a person who believes it is *through* the Son of God (*Joshua* to Joshuans; *Jesus* to Christians) that one is connected to the Son's Father; that is God; 5) a person who is free internally, alive eternally, forgiven completely, and delivered absolutely in a way that only those who have faith in the Son of God can be; 6) a person who behaves and operates based on what Joshua did and how he did it; and 7) someone who expresses all of these wonderful things through a life *reflective* of the one responsible for all of it: Joshua.

To be a Joshuan is to practice the same life-saving faith Christians practice but without many of the trappings that come with the name "Christian." To be a Joshuan is to gain new wings and lose old baggage. To be a Joshuan is to believe in the same God and same Messiah as Christians but with a new *mindset*, new *attitudes*, and new *priorities*. To be a Joshuan is to commit one's self to doing the things Joshua did in the *way* he did them. To be a Joshuan is to be about Joshuan Thought (which we will talk about soon). To be a Joshuan is to be a man or a woman living from the heart, constantly seeking a right perception of God, constantly pushing forward toward greater, authentic experiences with God. To be a Joshuan is to be free of all the negative things associated with "Christians." Now, you might say, "Who cares what the world thinks about us?" Well, you should care. You are here to show the world God's love. It therefore matters very much what the world thinks about you. Oh, and speaking of love…to be a Joshuan is to be about love. Always love. Incredible, boundless, contagious love. *Constant* love.

In short, to be a Joshuan is to follow a path beyond Christianity, a hybrid of sorts. What is this hybrid? Well, are you ready for another new expression? Now, I know that the last thing the world needs is another *-ism*. So you have my apologies in advance. But it just seemed like that is where this was leading. *Joshuan* and *ism* just seem to go together. Therefore, let us begin moving away from discussing Christianity, and let us begin talking about *Joshuanism*.

Michael Vito Tosto

Joshuanism: A Path beyond Christianity

There was once a time when some of the believers within the established institution of Christianity were unhappy with the direction their religion was taking. They were disillusioned with the way things were being done. They stood against some of the things being taught. They simply could not turn a blind eye to the blatant, glaring irrelevancy Christianity seemed to have regarding the way the world was evolving.

So, they fought back. They voiced their concerns. They were bold enough to take issue with the problems others were too frightened even to acknowledge. They saw what was wrong, and they had the courage to *call* it wrong. They moved against the establishment. They *protested*. Enough people joined their ranks that eventually they had a movement on their hands, and because they were protesting, they were given a name that reflected their actions and their message: they were called Protestants. Thus, history tells us, the Protestant Reformation reshaped the course of Christianity (and it seems Catholicism has never quite forgiven this).

Now, let me ask you this: do you think the Reformation was easy? Do you think the men and women who pulled it off did so as an afterthought? I am not even talking about the threat of the Inquisition here, itself a formidable enough reason to keep one's mouth shut. No, I mean the tremendous *resolve* it must have taken to change something that had not been changed in centuries, something that most people thought *could not* be changed. Today, in our luxurious world of freedom and choices, where religion is not mandated or regulated, we have a hard enough time summoning the determination to change anything, big or small, and we forget, immersed as we are in our liberties and secularisms, that for the people of the 16th century (the age of the Reformation), Christianity (in the form of Catholicism) permeated *everything*, every single aspect of life and death, at least in the West. In view of this, how easy do you think it was to change all that? Can you imagine having to *protest* against that which your entire world revolved around, that which held your destiny in its hands from the moment of your conception? I cannot even fathom how difficult this must have been.

Here is another question: what else was going on in history at this time? To properly understand the Protestant Reformation (why it occurred, how it occurred, why it *needed* to occur), we need to place it in its correct historical context. So, think about it. It is the 16th century. It has been 200 years since the Black Death. The Renaissance is in full swing. Humanism is gaining widespread interest. Humanity has reawakened to things it has been dead to for centuries: the arts, science, medicine, technological innovation, educational reform, social equalities, and cultural advancement. The Enlightenment is just around the corner. In all of this, humans are changing. They are evolving in their consciousness regarding the world and their place in it. This is the historical context of the Reformation.

Is it surprising, then, that amidst all this change and evolution, the topics of God, religion, and humanity's relation to both should also fall under scrutiny? No! It would have been more surprising if this *had not* happened, that if somehow all of this incredible cultural upheaval failed to infect the realm of the religious. The Reformation was therefore *bound* to happen. It was certain to occur because the minds and cosmological perceptions of that period's religious consciousness were evolving *beyond* the answers and attitudes of that same religion. What just 200 years prior was considered completely adequate and understandable to the adherents of Christianity was now, in view of humanity's evolution, looking quite archaic indeed.

Now, which period of change do you think is greater: the Renaissance or the present day? Is there even a comparison? Sure, humanity's inner light bulb switched on during the Renaissance, but today the bulb itself is obsolete. Leonardo da Vinci could draw flying machines, but he never taxied to a stop on LaGuardia's tarmac. Michelangelo could sculpt the human body in a way no one had ever witnessed before, but he never saw it in an MRI. Copernicus could postulate new ideas about the solar system, but he never stood on the Moon. No matter how urgent the scientific discovery was, no matter how Earth-shattering its scope, the discoverer still had to hand the message of it to a horseback rider, who would then spread the news. Today we just write an email, and the news is instantaneously delivered. No, there is no comparison. Today we are living in a Renaissance-To-The-Millionth-Power.

And just as Christianity was not immune to the radical changes of the 16th century, so it is not immune today. It's time for a new reshaping. Just as there was once a Protestant Reformation, so now there is *the Joshuan Revolution*. The result is a hybrid of Christianity: Joshuanism. Hence, there is now a new identity for believers: Joshuans.

Consider the definition of the word *hybrid*:

> [*Hybrid*] – 1) biological offspring resulting from cross-breeding different entities, e.g. two different species or two purebred parent strains; or 2) something of mixed origin or composition.

That is what Joshuanism is. We are *drawing from* Christianity, while also *adding* new expressions, new identities, new ideas, and new possibilities to create a hybrid, something truly *post/Christian*. It could just as easily be called neo/Christianity. But Joshuanism fits better because it reflects this unique, organic way of looking at our Savior as Joshua.

> [*Joshuanism*] – 1) a *path beyond* Christianity, existing specifically for those people who want to go on living for God through faith in his Son but who no longer find Christianity a satisfactory way of doing that; 2) a *way of life* that reflects a commitment to believe in Joshua, love Joshua, and live *like* Joshua; 3) the summation of Joshuan Thought,

Joshuan theology, Joshuan practice, and Joshuan expression; and 4) a spirituality based on Joshua.

In other words, Joshuanism is a new avenue for people who are perhaps a little disillusioned with institutional, organized Christianity. It seeks to bring a new conversation to the table; it endeavors to open the mind to new possibilities. Joshuanism is a *lifestyle*, or an *alternate approach* to "living daily life" as a believer (one we will discuss in great detail later). Joshuanism is a way of thought, a deliberate, stubborn refusal to allow the dynamic of our faith and our experiences with God to be extinguished by institutionalism, legalism, dogmatic zealotry, or merely a diffused, deadened irrelevancy. Joshuanism paints a new picture of the Savior, not by taking away or adding to who our Savior is but by revitalizing our vision of him, furthering our perceptions of him, relentlessly renewing our passion for him, asking new questions about him, seeking new answers, and daring to believe that God still has much to reveal to us. Joshuanism offers everything Christianity offers, just in a *different* way. That is what I mean when I say it's a *path beyond* Christianity.

"A path beyond Christianity?" You might say. "That sounds like a cult."

Joshuanism is not a cult. No one is making any crazy claims about obedience or spaceships hovering behind comets. No one is spiking punch with poison. No one is changing the complexion of Biblical thought. No one is undoing the last twenty centuries of Christian belief. Joshuanism simply offers a new context to continue those beliefs.

Nevertheless, I have no doubt that some people will be determined to view Joshuanism as a cult. That is unfortunate because it is erroneous. It would be another stunning example of missing the point, something humanity does all too often. At any rate, consider that Christianity itself began as a reshaping, to some degree, of Judaism. Does that mean the apostles were cultists? Were the Protestants of the 16th century cultists? When Martin Luther, John Calvin, and John Wesley proposed new, interesting, or even radical ideas into the mainstream of Christianity as it existed in their time, were they creating a cult? Or were they merely bringing something new to the table, thereby changing the complexion of Christianity?

"But this is *too* revolutionary," you might say.

Really? We have already established that Christianity changes. Sometimes that change has been minor, barely perceptible, but other times the change was unquestionably revolutionary. For instance, it was revolutionary to the Jewish thinking of the time to begin bringing the Gospel to the Gentiles (non-Jews). It was revolutionary to compile a "new" Testament, adding to what was already considered accepted scripture (the *Old Testament*). It was revolutionary to print personal *Bibles* that could be owned and read by those not of the clergy. It was revolutionary to suggest that one is saved by faith alone and not by deeds (the impetus for the Reformation) because for centuries Christianity had been a religion based almost solely on good or bad behavior. It was revolutionary, too, to bring the electric guitar, drum set, and projector into the church worship service, where for hundreds of years only organs and hymnals were considered suitable. Besides, *revolutionary* does not mean *rebellious sedition*; it means *radical change*. Sometimes radical change is exactly what is needed.

Is Joshuanism too revolutionary? Perhaps for some it will be, but others might see its value and find within its expressions a vast potential.

"But you're causing divisions! You're separating Christianity into two distinct sects!"

Two sects? If you really think the distinction in this conversation is merely between Christianity and Joshuanism, you might want to take another look at the religion you profess (if you're a Christian, that is). First, there are three main divisions of Christianity already (Orthodox, Catholic, and Protestant). Moreover, within those three divisions, there are hundreds of denominations, splinter groups, and warring factions. Christianity is already a severely divided entity to the umpteenth degree. Joshuanism seeks to divide nothing but rather to offer a home to those who, through Christianity's preexisting divisiveness and dissension, may have become disillusioned with the faith they once found so refreshing. In that sense, Joshuanism becomes a *unifying* factor, not a dividing one. Unlike some Catholics and some Protestants, who at times seem to be at war with each other, Joshuanism is *not* at war with Christianity. Further, Joshuanism is not a sect of Christianity at all. It exists *outside* of Christianity, *alongside* Christianity, but in a decidedly *post/Christian* state. There will be those who prefer to remain within the expressions of Christianity. That's okay. However, for those who would be interested, I have proposed Joshuanism as a new route.

Is having an alternative to the way we have always done things really such a terrible idea? Is it really blasphemous? Is it really so evil to aspire toward a new, fresh, relevant, connective, intriguing, revitalizing expression of our faith? I say no.

Doesn't the *Bible* say *all* who call on the name of the Lord will be saved? Joshuans call on his name. His *Hebrew* name. Doesn't the *Bible* say that those who do not regard Joshua (Jesus, to you) as the Son of God will not be saved? Joshuans regard him as the Son of God. Does not the *Bible* say that those who believe in him will not perish but have eternal life? Joshuans believe in him. Joshuans believe in the *same resurrection*, they nurture the *same faith*, they read the *same scriptures*, they worship the *same God*, they hope in the *same heaven*, they experience the *same forgiveness*, and they seek to express the *same love*.

Joshuans just do it all differently, just as the Protestants started to do things differently from the Catholics against whom they protested. Moreover, to be a Joshuan does not mean to protest against Christianity. No one is protesting anything here. Joshuans simply choose an alternative because, for them, Christianity and its expressions no longer match where their souls are moving, but they are not protesting anything. Joshuans merely endeavor to evolve peaceably in a *different direction*.

In other words, Joshuanism is not something *set against* Christianity. It is not some subversive, anti-Christian ideology. It's not a rejection of Biblical ideals. It's not an evil attempt to undo the Christian message. It's not a competing religion, vying for an entry into the record books next to Christianity. Joshuanism, in fact, is not a *religion* at all. It's merely a spiritual way of life based on the Son of God.

Christianity and Joshuanism

That said, let's explore how Joshuanism does contrast with Christianity.

I was going to take some time to go into great detail about the ragged state of Christianity in the 21st century. I wanted to explore the problems, the complaints, and the irrelevancy. In the end, however, I chose not to. Why? Well, first, that in itself could take an entire book. Second, I am sure most of my readers can read the writing on the wall for themselves. Third, I wanted this to be a positive message about a new direction, not a negative rehashing of the old direction. Fourth, I have no doubt that, as this book unfolds, I will have many opportunities to make relevant comments about contemporary Christianity, where necessary. But I will say this: my personal opinion is that Christianity has wandered extremely far from its original design and purpose. You may disagree. Either way, others have written better books than I could about what is happening in and to Christianity. Besides, I assume this book is in your possession because you have seen on your own the total disconnection Christianity seems to have these days with the world it's supposed to be reaching. If you want to explore this disconnection on your own, you should do so, by all means. At any rate, I wanted this to be a book not about Christianity as much as a book about Joshuanism.

We must, however, form a context in which to place our discussion. So, let's ask this question: what exactly *is* Christianity? Is it a religion? A relationship? A lifestyle? All of the above? None of the above? Well, the definition of Christianity, according to the Webster Dictionary, is this:

- the religion derived from Jesus Christ, based on the *Bible* as sacred scripture, and professed by Eastern, Roman Catholic, and Protestant bodies;
- conformity to the Christian religion;
- the practice of Christianity.

Likewise, we could say this about Joshuanism:
- a spirituality centered around Joshua of Nazareth, based on the *Bible* as sacred scripture, derived from Christianity but seeking to engender to new expressions of those Christian ideas;
- conformity to Joshuan spirituality;
- the practice of Joshuanism.

There are other comparisons. Just as Christianity is a *religion* centered on Jesus, Joshuanism is a *spiritual expression* centered on that same Son of God: Joshua. Christianity is indicative of rituals, liturgies, sacraments, and observances. Joshuanism is a state of mind, heart, body, and soul. Christianity is a fixed *institution*. Joshuanism seeks to be a *movement*. In Christianity, the focus is on what you *do* (i.e. attempting to be morally "spotless" on a daily basis). In Joshuanism, the focus is on what you *are*, or *who* you are. In other words, while Christians busy themselves *doing* this and *doing* that in an effort to earn what is already theirs by faith, Joshuans *rest* in the knowledge that God has (past tense) declared them righteous. Does this mean Joshuans make no attempts to live well, to live blamelessly, to live in an upright manner? No! Joshuanism includes recommended daily practices (as we will discuss later). Nonetheless, while the emphasis in Christianity constantly revolves around your *performance* (even when you are alone, when no one is looking), the emphasis in Joshuanism constantly revolves around your *position* in God, regardless of what you do or how well you perform.

"Performance?" I can hear you say. "I am saved by faith, not by deeds. I don't worry about my performance."

Are you sure? Ever felt guilty for failing to pray in the morning? Ever felt guilty for skipping church? Every felt guilty for letting a few days go by without reading the *Bible*? Ever confessed and repented of a sin but continued to be dogged by a feeling of remorse, which, according to your own belief, should no longer be present? Ever felt bad for waking up and saying to yourself, "I just don't *feel* like nurturing my Christian walk today?" Christians will acknowledge that they are saved, justified, redeemed, and set free with a hearty "amen," then turn right around and squirm within themselves in an effort to earn all of these things anyway. Doing the right thing *is* important, finding time to spend with God *is* important, paying attention to how we live *is* important—but in Joshuanism, one realizes that it is better to celebrate what we *are* than it is to worry about what we *do*. There is no human alive than can go through a day without sinning even if they sin without knowing it. There is no human alive that can go through a day without stepping a wayward toe out of line even if they think they can (because even by virtue of *thinking* they can, they have committed the sin of pride). So, what should we do? Should we weigh down our wings by worrying over every little thing we screw up? Christianity might say so. Joshuanism says no. Joshuans prefer to fly, to revel in their freedom, leaving guilt behind. Isn't this what Paul was saying in *Romans*? "Where sin abounds, grace abounds all the more" (*Romans* 5:20). Some might want to focus on the *sin*. Joshuanism focuses on the *grace*. Now, should we take care not to sin? Absolutely! No one, Christian or Joshuan, who either chooses to live *in* sin, or makes no attempt to *avoid* sinning inasmuch as is possible can truly have God in them because to have God in you is to love him and to love God is to crave righteousness. But where Christianity spotlights sin and guilt, Joshuanism spotlights love and grace.

Mind you, this is just a cursory glance at the differences between Christianity and Joshuanism. I have taken the rest of this book to explore the other differences in greater detail. Nevertheless, I do not intend to focus only on the disparities between Christianity and Joshuanism. I will try to show how both are telling the same story and pursing the same end—just in different ways. I have also taken the rest of this book to explore how one *practices* Joshuanism and how one makes sense of the changes it brings. Joshuanism proposes all kinds of reforms, revisions, and revamps, as you will see. You have been exposed to only a few of the new expressions so far. There are more. Many more. And new ideas, too; such as re-imagined ways of conducting our daily walk with God, how we "do" church, what the church is, what worship is, what salvation is really all about, etc. Perhaps you will find all of this as exciting as I do.

However, not everyone will.

Opposition to Joshuanism

I just received an email from a guy who heard about what I was writing and apparently found it, to say the least, unsettling. In his long and somewhat heated email, he said a great many things I would expect to hear from someone in his position. What is his position? *Entrenched.* Entrenched in what? In the current expressions of Christianity. He is most likely quite comfortable there, as many people are, but he forgets that just as many people are not. Therefore, we must observe one crucial addendum to the aforementioned truth that humanity changes, and it's this: people *hate* change; especially change that threatens their comfort. It is ironic, isn't it? Humanity is in a constant state of change, and yet individual humans themselves find it very difficult to accept change in their own lives even to the point of violently resisting it. Yes, humans will often fight viciously against any kind of change in their world, big or small, even when they know deep down that they should not. Indeed, this man's email drives home to me that which I already knew but perhaps was too naïve to really grasp until now: some people are going to oppose this. That's okay. It's to be expected. Joshua was opposed, too. I am just a man with an interesting albeit controversial idea. Joshua was the Son of God, and so threatened were his contemporaries by the change he brought that they killed him. Surely I can put up with some jibes and jeers.

Among the same, tired arguments the man presented in his email was one particular statement that I found interesting. He said this about Joshuanism: "You cannot propose an alternative to Christianity because there isn't one and there could never be one." I believe the Catholic Church said the same thing to Martin Luther. What exactly does that statement mean, anyway? What is he really saying? When he refers to "Christianity," is he talking about what it means to know God through the Son of God by faith? Or is he talking about an institution, a religion, a set of expressions that he recognizes and is familiar with? I suspect it's the latter. According to his line of thinking, the truth is only the truth if we say it in a certain way, if we funnel it through a certain manifestation, if we carry it out through a certain method. Similarly, according to that same line of thinking, the truth is *not* the truth if we come in with it through the back door instead of the front, if we dress it in different clothing, if we give it a new face. Further, which of the following two statements is more accurate: *There is no possible alternative to Christianity* or *there is no alternative to faith in the Son of God?*

The question, then (this is what the entire matter hinges on), is this: can a person get to God through his Son *without* going through Christianity? In other words, can a person have the same faith, read the same scriptures, practice the same authentic love, pray with the same passion, avoid the same sins, worship with the same adoring heart, and thereby enjoy the same salvation, while *at the same time* wanting and having nothing to do with anything that is blatantly Christian in appearance and expression? If I thought so, I would not have written this book. Moreover, one hopes that if you thought so, too, you would not be reading it.

At any rate, here is a thought worth examination: Joshua said *he* was the way, the truth, and the life; he did not say that he was the religion that would be based on him. Joshua also said that on the last day many will say to him, "Lord, Lord, we did all kinds of good Christian things in your name," to which he says he will reply, "Go away, we never knew each other." The issue is the state of one's heart and the nature of one's faith, right? So, what does it matter if one approaches God through Christianity, or Joshuanism, or some other route altogether? The Son of God is still the same regardless of whichever route we take to come to him. The apostle Paul said all who *call on his name* will be saved, not all who *practice this or that religion*. To be a Joshuan *is* to call on his name just like to be a Christian is to call on his name. Christians call on Jesus, Joshuans call on Joshua, but the same Son of God answers both.

How do I know the same Son of God answers? The Son of God is the Son of God whether we call him "Jesus," "Lord," "Teacher," "Immanuel," "Rabbi," or "Christ." That's just in the English language. The second person of the Trinity, the part of God that entered the world as a human and died on the cross, existed in eternity long before he forced his way through Mary's womb and received from his parents the earthly name *Yĕhōšuă'*. He is who he is regardless of what we call him, or in what language we speak the name. The name Joshua points to the same person as the name Jesus. Why wouldn't it? As Shakespeare pointed out, a rose by any other name would smell as sweet. The flower in question is not altered whether we call it a rose or something else. Neither is the Son of God. Not only is this so, but as I have said before and will continue to say, the Son of God's earthly name was Joshua before it was Jesus.

I could go on saying this until my head falls off, but it will not change that which I now know to be true: I will be opposed. Joshuanism will be opposed. Throughout human history, innovations and the innovators who innovated them have always been opposed. Change is always opposed. The work of God is always opposed.

How do I know I am doing the work of God? Consider the story found in *Mark* 9. The disciples tell Joshua they saw some guy using his name to perform miracles and demanded that he stop, to which Joshua responds, "Do not stop him. No one who does a miracle in my name can in the next moment say anything bad about me, for whoever is not against us is for us." Therefore, is the issue really the *name*, or is it the *person* behind the name? Does the power come from the five-letter word "Jesus" or from the divine entity to which that word is attached? Moreover, if someone were to translate the *New Testament* (originally written in Greek) into Hebrew (there are, in fact, Hebrew translations), how would his name be translated? It would be translated as Joshua (or *Yĕhōšuă'*). But again, it's the *same* Son of God being referenced in either case. Are Joshuans for or against that Son of God? For! He himself said whoever is not against him is for him and should not be stopped. Joshua also said that the work of God is to love God and love humanity and to do so through and in and for and because of the Son of God. Joshuans can do that just as effectively as Christians can.

Another person read a small excerpt of my writing on Joshuanism and had this to say, "When I dig down deep into your work, heresy spills out." I was alternately bothered and thrilled at the mention of the word *heresy*. I was bothered because that word is almost on the level of an expletive in believing circles. Indeed, one of the worst things anyone who believes in God could be called is a heretic. I was also thrilled. Why thrilled? When I look back over the last 2,000 years of history and survey the wide range of people who have been accused of heresy, more often than not, history has proven the accused to be right and their accusers wrong. More than that, I was thrilled because it pleases me to be identified with something so far removed from the current conventions of Christianity that I would be seen in the eyes of people entrenched in the shipwrecked status quo as a heretic. Of course, they will see me as a heretic and Joshuanism as heresy. Not only is Joshuanism new and startling (strike one), it's also foreign and unfamiliar (strike two). Since by its very nature it is seen as a threat to the coziness of those comfortably rooted in Christianity's familiar expressions (strike three), these same people would, of course, brand it as heresy.

Perhaps heresy gets a bad rap. Throughout history, who was more in the wrong—the "heretic" who had ideas about God that did not fit the "approved norm" or the people who were rounding up these so-called heretics, persecuting them, torturing them, and killing them? Then, think about this: to most of his well-educated contemporaries even Joshua himself was considered a heretic and killed for it. Martin Luther, too, was considered a heretic, though he escaped martyrdom. Even Galileo was called a heretic merely for suggesting that the Earth was not at the center of the Universe. He was right, of course, and his accusers were wrong, but because they were not ready for the change he brought, he was declared guilty of heresy. What was Galileo's *real* crime? He was a threat. A threat to what? The establishment. The comfort of the status quo. Anything that threatens the comfort of the status quo will always be considered heresy. Sadly, that is just the way it is.

Nevertheless, the question is a worthy one: is Joshuanism heresy? The answer is both yes *and* no. Consider the Webster Dictionary's definition of the word heresy:

> [*Heresy*] – 1) adherence to a religious opinion contrary to church dogma; denial of a revealed truth by a baptized member of the Roman Catholic Church; an opinion or doctrine contrary to church dogma; 2) dissent or deviation from a dominant theory, opinion, or practice; an opinion, doctrine, or practice contrary to the truth or to generally accepted beliefs or standards.

Most people think the word *heresy* is synonymous with *evil* or *satanic*, but this is incorrect. Heresy is merely an idea that is either completely contrary or slightly deviant to mainstream thought. Where does Joshuanism fall in regard to accepted Christian thought? Somewhere in the middle but leaning more toward *deviant* than *contrary*. After all, Joshuanism does not deny the existence of God, the divinity of God's Son, the incarnation, the crucifixion, the resurrection, or any of the creeds associated with Christianity (although Joshuanism does propose an updated creed, as we will see later). Joshuanism merely attempt to *express* the *same things* as Christianity in a *different way*. Sure, there are new approaches, new theological ideas, new concepts about how to go about living out our faith, but there is nothing evil about any of this and certainly nothing satanic about it. However, the sad truth is that there will be those who oppose Joshuanism vehemently, branding it as evil and satanic, just as people have always done to anything that threatens them.

In view of that, think about this: is it possible that Christianity *as it exists today* and what Joshua (Jesus) *came to do* are no longer one and the same? Is it possible that Christianity has strayed *beyond* the apostles' original intent? Is it possible that after 2,000 years of being soaked in humanity's interference, Christianity has wandered so far from where and how it originated that it now fails to resemble anything in the realm of "good news?" Did the Son of God come to establish a World Religion? Is it possible we have completely missed the point? If these things are possible, if they are even remotely possible, who then is the heretic—the one who clings to Christianity as it exists today or the one who asks if there is a better way to do things? The question should *always* be this: what did Joshua do? What did Joshua say? How did he live? How did he operate? What did he say was important? What did he say was *not* important? What behaviors did Joshua stress? About which behaviors was he silent? While Christianity goes on doing what it has always done, Joshuanism asks whether it is possible to get back to the *original intent*.

That's all this is about, really. It may be different, it may sound revolutionary, it may carry startling implications. In the end, however, it's not really meant to be *new* at all. Joshuanism is, at its heart, an endeavor to get things back to how they started. That is really the alternative being offered here. Sure, it may have new expressions, new terminologies, and a fresh name for the Savior, but underneath all of that, Joshuanism is really a route back to the beginning, back to the original intent, back to the *movement* that existed before the *institution* killed it. (As I typed that last sentence, I was reminded of a great quote from the 1986 film *Labyrinth*: "The way forward is sometimes the way back.")

This doesn't mean there are no truly new ideas associated with Joshuanism. There are. Some of these ideas are going to go down easy. Others will be hard for some to swallow. Remember, though, what I said at the beginning: this is just a *conversation,* one man wondering out loud about some interesting possibilities. If that makes me a heretic, so be it. Perhaps the world today needs a touch of heresy because clearly the "accepted norm" is not working.

Now, one other thing bears mentioning before we move on. I am an unknown. By that, I mean that few people outside my family and friends know my name. I am not famous (nor am I certain that I want to be). Because of my obscurity, one particular editor who saw what I was writing about sent me an email, saying this: "It would take a much more famous name to create a new religion." Maybe she was right about the name and then again maybe not. What tugged woefully at my heart when I read her email was that she viewed my work as an attempt to create a new religion. While Joshuanism is definitely a new approach, I do not want it to be seen as a *religion*. It may embody some religious aspects, but it also embodies spiritual, philosophical, existential, and sociological aspects as well. Further, the word *religion*, like the name *Jesus*, is a loaded word, one that immediately brings to mind certain connotations, images, and stereotypes. The word can hardly be uttered by anyone anywhere without massive baggage instantly infecting the conversation and the thoughts of those involved. If I had my way, Joshuanism would be accompanied by no label, no title, and no category. It would just *be*. If anything, I would hope the world would see it merely as a way of thinking, a way of believing, and a way of living—or at best, an *identity* one *assumes* rather than a *religion* one *practices*. This is not to say Joshuanism is without its distinctive practices—for it certainly does have unique practices. However, my intent is not to create a new religion. I just want to offer something new, a path beyond that which currently exists, one that attracts both the religious and the nonreligious alike. If I had to choose one word that describes what I hope Joshuanism is about, it would be the same word Christianity was meant to be about but has somehow failed to achieve. You know what it is. *Love*.

There need be nothing *religious* about love. There does not even need to be anything *spiritual* about love. Love should simply be the most practical thing on the face of the planet. Love can and should be done like breathing, something that just comes out of us and goes into us so naturally we do it without even thinking. Love is more important even than faith, as the apostle Paul notes in *1 Corinthians* 13:13. "These three remain," he says, "faith, hope, and love. But the greatest of the three is"...what? *Love.* This means a person could completely lose their faith (and thereby their religion) and still hold onto that which is most important: love. Likewise, a person could lose all optimism and reside in the innermost pit of the deepest hopelessness imaginable and still hold onto that which is most important: love. If the world wants to see Joshuanism as a new religion, I suppose it's going to do that whether I like it or not. However, if the world looks at Joshuanism and fails to see love, then this path beyond Christianity I have created is not worth the paper these words are printed on.

If Joshuanism is about love, then opposing Joshuanism is the same as opposing love. Why would anyone want to do that? (I ask that last question knowing full well that people oppose love all the time, as sad as that is.)

Frequently Asked Questions about Joshuanism

Are Joshuans the same as Christians?
No. Christians are Christians, and Joshuans are Joshuans. They believe in and worship the same God and Messiah; they express it differently.

Do you believe in the Christ?
Yes.

And who is the Christ?
Joshua, whom you call Jesus.

Was this Joshua raised from the dead?
Yes, he is the same person/God you believe in.

So you believe in the resurrection?
Of course.

Do you believe in God?
Yes.

Do you have faith?
Yes.

Do you believe the Bible?
Yes.

Do you go to church?
Sort of...well, probably not the way you do.

What does that mean?
You'll see.

Is Joshuanism a cult?
No, no more than Christianity was to Judaism or the Protestants to Catholicism.

Are you a new denomination?
No, but some will probably see Joshuanism as such.

Well, if you aren't a new denomination, what are you?
Believers, like you. Joshuans love God, just as you do. Joshuans love others, just as you are supposed to do. Joshuans pray, just like you. Joshuanism is just a *new expression* of the same faith you have.

Now, perhaps I can guess what your next question is...

The Joshuan Pages

Yes, a Joshuan version of the *Bible* is in the works. Well, not the whole *Bible*. Just the *New Testament*. It's going to be called *The Joshuan Pages* (TJP), and it will be a paraphrase. The name *Joshua* will be taking the place of *Jesus* in this version of the *New Testament*, and the word *Deliverer* will be taking the place of the word *Christ*. Nothing will be taken away from the context of scripture. This is merely an aspiration to express the scriptures in a new way.

For example, consider *Ephesians* 2:10.

The ESV translation of that verse reads like this:
For we are his workmanship, created in Christ Jesus for good works, which God prepared beforehand, that we should walk in them.

The NIV translation reads like this:
For we are God's workmanship, created in Christ Jesus to do good works, which God prepared in advance for us to do.

And here is the TJP version:
We believe we are God's artisanship. He specifically created us to do good things in and through and for the Deliverer, Joshua. This was God's design all along. He set aside these good things beforehand, intending that we should carry them out.

This endeavor is being undertaken with much care, much thought, and, of course, much prayer.

Therefore, from this point on, any time the *New Testament* is quoted in this book, I will be drawing from the TJP version (which I have already begun work on), unless otherwise noted.

Now, some may wonder why the name *Christ* is also being replaced with a new expression. The reason is simple. Joshua Christ is so close to Jesus Christ that it does little to stimulate the imagination toward the new, fresh perceptions we discussed earlier. The word *Christ* comes from the ancient Greek word *Christós* (Χριστός), which means *anointed one*. *Christós* is a translation of the ancient Hebrew word *Māšîah* (מָשִׁיחַ), or *Messiah*, which also means *anointed one*. The word Christ was therefore never a name but a title. He was originally known in Greek as Jesus *the* Christ and in Hebrew as Joshua *the* Messiah. Over time, though, the article was dropped, and he became just *Jesus Christ* as though *Christ* was his surname.

To the mindset of the humans living in ancient Judea, the notion of a Messiah, or Christ (the anointed one) carried heavy historical, spiritual, and political undertones. The title was extremely culturally significant to these ancient humans, but in our day, it seems to mean very little. Indeed, *Christ* and *Messiah* point so blatantly to Judeo-Christian expressions that one can hardly hear either word and not be immediately faced with associations, images, and connotations that are decidedly *Christian* and *religious*. Because Joshuanism is meant to exist as a path *beyond* Christianity, embodying completely new and/or different expressions, the title *Christ* has been dropped. Now, does this mean Joshuans do not view Joshua (Jesus) as the Christ, or the Messiah? No. Joshua *is* the Messiah. Does this mean Joshuans are somehow rejecting something about the person of the Son of God? No. Are Joshuans ashamed of the word *Christ*? No. We just see it as useful to begin looking at the Son of God in a fresh, relevant way.

So what about the replacement word? Plenty of titles could have been chosen: *King, Savior, Exalted One*, and so forth. But when I honestly asked myself what word or title, if any, best represents how the world *needs* to see him, how he *should* be seen by a hurting world, and what God's heart toward that hurting world is, only one word came to mind: *Deliverer*. Joshua the Deliverer. Isn't that the essence of the good news, or at least, isn't that what it was supposed to be about? Freedom for the captives! Sight to the blind! Aid for the poor! Relief for the oppressed! Liberation from bondage to sin! What word better sums up all that Joshua was about and is about if not *Deliverer*? Sure, there will be those that don't like it, but these same people aren't really going to like anything about Joshuanism anyway, so we cannot worry about them.

"The Joshuan Pages will be free for all (as the scriptures ought to be) and available for download at Joshuanism.com (with each individual book of the New Testament offered separately as they are finished). Bear me with me, though, because this process is going to take a long, long time."

Thus far, you have been presented with the basics of what Joshuanism is. I hope you are still with me because things are about to get more detailed, more intense, and even crazier than this.

PART THREE: Joshuan Theology and Belief

When I talk to people about Joshuanism and the Joshuans who practice it (a conversation I rarely have), the question I am asked the most is this: what do Joshuans believe? Well, for the most part, Joshuans believe the same things Christians believe. Are there some differences? Sure. Most of them are subtle, but some are not. A few are downright extreme. If Joshuanism perfectly mirrored Christianity, it would not be much of an alternative. Joshuanism is different from Christianity in precisely those places it needs to be different to stay relevant where Christianity might no longer be. That is why Joshuanism includes 1) a new look at some *old* theologies; and 2) some *new* theological ideas. However, before we get into all of that, we first need to explore a mindset that I call "Joshuan Thought." Without this mindset firmly in place (it's not a wicked or sinful mindset, in case you were wondering), you might find yourself closed off to things you ought to be open to.

Joshuan Thought

When I speak of Joshuan Thought, what I am really speaking about is an *attitude* or a *mindset*. Our attitudes play an important role in the pursuit of God. That being the case, we cannot really begin discussing Joshuan theology without first talking about our minds.

I would like to let you in on a little secret: God does not frown upon you or me having an open mind. In fact, God likes open minds. Remember Requisite Desire? God *wants* to be known. Does anyone ever come to know God without first having an open mind (or an open heart)? The answer is no. It takes an open mind to know God. Closed minds and a knowledge of God cannot truly exist together. Therefore, if it takes an open mind to know God, then we must assume God likes open minds since he *wants* to be known.

Consider the twelve disciples. They needed open minds when they were plucked by Joshua out of their regular lives and plunged into this strange realm of God that included all sorts of bizarre and new ideas. Consider also the citizens of ancient cities like Rome, Ephesus, Corinth, and Thessalonica. They, too, needed open minds when the apostle Paul brought the story of Joshua to them, and they *did* have open minds. Otherwise, Christianity would never have taken root in those cities.

The simple fact is that it takes an open mind to know an invisible God. Why is it, then, that when we *do* finally meet God and become believers, we suddenly turn right around and close our minds off to everything else? If it takes an open mind to know God, then surely it takes an open mind to *go on* knowing him. Nevertheless, for some reason it seems that the instant a human being becomes a believer; he immediately rebels against his open mind and closes it, somehow convinced that this is what God wants him to do.

Joshuan Thought is therefore a willful determination to undo this obstinate tendency. It is a mental resolve to remain open to the unfamiliar and the discomforting. This is necessary because comfort is always indicative of apathy. Joshuan Thought is a refusal to allow a closed mind to block us from going where God would have otherwise taken us had our minds been open.

Joshuan Thought is also a continuation of *post/Christian*ity, which, if you recall, is an attitude that 1) presupposes we do not have all the information; and 2) maintains that as humans evolve, so, too, does God's revelation of himself. In other words, Joshuan Thought is the belief that the more we know about God, the more we are then *able* to know.

Think about it this way: you do not teach a baby how to drive a car. Similarly, Joshuan Thought wonders whether the humans living in the year 50 AD were able to know or understand or even fully receive *all* of God's revelation. Joshuan Thought admits the possibility that because humans know more now than they did in 50 AD (or even in 1400 ad, or 1800 ad), perhaps they are now able to gain access to a larger scope of God's revelation of himself than was previously available.

Therefore, Joshuan Thought is 1) a committed, relentless conviction that there is always more to learn, and 2) a constant, unyielding desire to evolve, to grow, to become more, to know more, to see more, to further our spiritual awareness, to push farther into the heart of God, to reach deeper into the well of revelation, to connect with all humans, from all walks of life, on a much larger scope.

Sometimes our attitudes as humans, and particularly as believers, can be the biggest hindrance to this. This is because we too often prefer being *right* (or, always correct) over being *righteous* (or, humble and holy). Most humans think their way of doing things is the *best* way, their way of thinking is the *only* way, their way of seeing the world is the *right* way. Believers who have their *Bibles* thoroughly memorized and who always seem to be armed with the "right" answers" can be decidedly guilty of having these bad attitudes. Why are these attitudes bad? Because anytime anyone believes that they know all they need to know, three things happen:

1. They commit the sin of pride (which comes before a fall).

2. They close their minds and cut themselves off from further knowledge.
3. Because they believe they are right and that they know all they need to know, they can no longer be shown just how wrong they actually are.

Why are they wrong? Because God is infinite, which means there is *always* more to learn, as we have observed many times already in this book. That is why to be a Joshuan is to be committed to Joshuan Thought. That is why to be a Joshuan is to make a deliberate decision to *open* your mind to new possibilities in God and to *keep it open*. Joshuans condition their minds to be receptive to thoughts or ideas that before might have been considered inaccessible, immutable, or, dare I say, taboo. *That* is Joshuan Thought. Therefore, if you proceed through the book in your hands *without* this openness in mind and heart and attitude, you may find yourself wandering in a wilderness of the downright bizarre. Forewarned is forearmed. Now, let's continue…

Joshuan Theology

Just as Christianity has Christian theology associated with it, so, too, does Joshuanism have Joshuan theology associated with it. Joshuan theology does not seek to undermine Christian theology, nor does it seek to overtly challenge any of the weighty specifics (i.e., who God is, who Joshua was/is, the crucifixion, the resurrection, the atonement, the Trinity, etc.). In some cases, however, Joshuanism does seek to find new expressions for many of these things, if only to reinvigorate them. In other cases, Joshuanism offers something brand new to the table.

Remember what theology is?

Theo = God

ology = the study of

Joshuanism maintains that no one has to go to a special school to be a theologian. Anyone who seeks God is studying him because no one *seeks* anything without also *learning about* that thing. Seeking God is more than just attempting to either hear from him or experience him. To seek God is also to learn *about* God, to discover who he is, how he acts, what he is like. That is why I submit that anyone who seeks God is studying God, and anyone who studies God is, by definition, a theologian.

Joshuanism also maintains that no one can study God without also studying *spiritual life*. They go together. If you were going to undertake a thorough study of the planet Jupiter, surely that study would inherently include an investigation of Jupiter's atmosphere, right? Just as a planet has an atmosphere around it, so, too, does spiritual life surround God. To study one is to study the other.

So allow me to introduce yet another new expression, a new school of thought: *Zoêology*, (pronounced zoh-ee-ology).

The word *zoê* (from the ancient Greek word ζωή), means *spiritual life*, just as the word *bios* is ancient Greek for *physical life* (as in the word *biology*).

zoê = spiritual life
ology = the study of
Therefore, we have a new definition:

> [*Zoêology*] – 1) the study of the spiritual life imparted to the individual by God through faith in Joshua; and 2) the study of how that spiritual life relates to both the individual and to the collective group.

Zoêology is a key component to Joshuan theology. Indeed, Joshuans believe *theology* and *zoêology* are two sides of the same coin. To study who God is automatically implies a study of his interactions with us. Moreover, a study of who we are automatically implies a study of our interactions with God. So, as you encounter more new ideas in this book, keep in mind not only the theological aspect of the idea (that which pertains to God) but also the zoêological aspect (that which pertains to your *experiences* with God since to experience spiritual life *is* to experience God). This will be a helpful mentality to adopt, as you will see. Having said all that, let's now explore some elements of Joshuan theology.

The first thing we must observe is that this theology is not an exact science. In fact, no theology—Christian, Joshuan, or otherwise—is an exact science. When the nature of the object in question, the object of our research, is something as infinite and ethereal as God, the data we accumulate through study and investigation can only ever be flawed at best. This relates to the very thing I have been saying over and over in this book, that the infinite cannot be finitely ascertained. Consequently, theology, which is a form a science (since science is the pursuit of knowledge and understanding), can never have a *definitive conclusion* as opposed to other branches of science (such as geology or anatomy) which *can* have definitive conclusions. Why can they? Because the object of study is tangible and accessible. Everything we need to know about the Earth or the human body is at our disposal. The data needs only to be obtained and inspected. But God is not that way. We cannot get our hands on God. We cannot subject him to a microscopic examination. We cannot attach gadgets to his being for the attainment of measurable data. He is unseen; and further, he is mysterious by nature. The realm of God, then, is not conducive to scientific research.[2] Oh, we can certainly try. We may even come somewhat close, but the final word on the nature of God (which is theology's main objective) can never be reached.

Therefore, Joshuan theology does differ from Christian theology in that while the latter claims to have the monopoly on what is correct and what is incorrect, the

---

2 This is not to say that Joshuanism rejects science, as is often the case in certain quarters of Christianity. We will explore Joshuanism's relationship with science later in this section.

former admits that the journey toward understanding is not yet over; nor will it ever be. Joshuan theology is an attempt to take the immeasurable and measure it insofar as is possible with our human understanding and stage of evolution. In other words, while God's ways could never be fully grasped, Joshuanism makes an effort to try, knowing ahead of time that a definitive conclusion cannot be attained. Why bother trying, you might ask? The theologian tries because he must. The theologian is driven by a need to know God. He must, therefore, shoot arrows into the dark, knowing he will not hit his target but hoping he might come close. The theologian admits that God could never be precisely expressed in a concise synopsis or a balanced equation but, by making an attempt to do so, he trusts that God will reveal to him that which he can know according to his ability and evolution at that time.

This is something that many in the Christian realm have not yet understood. Challenge the particulars of any Christian doctrine, and you are sure to be viciously attacked in some circles. Question any element of Christian thought, and the word *heresy* will be heard before very long. This is a shame because part of the beauty theology has to offer is that it's an ongoing adventure. It's an open-ended question to which many different answers can suffice, depending on where you are standing. It's a journey of discovery that evolves and unfolds, taking us from one epiphany to the next. The moment we proclaim to have "arrived" at a definitive conclusion (which Christianity seems to proclaim often), we have missed the point and circumvented our own progress.

Joshuan theology makes no definitive claims. It asserts no final words and it assumes no superiority. Yes, there *are* some particulars within Joshuan theology that distinguish it and add to its value as a new approach, and those things are present because they *might* seem to make more sense than their Christian counterparts (then again, they may not—that's for you to decide). Nowhere within these pages, however, will you see Joshuanism claiming to possess a monopoly on who God is or what God is like. No one could ever possess this.

That said, I do believe the elements of Joshuan theology I am about to share with you make sense and serve to spur the open-minded pilgrim toward a greater knowledge of God. I would not have included in Joshuanism anything that did not evoke such a conviction within me. At the end of the day, though, only you can square with God what you want to believe.

There is one other general point we need to observe about Joshuan theology before we begin exploring some of its particulars. I mentioned before that in certain areas Joshuan theology differs only slightly from Christian theology, while in other areas it differs greatly. In some cases, Joshuan theology merely aspires to take an accepted aspect of Christian doctrine and repackage it. To what purpose? Well, sometimes, it's good to see things in a new light. Sometimes, it can make all the difference in the world to look at something you have seen all your life through a new lens. In other cases, though, Joshuan theology proposes entirely new ideas, many of which might seem to *oppose* that which is considered Christian. There again, that is the very idea: to push through to a theological consciousness that is decidedly *post/ Christian*, or, in this case, *Joshuan*.

Let me give you an example of one such repackaged element. Among the most fundamental aspects of Christian belief is the doctrine of the Trinity (or, the triune God: one God existing in three forms: Father, Son, and Holy Spirit). You may be wondering whether Joshuanism forsakes a belief in the Trinity. It does not. Joshuanism maintains a belief in a triune God, but Joshuanism does choose to express this belief in a new and different way. What Christians call the Trinity; Joshuans call the Singular Fellowship.

> [*The Singular Fellowship*] – the Joshuan expression for the Christian doctrine of the Trinity. The Singular Fellowship is the only infinite, eternal, divine entity (or God) in the Universe, existing, or coexisting, as three distinct yet unified forms in a perfect, unbroken, singular fellowship: the Father (God), the Son (Joshua), and the Soul of Godliness (aka the Holy Spirit in Christianity, which we will talk more about later).

This is just one of the many new expressions Joshuanism brings to the theological table. Nevertheless, as you can see, the basic belief is the same. The new expression merely renders the belief *Joshuan* in nature and distinction rather than *Christian*. It also serves to stimulate the mind toward fresh reflections. But again, not all elements of Joshuan theology are as recognizable as this one is. Some of what you are about to read may seem like it comes out of left field. Give it a chance, though. Thoroughly digest it before making your judgment. Personal decisions of a theological nature should never be made in haste. Chew on the things you are about to encounter, and keep an open mind. Deal? Ready for more? Then let's move on...

The Dismantling

The Joshuan version of the Christian Gospel is another such repackaging. Here we see the same basic elements of the Christian Gospel communicated through different expressions. Here, again, this serves to open the eyes of those who would see and the ears of those who would listen in a *new way*, with new possibilities, new profundities, and fresh, innovative implications. The power of the Gospel could never go stale, but the communication of it certainly can. And the communication of the Gospel in the realm of Christianity these days usually comes with too much hell and not enough love. So, let's explore the Gospel according to Joshuanism, which is no less Biblical but perhaps a bit more provocative than what one usually hears from the Christian pulpit.

The first thing you need to know is that you are loved. *You. Are. Loved.* God loves you. And not only does God love you, he *likes* you. He is pleased with you. He ought to be; he made you. He designed you. He wrought you into the creation you are. That is why he especially likes it when you are just being you. God is not angry with you. He does not hate you. He is not against you. He is not plotting your demise. He is not keeping an accurate account of each blunder you stumble into; he is not that petty. In fact, God is not petty at all. Humans are petty, yes, but God is not. So, before you grapple with anything else, know this: you are loved. By God. Forever. Period.

Not only does God love you, he also *desires* you. Think about that for a moment. The God of the Universe, the Creator of all that is and all that will ever be, wants you. He wants to be with you. He wants you to be with him. He wants you to know him. He wants you to enter intimacy with him so that he may fill you up with the fullness of his presence. God knows your name. He knows what you have done. He knows all the bad things you're still going to do even after you promise him not to do them. He knows each and every secret thought you've ever had or ever will have. Yet, in spite of all of this, he wants you. God craves you on a level you could not even possibly fathom.

Now, what do you think life would be like for you if you really believed these two truths? If you really, truly believed that God unconditionally loves you and that he desperately desires to be with you, what would than mean for your mental and emotional health? What would it mean for how you approach living your life each day? How would you respond to the bad things that are going to happen in life if you measured them against an immovable conviction within that you are loved and you are desired? I once heard a man say that without a knowledge of how much God loves them, each human is an orphan in the Universe. What if you did not have to be an orphan? God's invitation to you is just that. You do not have to be an orphan. You can be part of a family.

I would never claim that Christianity fails to communicate God's love for humanity. I know for a fact that such a statement would be incorrect. Christianity *does* communicate God's love. Nevertheless, it just seems to me that something is getting lost in translation. I have spoken with many Christians over a course of almost 20 years and, more often than not, I hear them repeatedly question whether or not God likes them, whether or not he is angry with them, or whether or not he notices their pain or even cares about if he does notice it. Why haven't these questions been settled by now? I have heard more Christians than I could ever count communicate to me that while God may love some people, he certainly does not love them [the ones speaking]. This is most likely related to the way human beings filter their knowledge of God through their own earthly understanding. However, perhaps something else is going on here as well. Perhaps Christianity has blemished the power of God's love by acknowledging it verbally but failing to show it practically. Perhaps multitudes of Christians are being sent mixed signals. On the one hand, they are hearing from the pulpit that God loves them; on the other hand, they are also hearing that God is angry, that God is unhappy, that God hates this behavior and that behavior, that God is sending wrath and punishment for all the sins we go on committing, that God is fed up with humans and their immoral ways, that God does not tolerate weakness, that God is against the people we are against, that God only loves certain people who succeed in getting it together. If this mixed signaling *is* the case (in my personal opinion, I have witnessed enough evidence to be persuaded that it is), then what we have here is a love that is labeled *unconditional* but which is communicated and demonstrated as being very much *conditional.* No wonder so many Christians are confused and hurting and failing to make the lines match up in their lives. No wonder people are leaving churches by the score. So which is it? Which are we going to go with? Does God love us or hate us?

Joshuanism chooses to believe that unconditional means unconditional. While the communication of the Christian Gospel usually begins with sin, the Joshuan version of the Gospel begins with love. Now, this is not to say that sin does not factor into this story. It very much does. It's just that sin is not the *main* factor. Sin is not the reason for any of this. Love is. If you ask a Christian why God had to send his Son into the world, they would most likely say, "Because of sin." But that is wrong! Sin was not the reason for the God's invasion of humanity in the form of Joshua; love was! Love is the main factor here. What does *John* 3:16, the most quoted Biblical scripture in the entire world, have to say on this matter? "For God *so loved* the world, that he gave his only Son, that whoever believes in him should not perish but have eternal life" (ESV). Note that it does *not* begin this way, "For God so hated our sin that he sent his only Son..." The Gospel is about love, not sin.

Now, before we go any further, perhaps we should identify here and now what sin is. In the realm of Christianity, sin usually has to do with behavior. This view is not entirely incorrect, but it's not entirely correct, either. When most people think of sin (especially if they come from a Christian background), they usually picture something like murder, fornication, or even just the telling of lies. But whatever they think of, sin is usually identified with ugly, immoral, harmful, or selfish *conduct*. In other words, they see sin as an *action.* Now, they are not entirely wrong in that conclusion. Nevertheless, the truth is that long before a sinful action is committed, it was first a sinful thought. And before it was a sinful thought, it was a sinful inclination. What I mean by that is this: the true heart of sin lies not in the committing of a deed but in the harboring of a propensity. Which do you think God cares about more—the committing of murder or the desire within you to commit murder? You might think it's the former. I would say it's the latter. Why? Because whether or not you do the deed matters little when the desire to do deed *already lives in your heart.* If murder lives

Joshuanism

in your heart, you are a murderer even if you never kill anyone. If deception lives in your heart, you are a liar even if you never utter a single falsehood. Sin is a heart issue first, a behavioral issue second. Isn't that what Joshua was communicating when he said if that you look at a woman lustfully you have already committed adultery with her in your heart? In other words, why bother trying to avoid actual fornication when every fiber of your being wants to fornicate? If every fiber of your being craves fornication, you are going to fornicate eventually. Trying to avoid fornication at that point is like trying to avoid eating. Sooner or later, you will be hungry enough to break down and eat. And why not, when food abounds? Therefore, the actual outward expression or the behavioral manifestation of the sin that lived in your heart long before you committed the deed matters less to God. What matters more to him is that you harbored within your heart the desire and the intention to carry that sin out. You *planned* it. You *premeditated* it. You stroked it fondly within your mind and nurtured it to the point of fruition. In other words, you *loved* the sin. You cared for it. You choose to live in it rather than in the love of God. *That* is the true heart of sin. In Joshuanism, sin is identified more with an *attitude* or *disposition* within the mind or an *inclination* within the heart and less with a *behavior* or an *action*.

However, sin *does* play a role in the Gospel. A large role. Make no mistake about that. I am not arguing that we should reject the presence or importance of sin in the story of God and humanity. I merely assert that sin is not the most *important factor* in the story. Love is. But sin does play a role. Without sin, Joshua need never have come to begin with, and that is not God's fault, it is ours. We are the sinners. Nevertheless, when Joshua did come, he came for love first and sin second. Love always takes precedence over sin. Nevertheless, our sinfulness did create an obstacle that God ultimately had to deal with. Whether or not you choose to believe the story of Adam and Eve to be factual or merely allegorical, the point is that humanity *chose* to sin at some point in the primordial past. In this respect, Joshuan theology agrees with Christian theology: sin separated humanity from God and his love. In Joshuanism, we call this the Great Barrier.

> [*The Great Barrier*] – the idea that humanity's imperfection and sinfulness created a barrier between them and the only perfect, sinless God, thus cutting humans off from God and the life they so desperately crave.

That is why Joshuanism refers to the work of Joshua as the Dismantling, for what did Joshua accomplish through his life, death, and resurrection if not the undoing, or dismantling, of this Great Barrier?

> [*The Dismantling*] – the result of Joshua's work on Earth; that by his life, death, and resurrection, the Great Barrier was dismantled, allow-

ing for peace and reconciliation to occur between God and humanity; and granting salvation to the human who receives it by faith.

Therefore, Joshuanism is a spirituality (or, if you prefer, a way of thinking and a way of living) that theologically depends on these two ideas for its purpose of existence. In other words, without the Great Barrier and the Dismantling, Joshuanism is nothing (just as Christianity without the doctrine of original sin and the justifying work of Jesus is also nothing). Without the Great Barrier, the Dismantling was unnecessary. Without the Dismantling, we have no Savior. This is *cause and effect* on a grand scale: because "A" existed (the Great Barrier); "B" was destined to happen (the Dismantling). Christianity might not identify with this new terminology, but the ideas are nevertheless the same. Like Christianity, Joshuanism maintains that the Son of God's work was indeed accomplished, paving the way for salvation. Both agree that the Son of God (Jesus to Christians; Joshua to Joshuans) resides at the heart of these philosophical, spiritual, and theological beliefs. Christianity is a religion based on those beliefs, or more accurately, on the Son of God who undergirds those beliefs. Joshuanism is a spirituality based on that same Son of God. Perhaps now, viewing Joshuanism in this light, you can see that this new path beyond Christianity is not the evil, blasphemous, or satanic heresy you may have originally thought it to be. I hope this is the case.

Now, let's discuss salvation.

Absolute Deliverance

If asked, most Christians would most likely identify salvation as something having to do with either the forgiveness of sins or a secured seat in heaven. To a Christian, to be *saved* is to be considered pardoned in the eyes of God and spared from an eternal fate in hell. These both sound like very good gifts to be had. But does salvation begin and end there? Oh sure, other Christians might talk about *redemption* as an aspect of salvation, but few lead lives anyone would describe as *redeemed*, and few experience anything in the way of redeeming power. I cannot calculate the number of times I have heard Christians say something like this: "I thought becoming a Christian would bring change—*real* change—but it hasn't" or "If I have God in me now, why can't I stop living as though I don't?"

Perhaps the problem is that Christianity has forgotten the fullness of salvation as offered by the Son of God. Joshuanism seeks to remedy that.

Joshuanism remembers that when Joshua was alive in the first century, he did and said some very interesting things concerning salvation. In fact, read through the four Gospels again, and you might be surprised to note how infrequently he actually mentions the forgiveness of sins. He does mention it, to be sure, but notice also how much more he mentions *other* things, such as: brokenness, restoration, oppression,

Joshuanism

relief, captivity, freedom, light, darkness, good, evil, sickness, and health. Joshua seems to be demonstrating on an astonishing scale that salvation is a multifarious experience that comes in many forms, with many diverse rewards, and which, at times, almost appears to have a yin/yang element. Joshua seems to be communicating a salvation that speaks to every ailment of the human condition, not just the *sinful* ailment.

Therefore, salvation according to a Joshuan mindset involves *all* of the following:

1. The complete, irrevocable forgiveness of specific sins (including past, present, and future sins);
2. The instant removal of a sinful nature in theory and the ongoing removal of a sinful nature in practice;
3. A secured place in the eternal presence of God (or, eternal life in heaven);
4. The instantaneous and permanent indwelling of God in the heart of the believer (carried out by the Soul of Godliness, the third person of the Singular Fellowship);
5. A spiritual connection with God where previously none existed (i.e., friendship with God, knowledge of God, fellowship with God, ongoing communication with God, etc.);
6. An awarded and irreversible status of "holy in the sight of God;"
7. The inception of spiritual life where previously only physical life was present;
8. The immediate instillation of meaning, purpose, and direction in the life of the believer;
9. The immediate extraction of the believer *from* the world and the immediate transfer of the believer *into* the community of those set apart (what Christianity calls The Church and Joshuanism calls The Extraction[3]);
10. A transference from slavery to freedom;
11. Relief from all aspects of oppression;
12. Freedom from all manner of addictions;

---

3   See Part Four.

13. Healing for all forms of pain[4];
14. Power for godly living;
15. The restoring of the believer to God's original design for humanity; that is, to be made in God's image;
16. Inclusion into all the wonderful blessings of God;
17. The ability to begin seeing through God's eyes rather than just your own;
18. A renewed sense of health and wellness;
19. Instant and constant access to the spiritual realm through faith; and
20. Instant and constant access to the redeeming, refurbishing, revitalizing, power of God.

As you can see, to experience salvation as a Joshuan involves more than just having your name written down in some heavenly ledger so that on the last day, when the trumpets sound and the books are opened, your name will be called. To experience salvation as a Joshuan is to be transferred from death to life, from nothing to something, from evil to good, from sickness to health, from oppression to liberation, from captivity to freedom, from old to new, from futility to meaning, from pointlessness to purpose, from sinful to righteous, from condemnation to total clemency, from darkness to light, from no to yes, from left to right and from right to left, to be established in the sight of God, needing nothing, owing nothing. Free and clear. Fully alive. Restored. Renewed. Repaired. Reborn. Relieved. Released. Reclaimed. *That* kind of salvation seems quite encompassing. That is why, when referring to salvation as it's expressed in Joshuanism, I sometimes (though not always) use the term Absolute Deliverance.

> [*Absolute Deliverance*] – The Joshuan expression for salvation, implying that to "be saved" is to experience not just forgiveness of sin and eternal life but also absolute, indubitable, immutable, interminable *deliverance* through faith from every possible aspect of *spiritual* oppression, captivity, defect, unrest, desolation, meaninglessness, and human dysfunction.

I don't know about you, but the prospect of all that sounds pretty good. Just being a human and moving through this world can be so hard sometimes. In fact, there are times when it seems like being a human is the very definition of what it means to hurt. Sometimes, just moving through this world without being wounded daily

---
4 God does not always see fit to deliver us from physical pain (or disease and death), though he does sometimes. We must assume that the physical aspect of salvation will be manifested in our new, resurrected bodies.

seems impossible. When you wish and hope and pray for an answer to all of this, isn't it deliverance you are really seeking? When you pursue salvation, when you cry out for God to save you, aren't you really asking to be delivered? When you strip away all the materialism and triviality from your human existence and get down to the truest, most basic raging desire within, the one that lurks underneath all others, the one that truly craves an answer in a way that no other desire does, isn't it deliverance you are longing for? Joshuanism says that you *can* and *will* be delivered. How? By faith. Faith in whom? Joshua.

That is why Joshua is called the Deliverer in Joshuanism, rather than the Christ, because to be "saved" by Joshua is to be absolutely delivered.

Doesn't that sound like good news? It ought to. The good news is supposed to be good news. In fact, it's supposed to be *astonishing* news. As much and as deep and as violently as you crave life, so, too, does God crave to give it you, and he will give it to you through faith in Joshua. Likewise, as much and as deep and as violently as you crave deliverance, so, too, does God crave to give it you, and he will give it to you through faith in Joshua. That is astonishing news for humanity.

Joshuanism is a spirituality through which this salvation (or Absolute Deliverance) that God offers is experienced by those who believe and presented to those who do not yet believe.

In view of all this, let's now construct a list of ten theological observations that document what we have already discussed about the Gospel, salvation, and the progression of thought that explains how these things fit together in Joshuan theology.

These are the Ten Tenets of Joshuanism:

1. God exists, God is good, and God can be known;

2. God has chosen to make himself known through *revelation*;

3. This revelation is manifold, presented to humanity through three channels: a) through Joshua; b) through the scriptures; and c) through our ongoing experiences with God;

4. God's revelation of himself to humanity is not complete (or finished) and never could be (Perpetually Incomplete Revelation);

5. God *wants* humanity to know him inasmuch as humanity is able to at any given time (Requisite Desire);

6. Despite this, humanity could not know God because of the Great Barrier;

7. Because of his love for humanity, God *entered into* humanity in the person of Joshua to dismantle the Great Barrier and succeeded in doing so;

8. With the barrier thus dismantled, humanity and God are able to have fellowship; God can now be known;
9. The individual human enters into this fellowship through authentic belief and faith in Joshua (the believer now *knows* God); and
10. Once in this fellowship, the individual is now a partaker of God's irrevocable salvation, including all the benefits therein (Absolute Deliverance).

There you have it. These are the essential elements of Joshuanism. Again, much of this is similar to Christianity. Nevertheless, some of it is quite different indeed. Christians, for example, do not usually consider God's revelation of himself to be incomplete or unfinished. They also seem to have a hard time with the idea that God reveals himself not just through his Son and not just through the scriptures but also through our continuing experiences with him, or perhaps it might be better to say that Christians afford their experiences with God a very low status concerning revelation, preferring almost always to defer to the scriptures. Joshuanism, on the other hand, encourages one to learn from their experiences with God because Joshuanism affords our human experiences with God a very high status. What does this mean, exactly? It means that as humanity evolves and continues to experience God, we gain new insights into what God is like, how God operates, how much we can know about God, what is right and wrong (because right and wrong *do* change—ask any Christians who were alive during segregation), and how and where our conventional thinking needs to change, if indeed it *does* need to change. And I think the answer is obvious. Change is definitely needed.

The Invited and the Respondent

One major theological breakaway in Joshuanism concerns the idea of *predestination*, a belief rampant within Christianity that says God has predetermined some humans for salvation and others for destruction (although not all Christians subscribe to predestination). Joshuanism does not agree with this belief or the faulty logic behind it. Yes, faulty. Consider that the idea of predestination implies the following things: 1) God specifically creates and designs certain humans with destruction in mind; 2) God knows ahead of time these humans are destined for destruction (hell) and, contrary to the love he supposedly possesses and indeed *is*, he goes ahead and creates them anyway; 3) God must therefore *desire* that some people experience eternal destruction because if he did not desire it, he would not and could not carry out the deed of creating them for that purpose, and if God violates his own desire[5]

---

[5] The question is this: can God desire one thing and yet behave in a manner contrary to that desire? In other words, can God do that which he does not want? The answer would seem to be no.

and his own loving nature, he ceases to be God; and 4) if God has predestined some for this purpose and others for that purpose, what *we* do actually means nothing and we are therefore absolved of any responsibility in the matter (which then means we can live any way we like). Joshuanism finds these implications unacceptable.

Before we go any further in this discussion, though, let's talk about hell. Christians believe in a hell. You may be wondering whether or not Joshuans do. The answer is complicated. Joshuans certainly acknowledge that the scriptures speak of such a place, but Joshuans are not obsessed with it. What do I mean by "obsessed?" Christians tend to view all of humanity through a lens that divides people into two categories: *the lost* and *the saved.* In other words, they see everyone in terms of who is going to enjoy eternal rewards and who is going to suffer eternal punishment (i.e., "*We* are going to heaven, *they* are going to hell"). By doing so, they take out of God's hand a pronouncement and a judgment that should be his alone. No one fully knows what goes on in the heart of God, and no one fully knows what goes on in the heart of another human. Moreover, by assigning heaven to some (usually "us") and hell to others (usually "them"), Christians cheapen the quality of *this* life and focus too much on the *next*. This is because Christians usually see *eternal life* as something having to do with *time*, something that begins *later* (after death). However, *eternal* does not mean *later*, it just means *unending*. Being given eternal life by God through faith is a great and precious gift, but it does not mean we should suddenly forget about life *now* or become obsessed with heaven and hell. Joshuans choose not to. Joshuans choose to see *now, today, this moment* as sacred. Didn't Joshua say tomorrow would worry about itself? So, while Christians are obsessed with heaven and hell (particularly hell, which is extremely bizarre and nothing if not counterproductive), Joshuans are obsessed with life, not death. Joshuans refuse to view another human being through a perceived judgment of their eternal destination. Why should anyone dwell on matters no one can even begin to fully understand? For that matter, why should anyone dwell on death?

However, the question probably won't go away, so I suppose we must answer it: do Joshuans believe in a hell? Does Joshuanism subscribe to a belief in hell? Yes. Joshuanism does not reject or discard the idea of hell. Joshuans just afford it little attention because, if we are doing our job, no one should go there, anyway. The Great Barrier has been dismantled, so if there is a hell, no one ever need go there. *That* is what we should be concerned with, is it not? The *life* God offers, not the *death* he sent Joshua to defeat.

Now, as for predestination, there is certainly no argument that the word appears in the *New Testament*. However, in each case, there seems to be no link between predestination and an *individual*. The text instead seems to be focusing on *a people* who were predestined, not that certain individuals were specifically designed for heaven and others specifically designed for hell. What people? The believers.

The Church in Christianity and The Extraction in Joshuanism (we will get to that). The called-out ones. The set-apart ones. The extracted ones, who, by faith in Jesus (if they are Christians) or Joshua (if they are Joshuans), have experienced salvation and are thus separate from those who have not yet experienced that same salvation. These are the people who are predestined, the ones who believe. Now, of course, not everyone believes. Nevertheless, Joshuanism maintains that those who don't believe weren't predestined *not* to believe because Joshuanism also maintains that *everyone* is predestined to believe. It's just that not everyone fulfills his destiny. The ones who do not are given the same invitation as those who do believe were given; but these persons have not chosen to believe yet. Maybe they never will. Still, predestination has to do with the believers as a whole, not the unbelievers and certainly not the individual. Some Christians, like the Arminians and the Wesleyans, agree with this assessment. Other Christians, like the Calvinists, do not.

For all of these reasons, Joshuanism prefers not to see people as *the lost* and *the saved*, or *the predestined for heaven* and *the predestined for hell*. No one is predestined for hell. God does not want a single soul sent to hell. If he did, he would be evil. If he is evil, he is not God. But he *is* God, and he's *not* evil. Therefore, we are *all* predestined for heaven. That is the only conclusion that makes sense. Everyone's destiny is heaven, but God does leave it up to us, each individual, to decide whether or not to fulfill that destiny. So, while Christianity sees people as belonging to either *the lost* or *the saved*, Joshuanism sees people instead as belonging to either *the Invited* or *the Respondent* because, you see, *everyone* is invited. Not everyone responds.

> [*The Invited*] – those to whom God's invitation for life and Absolute Deliverance has been given (everyone).
>
> [*The Respondent*] – those who, by faith, have responded to that invitation (the believers).

God never stops inviting. He is constantly putting out his invitation to those who have not yet responded. God gives up on no one. Who, then, are the Invited? Everyone! Everyone is invited: Those who believe, those who do not yet believe, and those who will never believe are all included in the Invited. Not everyone, however, is included in the Respondent. Who are the Respondents? Those who have responded to the invitation, those who by faith have received Absolute Deliverance.

The terms *the Invited* and *the Respondent* work better in this capacity than *the lost* and *the saved* do. Why? Because the term *the lost* implies futility and finality as though there is no hope, and the term *the saved* makes salvation sound like an exclusive secret society, an elite club reserved only for special people. On the other hand, the term *the Invited* implies hope and inclusion as though there is still a chance for people Christianity would consider lost. Likewise, the term *the Respondent* removes any hint of elitism and superiority regarding salvation, reflecting the truth that everyone is invited but not everyone responds.

The *New Testament* confirms this. Again, remember *John* 3:16? "For God so loved *the world*, that he gave his only Son, that *whoever* believes in him should not perish but have eternal life (ESV)." That passage does not say, "For God so loved those he *predestined*;" it says, "For God so loved *the world*." Likewise, the apostle John says in his first epistle that Joshua was/is the atoning sacrifice for *the entire world* (see 1 *John* 2:2). If God has predestined some for unbelief, meaning that they were specifically designed and created *not* to believe and therefore to suffer punishment and death, then the gift of God's Son could never have been meant for the whole word, that is, *everyone*. Now, does God know ahead of time who will believe in his Son and who will reject his Son? Of course. Can it be said, then, that God predestines for life those he already knows *will* believe and predestines for death those he already knows *will not* believe? Maybe. The scriptures seem to indicate something along those lines (see *Romans* 8:29), but there again, the text does not seem to be speaking of the individual but rather the collective group. At any rate, the invitation to believe, the invitation for life, must be meant for everyone. Otherwise, *John* 3:16 would read like this: "For God so loved *those who would believe in him* that he gave his only Son, that *those he designed to believe in him* shall not perish but have eternal life *while those he designed not to believe in him* will perish."

The Christian view of predestination falls apart when we consider that 1) God *is* love and therefore *could not* and *would not* design a human being with hell in mind; 2) God does not and could not ever *desire* that anyone be destined for death; and 3) God has given to the human race to opportunity to decide its destiny by choosing to remove himself from the decision-making process (meaning that he has given human beings free will, and if free will isn't *totally* free, it really isn't free will at all).

Now, does God know when he is creating a specific person that this person will choose to reject him and therefore ultimately suffer eternal punishment? Of course. He would not be God if he did not know that. Does this mean he is evil if he goes ahead and creates them anyway? No. Why not? Because he creates them with life in mind. He creates them knowing he will offer them every chance to choose him, to accept his invitation. He creates them hoping they will come to him. Yes, God hopes. Does he know his hope is in vain in certain cases? Of course, he does, but he hopes nonetheless. He hopes you will choose the destiny he has in mind for you, a destiny that leads to life, but he leaves that choice up to you. That is the definition of free will.

Speaking of free will, I'd like to tell you a little story. My wife and I were driving home the other day when she said something so profound I almost spit out the Dr. Pepper I was drinking. I immediately grabbed my phone and texted her statement to myself so that I could remember it later. This is the conversation that transpired in our car:

"Vito," she said (my wife calls me by my middle name), "I've been thinking lately about free will."

"What about it?" Said I.

"Well, God loved us enough to give us free will, right?"

"Truer words were never spoken," I said…and then she blew me away.

"I guess the question is whether or not *we* love *him* enough not to use it."

I was absolutely stunned. What a beautiful, simple, yet insanely profound thought to have. We have free will, yes. But do we have to use it? Is that not what surrendering to God means, when you really get down to it? Perhaps the sin of pride is *using* our free will instead of surrendering that gift back to God. Perhaps the act of humility is saying (and meaning) something along these lines, "God, you gave me the power to choose, but I relinquish that power back to you and prefer to choose what *you* would choose for me." What is it that God would choose for you? Salvation. Absolute Deliverance. That you would *respond* to his *invitation*. In other words, God hopes you will lay down your right to choose for yourself and take up the choice he has already outlined for you, a path that leads to him, to life.

God's choice for you is never death. God's choice is never hell. God does not and could not destine anyone for anything other than life. Yes, you have free will, but you don't have to use it. If you truly trust God, then let him decide for you. He will never decide that your fate should be death. He will always choose life for you; otherwise, he would not be love.

Joshuanism, therefore, rejects predestination because, in view of God's love, it simply does not make any sense. Now, I can already hear certain Christians saying, "Well, a lot of things don't make sense, but we accept them by faith." I don't disagree with that statement; however, I want to make one thing quite clear: while Christians too often swallow everything their dogma has taught them over the last two millennia with a shrug of their shoulders, resigning themselves just to have faith in teachings that make absolutely no sense, Joshuanism believes human beings ought to use the minds God has given them. Logic gets a bad rap in Christian circles because of how much emphasis is placed on faith. Of course, faith is important (though it is not the most important thing, according to the apostle Paul's statement in *1 Corinthians* 13:13), but faith ought to be used in conjunction *with* the mind, not *without* the mind. Instead of blindly accepting ideas and teachings that make zero sense, we ought to ask ourselves if our information is faulty. We ought to ask ourselves if our theology needs an update.

Does this mean we will comprehend everything? No. Are there going to be things we do not understand and could never understand? Of course. Theology is not an exact science. Does this mean we should we accept by faith everything we do not understand? It depends. On what? On what we continue to learn about God. Is God's mind above ours? Certainly. Does he know more than we do? Absolutely. That goes without saying, but this just means God has *more* logic than we do, not a *different* or a *competing* logic (after all, he created us in his image, and that includes our minds). By giving us intelligent minds, God has endowed us with a wonderful tool to be used in the study of both him and his ways. Faith may dwell in the *heart* and in the *soul*, but faith without a sound *mind* that intelligently grapples with the mysteries of God is a shallow faith. If you do not even somewhat understand that which you believe in, how authentic is your belief? Accepting bad information by faith benefits no one. Seeking good, right information by faith, using our minds as well as our hearts, benefits everyone. In Joshuanism, we maintain that though God's ways are above our ways and though his mind is above our minds, he wants us to have right information, not just right faith. Joshuanism also maintains that we are able to handle more information as we evolve in our capacity to do so, which means that previously held notions should always be re-evaluated.

Do not be afraid to use your intelligence. After all, God gave it you. It is therefore a gift. It is therefore something he intended for you to use and use often. He gave you the ability to comprehend because he obviously *wants* you to comprehend. He wants you to understand. So, why hold yourself back?

Scriptural Relegation

This might be the hardest pill to swallow in all of Joshuan theology. Therefore, I am going to try to express this idea carefully and delicately so as to make sure readers understand precisely what I am saying.

Scriptural Relegation has to do with the inerrancy of scripture. In other words, Scriptural Relegation questions whether all scripture is, in fact, inerrant, specifically the *New Testament*. Now, before you write this idea off as heterodox or just completely blasphemous, consider the following facts:

1. **Some scriptures disagree with each other.** There are many examples of this. The genealogies of *Matthew* and *Luke* contradict each other. The final words of Joshua, just before he dies on the cross, are different in *Matthew*, *Luke*, and *John*. *Matthew* and *Mark* disagree about what drink was offered to Joshua on the cross. Judas Iscariot hangs himself in Matthew's account, but the book of *Acts* says he fell into a field where his body burst open and his intestines spilled out. Joshua tells his followers never to judge another human being in *Matthew*, yet the apostle Paul says in *1 Corinthians* that he has passed judgment on a particular sinner in Corinth. In *Acts* 9:7, Luke says that the men traveling with Paul on the Damascus Road (when Joshua appears to him) did not see the vision but did hear the spoken words. Some chapters later, in *Acts* 22:9, Luke says the men did not hear anything but did

see the vision. So, which was it? Now, these are just a few of the many instances we could point to in the *New Testament* where one verse seems to contradict another. What conclusion can we reach except to say that perhaps the *Bible* is not as faultless as we have been told?

2. **Some scriptures display human imperfection.** For instance, when Paul is recounting to the Corinthians the number of believers he has baptized in the city of Corinth, he begins by saying he only baptized two individuals. Then he says he forgot that he also baptized an entire family. After that, he adds that he does not quite recall if he baptized anyone else (see *1 Corinthians* 1:13-17). Now, if every single word of the *Bible*, though penned by humans, originates ultimately from the mouth of God and is therefore utterly and irrevocably inerrant, does this mean that it was not really Paul forgetting how many believers he baptized in Corinth, but that, in fact, it was actually God forgetting this information? Clearly, God cannot forget anything. Thus, we must assume that the human (and therefore *errant*) fingerprint in scripture is much greater than we previously were willing to admit and that perhaps God's fingerprint in scripture is not as strong as we once thought.

3. **Some scriptures are factually incorrect.** There are many historical inaccuracies in the *Bible*, even in the *New Testament*. For example, King Herod's infanticide is found nowhere in the historical record. Similarly, Caesar's census, cited in both *Matthew* and *Luke*, is not mentioned in any historical text of that time and is considered by historians to be dubious. More than that, though, consider these factual errors: 1) in *Matthew* 27:9, the writer quotes an *Old Testament* prophecy and attributes it to Jeremiah when, in actual fact, the prophecy in question is found in *Zechariah*[6], not *Jeremiah*; and 2) in *Matthew* 23:35 the writer has Joshua (Jesus) mistakenly confusing two *Old Testament* characters, speaking of a person named Zechariah who was killed in the old Hebrew temple, calling him the son of Berekiah when, in actual fact, there were two Zechariahs, and the one killed at the temple was the son of Jehoiada; the other Zechariah, who was not the person killed at the temple, was the son of Berekiah. So what should we conclude then? Did the Son of God remember incorrectly? Or did the writer record the quote incorrectly? Obviously, the latter must the case. Now, if there are clearly errors in the *Bible*, how can we go on calling it inerrant? Moreover, if these are examples of scribal errors, as some say, made by those translating the texts over the centuries, why

---

6   Zechariah 11:12-13.

would God have allowed the scribes to make errors while not allowing the original writers to do so? Did God render only first draft inerrant and then step away from the scribal translations, allowing them to err wherever they might?

4. **Some scriptures promote ideas and practices that today we no longer observe or find acceptable.** The most hardcore of fundamentalists will profess that each word of the *Bible* is sacred and that no one can pick and choose which scriptures to follow and which to ignore. Yet there are several verses of the *New Testament* that are almost universally ignored, even by fundamentalists, because they point to practices that no longer have any cultural significance. For example, in *1 Corinthians*, the apostle Paul declares that 1) women should cover their heads when they worship God; and 2) women are not permitted to speak when the believers gather together; they must remain silent. Neither of these practices is much observed anymore, except in certain quarters of the Orthodox Church and to some extent in Catholicism's Latin mass. And why not? Our culture is different from the culture of Paul's time, the culture of first century Corinth. Culture changes. Humanity changes. The role of women has evolved to the point that Paul's words about women keeping silent, while appropriate in his day, are considered chauvinistic and sexist today. If you were to ask a Christian why these verses are ignored in today's Christianity, they would most likely say something like this: "Well, that's Paul referring to things that were considered right and wrong in his day, but today we know better." Now, these same Christians will then go on to tell you that the *Bible* is 100% the Word of God and 100% inerrant. But you cannot have both! Either the *Bible* was written by humans who filtered their writings through what was acceptable *at that time*, or it was written completely by God, who would have made statements that were *timeless*. Further, if we decide that certain scriptures are no longer applicable when it suits our fancy to say so; doesn't that demote, or relegate, the sacredness of scripture to the point where any verse could be rejected if we deem it culturally acceptable to do so?

The point I am trying to make here is this: for so long we have viewed the *Bible* as inerrant because that is what we were taught to do, but perhaps it's time to begin questioning whether this is actually the case. Hear me; I am *not* trying to defeat the scriptures, blacken them, or cheapen them. I am not saying they are not important. I am not even saying they are not *of God*. But what I *am* saying is that perhaps God was not actually responsible for each and every word. Perhaps God was moving in the lives of those writing the words, but does that mean he made the words inerrant? Not necessarily.

Here is a question: Does the *New Testament* itself ever make a claim about its own inerrancy? I would say no. The two scriptures that most people point to when making the case for inerrancy are *2 Timothy* 3:16-17, and *Hebrews* 4:12, as quoted below:

> The scriptures were breathed into existence by God. They are beneficial for our spiritual education, for the adjusting of our behavior, and for our preparation to become thoroughly equipped, holy people of God, able to handle any task. (*2 Timothy* 3:16-17)

> The word of God is alive and energetic. It is as sharp as a double-edged sword; it penetrates everything, separating the soul from the spirit, the marrow from the bone; it evaluates the thoughts and the attitudes of the human heart. (*Hebrews* 4:12)

These verses certainly make a case that the scriptures are special, to the point of enjoying a status above other writings (writings that are not considered to be scripture). But nowhere in either of these two verses does the *New Testament* say of itself: "I am flawless, without factual or conceptual error, lacking any defect, completely and totally perfect." First of all, the context of the fourth chapter of *Hebrews* has nothing to do with scripture (read it for yourself). The "word" of God mentioned here has to do with the hearing of God's *voice* when he calls his people to rest. Moreover, even if one interpreted this passage as having to do with the written scriptures (which would be incorrect), the passage still does not indicate inerrancy. Living, yes. Active, yes. Powerful, yes. However, you could say the same things about human beings. Humans are living, active, and powerful—and errant. *Hebrews* 4:12 has some interesting things to say (even though, in its context, this passage does not specify written scriptures), but one thing it does *not* say is this: "the *New Testament* is flawless."

What of *Timothy* 3:16-17? Consider the phrase "The scriptures were breathed into existence by God." In the ESV, that phrase reads like this: "All Scripture is breathed out by God." Notice, however, that saying the scriptures are "breathed out by God" is not the same as saying "All scripture is perfect and inerrant." God-breathed means *inspired by God*. The word used here in the Greek is *theopneustos*, which literally means, "blown into by God," or "God-breathed." The meaning is that God inspired the writing of the scriptures. But does this mean he guided the usage of each word, the execution of each thought, the direction of each theme? That is certainly not what the text says. Further, God did more than *inspire* the creation of the Earth; he created it outright, and yet it's not without flaws. The human body, too, was created by God, not just inspired. It, too, is not without flaws. Humans can be born deformed, disabled, and defective.

Another lesser known passage that some identify as saying something about the inerrancy of scripture is found in 2 *Peter*, quoted below in the NASB version (widely considered to be the most accurate English translation available).

> But know this first of all, that no prophecy of Scripture is a matter of one's own interpretation, for no prophecy was ever made by an act of human will, but men moved by the Holy Spirit spoke from God. (2 *Peter* 1:20-21)

The zealous faithful will, at first, read that passage and see within it confirmation that the scriptures are infallible. But look again. Is that really what this passage is saying? First of all, this passage is referring to the writings of the Old Testament. It therefore has no bearing on the status of the New Testament (which, as the compiled selection of books we know of today, did not exist at the time Peter penned his second letter). However, even if we put that point aside, we still have to read the passage for what it says, not what we want it to say. What does this passage say? This: 1) the scriptures are not a matter of one's own interpretation (in other words, you have to let the scriptures interpret themselves, you cannot make them mean what you want them to mean, you cannot bring your own agenda to them); 2) the writers didn't just dream the scriptures up, pulling the ideas out of their own mind and putting them on paper because they sounded good; and 3) God spoke through the writers, or inspired them, if you prefer. These last two points are in agreement with 2 Timothy 3:16-17. Indeed, we have already observed that God spoke through the writers of the New Testament, that God used humanity, or partnered with humanity, in the writing of the scriptures. What 2 *Peter* 1:20-21 does not say, however, is this: "the New Testament if flawless."

Now, no one is trying to reduce the wonder of God's work; all I *am* trying to do is make the case that just because God *inspired* the scriptures, this does not mean he guided each word, each sentence, each statement, each concept, and each idea into a state of infallibility or inerrancy. If he had, the errors, discrepancies, and contradictions mentioned above would be absent. Thus, we must conclude that anytime God works in tandem with humans to accomplish a goal, the finished product is never perfect, and could never be perfect. The writers of the *New Testament* (Matthew, Mark, Luke, John, Paul, James, Peter) may have been inspired by God, but this did not keep their own imperfections, preferences, cultural ideologies, and personal biases from seeping into the pages of what would eventually be known as the canonical *Bible*. What's more, being inspired by God did not seem to keep the element of human error from seeping in, either.

Therefore, the idea of Scriptural Relegation in Joshuanism asserts that the scriptures are God-inspired but not necessarily inerrant. In other words, Joshuanism relegates, or demotes, the scriptures from the realm of the inerrant to the realm of the "possibly fallible."

> [*Scriptural Relegation*] – the idea that 1) while scripture is sacred, useful, and transformative, it might not be infallible or inerrant; and 2) if it isn't infallible or inerrant, it is therefore subject to amendment *where necessary.*

Now, I said in an earlier section that Joshuanism does not seek to change the complexion of Biblical thought. By Biblical thought, I mean the basic essentials of what we believe: the weighty portions of our theology that cannot be denied, augmented, or abolished lest we lose the reason for these beliefs in the first place. However, there are certain elements of the *New Testament* that simply must be re-evaluated in light of what humanity has come to know and understand about ourselves, the world, and God. For example, in *New Testament* times (the first century) it was considered shameful for a woman to speak when believers gathered together (as we have already noted). Today, this is not the case, and as a result, that particular aspect of Paul's teachings is casually but quietly ignored. If it's okay to do that with one aspect of the *New Testament*, is it okay to do that with others? If we admit that humanity has changed to the point where a woman speaking in a public setting is no longer sinful where it once *was* considered sinful, can we treat other admonitions in the *New Testament* with this same liberality? Can we, in view of 1) how humanity has evolved; and 2) what we now know medically and scientifically (concerning information unavailable at the time the *New Testament* was written), begin to question whether certain other Biblical precedents are subject to modification or repudiation? Obviously, issues like homosexuality and divorce, among others, would be affected by such an approach. That is precisely the point of Scriptural Relegation: to move our minds, our ideas, and our concepts of right, wrong, acceptable, and unacceptable into the realm of that which is truly *post/Christian.*

In Joshuanism, we find that it is okay to wonder about these things. Indeed, it's even okay in Joshuanism to experiment with new ideas, beliefs, and attitudes regarding the scriptures. Does this mean Joshuanism rejects the *Bible*? Of course not. Does this mean Joshuanism rejects the idea of sin? Not at all. Joshuanism merely asks whether the definition of what constitutes a sin can change as humanity changes. If we maintain that sinfulness has more to do with attitude and less to do with behavior (as we observed earlier in this section), perhaps what constitutes a sin *can* change. After all, attitudes of right and wrong evolve alongside humanity. Do you disagree? Consider this: when was the last time you burned someone at the stake for contradicting your theology? When was the last time you accepted a slave into your godly household? When was the last time you committed genocide in the name God? When was the last time you bought an indulgence from the local priest? When was the last time you waged a bloody war to reclaim holy relics? When was the last time you seared a scarlet letter into the breast of a prostitute? When was the last time you hung a man for the color of his skin while the preacher stood by and condoned the act? When was the last time you cut off the hand of a child who stole from you? When was the last time you put to the sword those you caught worshipping idols? When was the last time you put a man on trial for daring to read the scriptures in the privacy of his own home? When was the last time you beheaded a man for being a scientist? All of these things were at one time done by Christians who viewed this behavior as perfectly normally and unquestioningly acceptable. Obviously, what constitutes a sin *can* change over time.

If a Christian tells you that, no, the definition of sin cannot change over time; humbly inquire why women speak in their churches with their heads uncovered. Ask them why they get divorced when the *New Testament* specifically tells them not to. Ask them if they support the abolition of slavery when the *New Testament* says slaves should stay in the keep of their masters. Ask them if they are treating sickness with prayer, as James said they should, or if they are seeking the treatment of a doctor. Ask them if, when someone assaults them, they just stand there and silently turn the other cheek. Ask them if they pray in public when Joshua explicitly told them not to. Ask them if they have given up all their possessions in order to follow the Son of God, since that is what he said they should do to follow him. The truth is this: Christians ignore all kinds of *New Testament* scriptures when it suits their fancy to do so. At the same time, the ones that speak of things they do not understand or are threatened by (like homosexuality, for example) they zero in on as absolutely immovable.

The question is this: how do we know when and where we need to reconsider the continuing validity of certain scriptures? In other words, who is to say what should be ignored and when it should be ignored? Joshuanism has an answer for that, and it has to do with what Joshua said were the two greatest commandments in existence: 1) to love God with all our heart and soul and mind; and 2) to love our neighbors as we love ourselves. Not only did he say these were the two most important commandments, he basically says in *Matthew* 22:40 that if you are doing these two things you are automatically doing *everything*. To fully and deeply love both God and every other human being (even the ones that make you uncomfortable), Joshua says, is the summation of all scripture. Therefore, if at any time we, by observing one particular scripture, can no longer be loving to another human being *because of that scripture*, that particular scripture should be subject to re-evaluation. If some aspect of Biblical teaching becomes, by virtue of its own meaning, antithetical to a loving spirit and a caring attitude among the believers, perhaps that scripture has outlived its usefulness. The question should always come back to whether any one thing is helpful or detrimental to the execution of those two greatest commandments: to love God (which is sometimes the easier part) and to love *everyone else* (which is usually the harder part). If it fosters hatred, prejudice, judgment, division, hostility, or in any other ways inflicts a wound upon those whom we are supposed to love, the scripture is no longer beneficial.

And in case you were wondering whether or not Joshua has anything to say on the matter, consider what he told the Jews who were grumbling against him in the book of *John*: "You meticulously keep your noses buried in the scriptures because you mistakenly think that those written words save you. But you're wasting your time. Those written words point to me, but you refuse to see me for who I am, and by your refusal you miss out on the life you're searching for" (*John* 5:39-40). Even the Son of God himself seems to be saying that we take the scriptures much more seriously than we ought to. It's as if he is saying, "You think it's these writings that have the power, but they're just words that speak of something greater than the writings themselves: me." In other words, the scriptures exist to point humanity toward the Son of God. Now, if the Son of God *is* God, and God *is* love, then the purpose of scriptures must be also be love. If this is so, then it stands to reason that any one passage of scripture that can longer serve in this role (that is, to stimulate us toward love) and prevents us from accomplishing the two greatest commandments is obsolete.

Are the scriptures important? Yes. Are they fallible? Joshuanism does not definitively say *yes*; it just says *maybe*. Joshuanism is willing to admit the possibility. Are the scriptures useful for teaching and training us in God's ways? Yes. Can certain scriptures lose their relevancy? Joshuanism says yes. How do we know when and if this has happened? It has happened any time the observance of a certain scripture bars us from expressing the love that Joshua said is more important than everything else—even the scriptures themselves. Do Joshuans read the *Bible*? Of course. Do they believe every word in the *Bible*? That is between the individual Joshuan and God. However, Joshuans would rather err in scripture and be powerful instruments of love than err in love and be rigid adherents of scripture.

Recall, if you will, the Ten Tenets of Joshuanism. Let's briefly discuss the Third Tenet, as quoted here: *This revelation is manifold, presented to humanity through three channels: a) through Joshua; b) through the scriptures; and c) through our ongoing experiences with God.* Now, if we contend that the scriptures might not be inerrant, how can we say that God reveals himself through them? The answer is simple. We know God is perfect, but his revelation is received by humanity, interpreted by humanity, and filtered through humanity's imperfection. God's revelation of himself may be perfect when it leaves his mouth, but it becomes imperfect the instant it touches the ear of a human. As I said earlier, nothing imperfect issues from God, but nothing perfect passes into the mind of a man. Whenever humans are introduced into any equation, that equation ceases to be perfect. The scriptures are one such equation. Does this mean God cannot and does not use the scriptures in revealing himself? Of course not. He does use them, just as he uses individual humans (who are definitely *not* inerrant). The Joshuan must therefore assemble the larger picture out of all three channels rather than depending only on one. God knows and fully understands that human imperfection will always limit how his revelation is perceived. If he had chosen only to use perfect means of conveying his revelation (such as inerrant scriptures), humanity would never know God. The perfect God must therefore use imperfect means to reach us. In other words, he must come to our level (which he did in the ultimate example of Joshua's invasion of humanity) rather than expecting us to go to his. In view of this, God not only *can* use errant scriptures to communicate with humanity (if indeed the scriptures are errant), he *must* do so.

> *This is a good place to pause and take a breather as much of this material is quite heavy. So, put the book down, and go take a walk or get some coffee. Ponder these things if you feel you must, or push them from your mind altogether and focus on something else for a while. Sometimes, it's good to give our minds a rest. When you feel you are ready to delve even deeper into these new ideas, move on.*

Diversiffed Uniformity

One of the main reasons I felt a path beyond Christianity was needed has to do with the rampant discord found in it. Christians disagree about everything from essential matters down to the lowest of the most insignificant matters. Churches often divide into two factions over these disagreements, with half the congregation leaving in a mass exodus and starting their own group. Denominations fight over who has a better approach to this or that aspect of theology, and as a result, the nonbelieving world looks at Christianity and sees something that resembles a nation in the throes of a civil war. They see within Christianity the very same destructive patterns that characterize the rest of the world. While Christians talk extensively about how they no longer belong to the world, they continue to operate in a manner that does little to distinguish them from everyone else. I do not say these things to paint an ugly picture of Christianity or the Christian. I say these things to illustrate the unfortunate truth that those who might otherwise come to Christianity and find the answers they seek do not come because they see nothing attractive there. It's a sad fact, to be sure. However, it *is* a fact.

I do not take issue with the disagreements. I take issue with how Christians *respond* to them. There is nothing inherently harmful about having differing opinions. In fact, differences of opinion can be a strength that draws us together. We can find common ground on which to stand while at the same time bringing our differences to the table so that what we have to offer the world is diverse and manifold, covering a wide variety of questions and pursuits. For too long, however, Christians have failed to do this. They have instead allowed their differences to drive them apart.

Joshuanism, on the other hand, is specifically meant to be a tapestry of diversity, a place where believers can freely agree on the essential elements of belief and freely disagree on the nonessential elements of belief, with each differing mindset bringing something interesting, beautiful, and beneficial to the discussion.

What do I mean by the essential elements of belief? Those things that cannot be rejected. No one is forced to believe in God, his Son, or anything having to do with either one, but to be a Joshuan *is* to believe certain immovable things. No one has to be a Joshuan any more than anyone has to be a Christian. You can be anything you want to be. To be a Joshuan, though, is to accept by faith certain beliefs that are not subject to rejection. Otherwise, you would cease to be a Joshuan at that point, just as you would cease to be a Christian if you rejected the basic beliefs of Christianity. If you want to reject any part of any teaching, that is up to you, but to belong to Joshuanism is to accept certain Joshuan beliefs and expressions. There are only eight of these essential elements of belief, called the Eight Immovables of Joshuanism.

> [*The Eight Immovables*] – 1) those fixed, essential elements of belief in Joshuanism; and 2) eight nonnegotiable stipulations that must be accepted in order to render one an authentic Joshuan (as opposed to a Christian, or something else altogether).

However, under the umbrella of the Eight Immovables, there is room for diversity and disagreement about the nonessential elements of belief. You can disagree about peripheral issues and still be a Joshuan. You can hold a different opinion on this or that interpretation of scripture or theology (providing it does not violate any essential elements of belief) and still walk side by side with your Joshuan brothers and sisters. No one has to seclude themselves into warring denominations in Joshuanism. Some Joshuans are going to do things one way, others are going to do things another way, and still others are going to do things a third way. Some are going to emphasize one thing over another, while others are going to focus on something else altogether. The point is that all of this okay. We all come from different walks of life and have different backgrounds, different mindsets, different worldviews, and different strengths. Nevertheless, we can continue in these differences and still agree on the things that matter most: God, Joshua, love, faith, etc.

Perhaps this is a good time to talk about unity and uniformity. Unity is not the same thing as uniformity. *Unity* implies two or more different elements joined together in union. *Uniformity* implies that each separate element is identical whether they are joined together or not. Neither word, however, accurately depicts the vision I have for Joshuanism. Uniformity would mean we are all carbon copies of each other, which, of course, we could never be. Moreover, unity, by its very nature, is subject to disunity. If something is joined together, it can be taken apart. So, what is the vision I have for Joshuanism? It should be 1) a place where our differences are as celebrated as our similarities (extinguishing the possibility of *uniformity*); and 2) a place where disunity is incapable of surviving (extinguishing the possibility of *unity*, because as soon as we are united we can be divided).

Therefore, Joshuans must exist in a perpetual state of both diversity *and* uniformity. In order to express this paradox, I created a term that joins these antonyms:

[*Diversified Uniformity*] – 1) a term expressing the paradoxical idea that Joshuans are different and yet they are the same; and 2) a proviso within Joshuanism, stating that aside from the Eight Immovables, the Joshuan can hold any theological or zoêological view and still be considered a Joshuan.

Diversified Uniformity is a Joshuan expression for the dichotomy of similarities and differences that will always characterize human beings regardless of the religion, spirituality, or culture to which they belong. No two humans are ever going to agree completely on any one issue. The point of Diversified Uniformity is to take the hostile element out of the equation. Diversified Uniformity automatically assumes that 1) we are going to disagree; and 2) even in our disagreement we are the same. How are we the same? Consider identical twins. They are different, and yet they are the same. They have two different names, two different minds, two different personalities, and two different sets of interests, and yet they are the same. You could mistake one of them for the other. They are two separate entities who share one appearance. Diversified Uniformity takes this idea and modifies it for the Joshuan. This means you can have two different Joshuans who represent two differences of opinion on a given matter, but who nevertheless share the same God, the same purpose, the same love, the same faith, and the same objectives. They are different (diversified), and yet they are the same (uniform).

I do not mean to downplay the importance of unity. We should stand united where we can. It's just that I know the human being's propensity for disunity is quite strong. It is easier to destroy than it is to create. It is easier to tear something apart than it is to put it back together. If unity is our goal, we might never achieve it. Diversified Uniformity, however, *is* achievable. It removes the weak spots in our armor by elevating our differences to a status of importance alongside our similarities. As a result, our differences cease to be a trigger for animosity and division, thereby making harmony possible. Diversified Uniformity changes the equation. It makes room for the obvious fact that Joshuans from different sectors of the world are going to go about their business, well, differently. Where that is not always considered acceptable in Christianity, it is always acceptable in Joshuanism.

What does this mean in practical terms? There may be Joshuans who want to go on seeing the scriptures as inerrant, choosing to reject Scriptural Relegation. There may be Joshuans who wholeheartedly embrace Scriptural Relegation, rejecting scriptural inerrancy. There may be Joshuans who want to go on believing in the Calvinist view of predestination. There may be some who do not. Some might favor the idea of Mosaic Theology (which we will talk about in a minute). Some will severely dislike it and subsequently have nothing to do with it. Some Joshuans will see science as a hindrance to their faith, while others will see it as an encouragement to their faith. Some Joshuans are going to love all the new expressions in Joshuanism. Others will love some of the expressions and be unsure about the rest. We could go on and on, but the point is this: just because I have laid out the basic theological ideas associated with Joshuanism, this does not mean there is no room for disagreement and discussion. Not everyone has to see eye to eye on every matter. I have laid these ideas out because I believe strongly that they should characterize Joshuanism and, in so doing, set Joshuanism distinctly apart from Christianity. Nevertheless, I have also created Joshuanism to be a tapestry of diversity where any of these ideas can and should be subject to an ongoing dialogue. Diversified Uniformity makes this possible, allowing for this dialogue of differences to continue, while having no divisive effect on our harmony.

These, then, are the Eight Immovables of Joshuanism:

1. A belief in God;
2. A belief in the Singular Fellowship (The Father, The Son, and the Soul of Godliness);
3. A decision to view God's Son as Joshua rather than as Jesus;
4. Acceptance of the Ten Tenets of Joshuanism;
5. Acceptance of the Joshuan Creed (found at the end of this section);
6. A decision to gather together with other Joshuans in a definitively Joshuan way (which we will discuss in the next section);
7. A decision to practice the Five Elements (which we will discuss later); and
8. A decision to primarily read *The Joshuan Pages* version of the *New Testament*

That's it. The rest is open to all kinds of diversity. Why? Because Joshuanism refuses to be threatened by opposing thoughts. If I created Joshuanism and then turned right around and closed it off to any kind of disagreement or discussion, I would be as guilty as those who drove me to create Joshuanism to begin with. That said, acceptance of the above eight items is sufficient to make you a Joshuan. Any deviation from any one of these eight precludes you from being Joshuan. Now, if you do not want to be a Joshuan, you do not have to be one. That is totally fine. But if you do, the above eight items are the only nonnegotiable essential elements of belief. Reject any one of them, and you cease to be a Joshuan at that point. If you do reject any or all of those eight items, though, no one here is going to oppose you. Joshuanism respects your right to make your own destiny with God.

Mosaic Theology

Another aspect of Christianity that Joshuanism hopes to counter is the widespread belief that other religions and philosophies are, at best, unusable and, at worst, evil. However, the attitude prevalent within Christianity that any and all ideas, values, viewpoints, and schools of thought that originated *outside* of Christianity (such as Buddhism, Hinduism, and Taoism) are in *opposition* to God reflects not a security of faith but an insecurity of faith. Those firmly rooted in what they believe should be able to move in and out of other mindsets without losing their footing. More than that, those with minds open enough to embrace Joshuanism are most likely also open enough to embrace the wisdom found in the other religions of the world.

Before we address this idea further, let's explore why Christianity is closed off to other religions.

The Christian religion is an exclusive entity. To belong to it means you cannot, for any reason whatsoever, blur the lines between it and its neighboring religions. Therefore, to be a Christian is to believe that Christianity is the only true religion; all others are false. Where does this attitude come from? A number of places, but primarily one particular verse, where Joshua makes one of his most famous statements and self-proclamations: "I am the way, and the truth, and the life. No one comes to the Father except through me" (*John* 14:6 ESV). This is an interesting statement not just for what it says but also for what it does *not* say. What doesn't it say? This: *Christianity is the way and the truth and the life. No one comes to God except through Christianity.* In other words, the question is whether the Son of God is synonymous with the religion that currently bears his name. Does the Son of God equal Christianity, or does Jesus Christ (known here as Joshua of Nazareth, or Joshua the Deliverer) exist apart from the human religion that has built up around him? I have asked the question before, and I will keep on asking it: can a person get to God through his Son *without* going through Christianity?

For instance, take the thief on the cross, who was crucified next to Joshua, the one to whom Joshua grants salvation, just before both men die. This thief managed to gain salvation and get to God without ever having done a single *Christian* thing. All he did was ask Joshua to save him (technically, he asked Joshua to *remember* him, but we must assume this was a plea for salvation). Joshua grants his request, though the thief never recites the Apostles' Creed, the Nicene Creed, or the Lord's Prayer. The thief never makes a monetary contribution to a church, never even sets foot in a church. He never has access to the *New Testament*, and he is not present when the Holy Spirit comes at Pentecost. He is never baptized, never takes communion, and we cannot say definitively whether he ever utters a single prayer. In fact, the thief does nothing *religious* at all. The best that can be said for the thief is that 1) he believed Joshua was the Son of God; and 2) he voiced that belief when he asked Joshua to save him. The thief was saved. Was he a Christian? No, he was not a Christian by the Christian definition. Nevertheless, he *was* a Respondent.

Consider these questions: can a Muslim believe in God's Son and still be a Muslim? Can a Buddhist believe in Joshua and yet never leave the realm of Buddhism? Can someone who has no affiliation whatsoever to any religion, spirituality, or philosophy believe in Joshua, thus be saved by God, and go on having no such affiliation? Can a person be a Respondent and never have anything to do with either Christianity or Joshuanism? The answer would seem to be yes. Why is it yes? Love. Isn't it interesting how everything always comes back to those two greatest commandments Joshua gave us? Remember what they were? 1) love God; and 2) love humanity. The point of all of this is love! Not this rule or that doctrine. Not this belief or that belief. Not this religion or that idea. Not who is right and who is wrong. But love! All of this (i.e., seeking God, finding God, becoming alive in God, living for God) is for and about love, in the end. Love for God and love for everyone else. Therefore, can a person love God, love humanity, and yet be a Buddhist? Can a person love God, love humanity, and yet practice Judaism, Shintoism, or even New Age spirituality? Can a person prize the elements of a differing religion, identifying with that religion in a way they do not and cannot identify with Christianity, and yet have the kind of love Joshua said would fulfill those two greatest commandments? The question is an interesting one because it challenges the long held attitude within Christendom that other religions are evil.

Martin Luther said we are saved by grace alone, through faith. The apostle Paul, however, said love was even greater than faith. So, can a person who never exercises faith in the Christian sense exercise an authentic love and, in so doing, please God? If you are wondering about the answer, consider this scenario: suppose two men are walking down Michigan Avenue in Chicago. One is a Christian; one is not. They happen upon a young homeless woman and her newborn baby. It is evident from her appearance that she is starving, hopeless, and desperately in need of help. The baby is thin and frail and dangerously close to succumbing to malnutrition. Now, suppose the Christian man sees this wretched sight, hands the woman a pamphlet about Jesus, says, "I'll pray for you," and then walks on. Suppose the other man, who is not a Christian, says, "Wait here, don't leave," then runs to his parking garage, brings his car around, puts both the woman and her baby in the backseat, and then drives her to the nearest restaurant. Suppose also that he arranges for her to have a meal and for the baby to be appropriately fed. Later, he arranges shelter for her and from then on checks up on her, doing what he can for her when he can. Which man did the work of God? Which man behaved with true righteousness? Which man fulfilled the second of the two greatest commandments (to love your neighbor as yourself)? It was the second man who did these things, though he is not a Christian. Joshua did not say that the world would know his followers by their *faith*. He said the world would know his followers by their *love* (*John* 13:35). Am I toning down the importance of faith? No. But I am making the case that the two greatest commandments can be observed by one who never sets foot in the realm of Christianity. If that *is* the case, then adherents of religions other than Christianity can bring authentic love to the table. If *that* is the case, perhaps they can bring other benefits to the table as well.

That is the idea behind *Mosaic Theology*.

> [*Mosaic Theology*] – a belief that though Joshua offers the only way to *salvation*, other cultures, philosophies and religions have some interesting *insights* into God and life which should not be rejected at face value.

Why the word "mosaic?" Well, what is a mosaic if not thousands of smaller images pieced together to create a larger picture? What is the larger picture we are after? Who God is, who we are, and what matters in this life. Christians believe they have the monopoly on those answers because the center of their religion happens to be the Son of God. Yet, there is more to seeking and finding God than just salvation. Joshua may be the only way to salvation, but is he the only source of wisdom and insight? If all humans are created in God's image (which the *Bible* teaches and Christians accept), then surely all humans, from all corners of the Earth, have something to say about God. If the law of God is written on the hearts of all human beings regardless of where they come from or what religion spawned them (which the *Bible* also teaches and Christians also accept), then surely any human being, Christian or otherwise, can lend something interesting to the conversation when it comes to things like who God is and what the purpose of life is. Mosaic Theology suggests that this is the case; that searching for God, finding God, and putting together this puzzle of life on Earth is a story that can be told from any standpoint, with any background, from the lips of anyone with a sincere heart to know the truth.

Joshuanism maintains the exclusivity of salvation offered by the Son of God. In other words, Joshua *is* the way, he *is* the truth, he *is* the life, and no one gets to God without going through him. What is the way of Joshua? Love. What is the truth of Joshua? Love. What is the life of Joshua? Love. As we have already discussed, it is possible to have love, be love, and operate in love without ever knowing a thing about Christianity or even the Son of God. If love is greater than faith, then could a

Native American man living in the tenth century who had zero exposure to Christian theology and teaching and therefore zero faith in the Son of God walk in a manner reflective of the love Joshua preached? If so, could it be said of this man that he was walking in the *way* of Joshua, the *truth* of Joshua, and the *life* of Joshua even though he himself never knew Joshua? Does the phrase "no one comes to the Father except through me" literally mean through personal knowledge *of* and faith *in* Joshua, or does it mean something less literal? Could it possibly be that when he says "through me," he is really saying "by doing what I do and living like I live?" After all, doesn't Joshua say in *Matthew* 25:40 that when a person is loving to another human being, it's the same as being loving to him or to God?

Mosaic Theology therefore finds value in the teachings of other religions. This is not the same as saying Joshuans must practice everything offered by every other religion. That is not possible and, at any rate, it's ridiculous. What this does mean is that Joshuanism has room for the ideas of those who reside outside the realm of Christianity. Joshuanism has room for the insights, the alternate perceptions, the discernments, and the wisdom born from centuries of spiritual thought found in other religions and philosophies. This is because Joshuanism sees the spiritual and existential history of humanity as a long, desperate, often painful search for God—a wandering and meandering through centuries of pondering and pining and grappling with the riddles of life. Moreover, even if we believe that only Joshua offers *salvation*, is it really so blasphemous to believe also that people like the Buddha or Confucius can offer something in the way of *understanding* and *encouragement*? Where Christianity says yes, it is blasphemous, Joshuanism says no, it's not.

So, what other religions should we draw from, and what aspects of those religions should we take? Well, there is no hard and fast rule except to say this: if it's counterproductive to love, damaging to faith, or indicative of immorality, it's probably not going to offer you much. If, however, it's none of these, perhaps it is worth investigating. You will never know unless you try.

Zen Joshuanism

One particular aspect I feel quite strongly should be grafted into Joshuanism is Zen; or at least, certain elements of Zen. Now, I am sure any fundamentalists reading this (if they have managed to condescend enough to do so) are probably shaking their heads and wagging their fingers at me (which I am sure they have been doing a lot since page one). Most Christians reject Zen at face value because 1) they are supposed to; and 2) Zen is not Christianity. However, if they would actually take the time to explore and investigate what Zen is about, they might be surprised how this curious Eastern mindset deals with many of the questions and problems of human existence.

Joshuanism

Zen is different from Christianity in many ways. One of the differences I want to focus on has to do with the objectives of each. Christianity, of course, aims for *salvation*. Zen, on the other hand, aims for *enlightenment*. What is enlightenment? Here in the West, our immediate reaction to the word "enlightenment" is to synonymize it with the word "knowledge." Enlightenment, to us, has to do with intellectual advancement. We even refer to a period in our Western history as the "Age of the Enlightenment," a time of great expansion in science, philosophy, and rational thought. However, in the East, where Zen originated, enlightenment has a completely different meaning. Here the word means *the end of suffering*, or *the absence of suffering*. Now, right away we have a problem because, on the surface, enlightenment would appear to be at odds with Christianity. How so? Well, first of all, the *New Testament* says in multiple places that it is *through suffering* that believers enter the kingdom of God. Second, it also says in multiple places that the believer should be grateful for suffering, find joy in suffering, and learn patience in suffering. Therefore, where Zen ultimately aims to eradicate suffering, Christianity finds suffering beneficial. However, notice that I said enlightenment would *appear* to be at odds with Christianity, *on the surface*. Maybe in reality, it's not.

The kind of suffering advocated as useful in Christianity has to do with what is going on *externally*. In other words, suffering that is happening *to* you because of outside forces (such as persecution, oppression, social conflicts, and even physical diseases, which may be happening *in your body* but are external in the sense that they are not happening in your mind). Learning the art of perseverance in the face of this kind of suffering is indeed beneficial to the sufferer because perseverance always leads to strength of character. The kind of suffering considered reprehensible in Zen, however, has to do with what is going on *internally*, in other words, *in you*, or more accurately, *in your mind*. This is the kind of suffering Zen targets, the absence of which is the definition of enlightenment. When we see that there are these two separate forms of suffering (the external and the internal), we can then see that Christianity is not at odds with Zen at all. In fact, the *New Testament* has much to say about the health of the human mind.

That's all Zen is about, really. The mind. Getting the mind healthy. Keeping the mind healthy. Ridding the mind of that which would harm it, twist it, or in any way add sorrow to it. Seen in this light, Zen would seem to be right in step with God's ways and the teachings of Joshua. How so? Again and again, it all comes back to love. The two greatest commandments. What could possibly be more loving for the world and those you know than to get your mind healthy? Think about it. If your mind is healthy, you will be a much better you, a much happier you, and a much more effective you. In turn, you will have a much more positive impact on those around you. It's paradoxical, but it's nevertheless the truth. The most loving thing you could do for another person is to first get yourself healthy. If you are suffering in your mind or in your spirit, how much help could you be to the hurting people of this world who are suffering along with you? In order to free them, you must first free yourself.

That is why I believe with a deep passion that Zen ought to be married to Joshuanism, hence, Zen Joshuanism. Some of you are going to love this. Others will be wary. That's okay. Remember, Diversified Uniformity means you can be Joshuan and decide you want nothing to do with Zen. It could be that for you the idea is just too foreign. Again, that's okay. I did not title this book *Zen Joshuanism*; I titled it *Joshuanism*. While I did want to devote an entire book to this idea, I chose instead to limit this discussion merely to a section. Joshua is still the main focal point of Joshuanism, not Zen. Nevertheless, for those who are keen to explore this interesting teaching from the East regarding the healing of our minds and the expulsion of suffering there, Zen Joshuanism is an avenue that I have made available.

So what is *Zen Joshuanism*? It is still fully Joshuanism, but it's not fully Zen. In other words, it's a Joshuan take on Zen. On its own, Joshuanism deals with *salvation*, or Absolute Deliverance.[7] When we attach Zen to Joshuanism, however, we have included *enlightenment* as a goal alongside *salvation*. Consider this definition:

> [*Zen Joshuanism*] – 1) a discipline within Joshuanism by which the Joshuan can use elements of Zen (such as meditation and the practice of the Now) to gain mental and emotional health in order to render them better equipped to fulfill Joshua's two greatest commandments; and 2) the addition of *enlightenment* as a goal alongside *salvation*.

So, let's talk about Zen. In its most basic form, Zen has to do with *this moment*. Now. Not yesterday, not tomorrow, not some future state of existence (the afterlife), not the past and all its mistakes, but *now*. For a mind-blowing investigation into this dynamic, read Eckhart Tolle's masterpiece, *The Power of Now*. It is truly an astounding work, one rife with fascinating nuggets of truth and wisdom. He articulates these matters much more effectively than I ever could. However, I will try to sum up these ideas, while at the same time imbuing them with a Joshuan twist:

1. There are two separate aspects to your existence: a) *You* (who you are eternally, the part of you that is either dead to God or alive to God, depending on your faith situation), and b) your *mind*.

---

7   You might be thinking, "I thought you said Absolute Deliverance included the same benefits enlightenment seeks to obtain. How then can you say we should add enlightenment to salvation? Are you contradicting yourself?" No. You are correct, Absolute Deliverance does include mental health, or rather, it ought to be said that it should include mental health. It is meant to include mental health. The fact is, though, it all too often is does not. This is not say God has held out some element of salvation. It's just that human beings don't always have access to the proper tools (such as Zen) because perhaps their religions prevents them from obtaining these tools. It can also be said that perhaps humans, even when they do have the proper tools, are not always faithful to use them.

2. These two separate aspects exist together but are nevertheless *not* one and the same. Or, as Tolle says, you are not your mind.
3. Your *mind* lives *in time*; that is, either in the past or in the future. It sees reality in these terms, measuring everything against what has already happened or what is to come.
4. Time is an *illusion*. Yesterday is gone, and tomorrow does not exist yet. The only thing that is real is Now. The past is just a series of former Nows. The future is just a series of coming Nows. All that ever really, truly exists is Now.
5. The mind is determined to avoid the Now at all costs and stay lost in the illusion of time because if the mind surrenders to the Now, it loses all its power.
    a. Guilt and sadness over what you have done *in the past* or what happened to you *in the past* keeps you in the past.
    b. Worry and anxiety over what will happen *in the future* keeps you in the future.
6. Guilt and sadness over the past form the basis of mental *pain*. Worry and anxiety over the future form the basis of mental *fear*.
7. When pain or fear infects your *mind* (one aspect of your existence), the diseased mind then hinders the ability of your other aspect of existence (You) to live fully in the Now.
8. Thus, you are unhealthy, dysfunctional, depressed, burdened by pain, and burdened by fear—the very definition of *suffering*.
9. From a Zen perspective, the *absence* or *end* of suffering of this kind is *enlightenment*.

In other words, the goal of Zen, the aim of enlightenment, is to bring you *into the present*, to bring you *into the Now*, so that the past (with its pain) and the future (with its fear) collapse to their mutual destruction, liberating you from their power. This is the very essence of Zen: to be fully present, fully in the Now, free from the illusion of time and its infections.

So, how can we apply these ideas to Joshuanism?

Tolle speaks often in his book about the *noise* of the mind, that we are habitual thinkers who have lost the ability to turn our minds off. He also has much to say about the remedy for this. What is the remedy? Meditation. Now, *meditation* is one of those words that carry associations. I don't know about you, but as soon as I hear or read the word *meditation*, I think of the Beatles sitting in a circle around the

Maharishi Mahesh Yogi, chanting mantras and being cool in a way only the Beatles can. At any rate, Zen's take on meditation is very simple. Meditation, in this sense, is simply *bringing yourself into the present.*

Let me explain. Because Zen suggests that there are two parts to your existence (You and your mind), it is therefore possible for *You* to watch *the thinker*. Tolle talks extensively about this as well. That is what meditation is in the realm of Zen: watching the thinker. Meditation is making a concerted effort to observe impartially what the mind is doing, what the mind is saying, how the mind incriminates you, and how the mind refuses to be quiet. As soon as you do this, Tolle says, a dimension of consciousness has come into being. You are now *present*. You are now *aware* of the separation between You and your own mind. How so? If you are watching the thinker, or observing the mind, you have thus confirmed that You and your mind are not the same. Do this long enough and often enough, and eventually it becomes natural to quiet the mind and live in the Now. If you can achieve that, you can end your suffering. *That* is enlightenment. I recommend a thorough reading of *The Power of Now* to obtain the full effect of these teachings.

Zen Joshuanism is an adaptation of this kind of meditation. The Joshuan practices Zen Joshuanism (if he or she wants to) by 1) making a daily determination to meditate, or to become present by watching the thinker; and 2) to practice living in the Now. The more present you are, the quieter your mind is. The quieter your mind is, the better disposed you will be to *communing* with God (i.e., talking to God, hearing God, and sensing God). That is all there is to it. There is nothing *religious* about Zen. Even Christians could practice Zen and still maintain the purity of their Christian faith.

Are these ideas contrary to the Son of God? Not at all. Joshua himself told his followers in *Matthew* 6:34 not to worry about tomorrow (the *future*). He also told his followers in *Luke* 9:62 that no one who puts his hand to the plow and then looks back (focuses on the *past*) is fit to serve him. That, by the way, is the whole point; being *fit* to *serve* him. How do we serve him? By carrying out the two greatest commandments: love. It always comes back to love. No one who is lost in the throes of mental suffering is fit to love anyone. They cannot even love themselves. It is therefore interesting that Joshua phrased the second of the two greatest commandments in this manner: "love your neighbor as *yourself*." Or put another way, "love your neighbor the way you love yourself." If you do not love yourself, you are not going to love your neighbor, and you are certainly not going to love God. Love, by definition, must be free and unburdened. Love and oppression cannot exist together any more than light and darkness can. If you are living under mental oppression, you cannot love, at least not authentically. Therefore, you must have a healthy *self* in order to love *yourself*. Zen is a great tool for getting healthy. It's very zoêological.

If you are sitting there thinking that this is all extremely unorthodox, perhaps even sinful, consider that if Zen *is* helpful in bringing peace to the human mind, how could God frown on that? Ask yourself, do you really think he is up there fuming and having a fit because you are using Zen to improve the quality of your mental health? Do you think God is pouting that you are using a route that is *not* Christian? Or does God approve of any method that brings health to the human? Health is health, regardless of where it originates. God knows that. The question is whether you do. Therefore, any tool that is beneficial to the mind or soul must surely have God's stamp of approval on it. It would have to. If this were not the case, we would have to assume that God opposes healthy humans. I do not believe that. Do you?

Try Zen, or do not try it. Embrace it, or do not embrace it. In Joshuanism, the choice is *yours*.

The Fusion

Just a few moments ago, I was sitting at my desk, when I noticed that some people were on my front porch. I went to investigate and found that a young girl was moving into the apartment above mine. There was an older woman with her who turned out to be, oddly enough, her guru. I chatted with them for quite a while, asking all the requisite questions one asks when meeting someone new.

After a while, the older woman said to me, "What do you do?"

"I am a writer," I answered.

"Oh, really? That's great. What do you write?"

My customary caginess overtook me, and I replied with two very ambiguous words: "Spiritual stuff."

Right away, I could tell the older woman was intrigued. She wanted more answers about my work. I gave her some. Then, she wanted even more. So, I broke down and told her all about Joshuanism. I explained the necessity of moving away from "Jesus" and toward "Joshua." I told her about Tables and Zen Joshuanism and Mosaic Theology and the rest. I gave her all the information as succinctly as I could. When I was finished, I expected the usual hostility and condescending explanations about how "mistaken" I am and how I have "missed the point," but she surprised me. She just watched me silently for a moment, her eyes almost scrutinizing me. Then, she clapped her hands together and beamed with approval. "That is the most amazing thing I have ever heard," she said. "It makes complete sense!"

I was shocked. I am so used to a wave of hatred hitting me the instant I speak the "J" word that I forget that there may be many people out there who will read this book and view it like a drop of cool water on the parched tongue of a man lost in a desert.

She began to ask me relevant questions about all of this, and I answered her to the best of my ability. Then she asked, "What about science?"

"What about it?" I replied.

"You need to wed science to this," she said. "That's the only way it will survive where the world is going."

I smiled and said nothing at first, regarding her silently and intently. "What?" She finally asked.

"It is just weird," I answered. "That's the very thing I was typing when I noticed you two on my porch."

It *was* weird. I got the feeling that somehow this encounter was planned, that this woman on my porch was meant to be an agent of encouragement to me. God knows I have needed it. Some encouragement, I mean. I have written most of this book under the impression that much of the world will hate every word I type.

So, what of science? What about her advice to wed science to Joshuanism? What is your first impression of that idea? Mine was the same as hers. I knew instantly that it was necessary. Moreover, it had been my plan all along. I just think it is uncanny that she should have made such a statement on the very day I was writing about how science fits into Joshuanism. However, all spookiness aside, we have some issues to address.

Albert Einstein once said that religion, art, and science are all branches of the same tree. Maybe that is true. The discussion is an interesting one. Let us shelve art, though, and talk about the strange, troubled relationship between religion and science.

It would seem to me that the human beings of the 21st century have more reason to discard the belief in God than any other generation ever has. Where before God was a blanket solution to any mystery, a universal explanation for the unknown, we now have answers. *Solid* answers. So many of life's ambiguities seem to have been obliterated as humanity has pushed forward in science, mathematics, and technology. It's almost as though the need for God has been eliminated. Almost. But not quite.

A friend of mine once told me the story about how he came to believe in God. He was ten years older than I, but we shared a common interest in certain spiritual and theological matters. We were partners in crime for a while, stirring the Christian pot whenever we got the chance. In view of the spiritual depth and tangible godliness of this guy, I was stunned to learn that only five years prior he was the staunchest of atheists. Not only that, but he had been writing a book about science, calling science the "new God." It was a vehement attack against spiritual faith, he told me, using every piece of weaponry in the arsenal toward the disproving of God's existence. He already had several publishers interested in the work and was close to finishing it when an accident happened. His SUV flipped on a mountain road. He had apparently lost control of the vehicle in the rain just as he was rounding a sharp curve. The car skidded, flipped, and tumbled down the side of the mountain. When rescuers appeared on the scene, the SUV was mangled beyond recognition. Yet, my friend somehow walked away from that wreck with only a minor cut above his eye. As he was telling me this story, I asked him how in the world he had survived. He said this: "The moment I lost control of the car I knew I was dead. I knew I was facing the bitter end. All I could do was call upon the very one I'd spent my life hating. All I could do was say four words, and so I said them. 'I believe in you!' I screamed just as my car flipped over the side of the cliff. The police told me no one could have survived that fall. It was impossible, they said, but I knew how it was that I survived. And I gave my life to the one who had saved me." I have never cared for the cliché, but I suppose the point is a good one: are there any atheists on an airplane when it's crashing?

The point is this: we have no shortage of scientific explanations for whatever you want to explain from the creation of the Universe to the hatching of an egg. We have monstrous mathematic equations that somehow unravel the riddles of life, gravity, relativity, time, and any other abstraction you can think of. We have technology that daily changes the way humans operate and react to the world. We know and can do so much more than we could ever know or do before. We are almost something like post/human. Yet even now, in the midst of this unparalleled evolution in mind and ability, the belief in God prevails. Why is it that, even now, when humans have more reason to turn atheist than ever before, so many of them refuse to let go of a belief in God? Is it merely a clinging to the comfort of the beliefs of old? Is it fear? Are humans afraid to discard God because a belief in hell persists despite all we have learned scientifically? What is it that keeps humanity still rooted in the unseen when everywhere we look science seems to be snatching away all our mysteries?

Maybe it's that science *is not* snatching away our mysteries. Maybe it's that the so-called "conflict" between religion and science, or faith and reason, only exists in the minds of those who want it to exist. Maybe in reality, it does not exist at all. Perhaps science does not seek to destroy faith the way so many people think it does. What if science and faith were telling the same story from different points of view?

Before we explore this possibility, let's revisit another time in history when it seemed science was working against faith. Remember that time machine we used earlier? Suppose we used it again to visit Europe in the late 16th century. We would find there a scientific atmosphere not unlike our own. What I mean is that we would encounter breakthroughs in rational thought and advancements in scientific knowledge that, on the surface, would appear to be in opposition to the faith and religious consciousness of the time. Just like today, we would find the proponents of the religious status quo digging their heels in, stubbornly resisting the change these breakthroughs imply, refusing to lay down old, comforting ideas and take up new, unsettling ideas. They violently oppose those new ideas they feel are threatening them and their worldview, and they violently oppose the men responsible for them.

Unlike today, however, the proponents of the status quo in the 16th century had the deadly Inquisition on their side and, consequently, the power to inflict terror and even death on anyone who championed these so-called "heresies." Meanwhile, the heretics, who turned out to be completely right (and who, in most cases, were deeply religious people), had no power to inflict torture or death on anybody; all they were armed with was the truth and their convictions. What was the truth? That the world *was not* flat. That the Earth *was not* at the center of the Universe. That objects like planets and solar systems and even other galaxies existed. That the Earth was just another one of these planets, fairly insignificant on its own, in submission to physical laws of a decidedly *scientific* nature—not a *religious* one. Therefore, the Inquisitors and the heretics squared off in an ongoing struggle for the monopoly on explanations to the mysteries of the Universe.

So, who won? The truth is that both sides won and both sides lost. How is that possible? Well, those ideas still exist today, right? We know the Earth is round. We know it does not reside at the center of the Universe. We know all about the physical laws and the scientific rationales for what is going on cosmologically. Science prevailed. Yet, faith did, too. Faith did not disappear. Religion did not crumble in on itself and cease to be. Men and women of God continue to be born, live, and die in the throes of spiritual conviction. The Catholic Church still exists. Protestantism still exists. Millions of people affirm the scientific discoveries and still say grace before a meal, still go to church, still study the *Bible*, still believe what they find in the *Bible*, and still look forward to the reward of heaven after death.

If we stood on a street in Florence in the year 1600 and surveyed the cultural atmosphere and observed the gathering storm that pitted the clergy against the scientists, it would probably feel like one was going to vanquish the other. It would probably feel as if everything known and accepted and comforting was being called into question and that when the smoke cleared, only one would remain standing: faith or science. However, when the smoke cleared, both remained standing. Both survived. It's now 400 years later, and the world is still filled with champions of faith *and* champions of reason. In fact, the world is filled with millions of people who champion both at the same time.

Sometimes, it seems like we are still fighting that same battle. We are still looking for one clear victor. We are still operating as though science opposes faith, faith opposes science, and in the end, only one will be proven correct to the utter destruction of the other. We have the religious camp on one side, be they Christians or of some other conviction, clinging to creationism and traditional explanations for the origins of humanity and civilization. We have the scientific camp on the other side, clinging to evolution, mathematical theories, abstract equations, and the perpetuation of further discovery through the scientific method. Both sides are vying for dominance; yet, neither one will ever have it. Why not? Because one side of a coin cannot do battle against the other side. If they try, the result will be a useless, meaningless, ongoing spinning to no end (which is exactly what we have with the so-called "conflict" between faith and science). The only thing each side of that same coin can really do is attempt to coexist peaceably with the other side. After all, there may be two sides, but there is only one coin. Likewise, there may be two points of view (faith and science), but there is only one story (God).

Therefore, Joshuanism marries faith and science together, once and for all. Joshuanism maintains that both are telling the same story of the same creative, wondrous God. Joshuanism asks what difference it makes whether we believe in creationism or the Big Bang, the Garden of Eden or the theory of evolution. If God initiated one, he certainly could have initiated the other. Remember, even evolution had to be designed and set in motion by someone. Even the Big Bang had to be triggered. Both points of view spotlight the same creator and same designer: God. Consequently, Joshuanism allows the Joshuan to lean to whichever side seems right to them, first through Diversified Uniformity and second through the *Fusion*.

> [*The Fusion*] – the Joshuan expression for the marriage between faith and science; 2) the end result of this marriage; 3) the Joshuan belief that faith and science are telling the same story of the same God; and 4) Joshuanism's contention that the so-called "conflict" between faith and science is over and never need have existed in the first place.

You might as well get used to science because it's going to keep on advancing. You cannot fight it. Why would you want to? Science is an incredible thing. It is no small accomplishment to be able to finally start answering some of the questions that have dogged humanity for thousands of years. Some people, however, say that the power is not found in the obtaining of an answer but in the asking of the question. Well, there will never be a shortage of questions. In most cases, each new answer only leads to more questions. Why shouldn't this be an exciting prospect? Why shouldn't we look upon our future with wonder at what we will become if we keep on down this road of discovery? Why do we have to view each new scientific breakthrough as another nail in the coffin of faith? Who says faith cannot evolve alongside these breakthroughs and discoveries? It can. It should. It needs to. Why? Because science is not going to stop. You cannot fight it. Pending some apocalyptic end to the world as we know it, the evolution of knowledge is going to mushroom. As they say, "if you can't beat them, join them."

That is the idea behind the Joshuan Fusion. The word "fusion" means merging two separate entities together to form one single entity. Like milk and chocolate syrup. You start out with two separate entities, but when you combine them (or *fuse* them); you end up with one single entity: chocolate milk. That is precisely what

Joshuanism does with faith and science; it fuses them together to form one single mindset that accepts the separate but equal evolution of both.

The two separate elements in this case, faith and science, come together in Joshuanism to form something entirely new, different, and singular: a spiritual "coin" of sorts. One side is faith; the other side is science. Two sides, one coin. Two channels, one truth. Two atoms, one molecule. Two elements, one entity.

Now, let's discuss some of the differences between faith and science. Faith, by its very nature, seems to breed insecurity. The more some people believe in something, the more they feel the need to guard it as though the very mention of an opposing idea will cause all they believe in to shatter. I have a hard time understanding this. I would think it should be the other way around. Faith should breed security; doubt and uncertainty should breed insecurity. The more we believe something, the surer of it we ought to be, to the point where very little could shake our conviction. The less sure of something we are, the more vulnerable to foreign ideas or opposing explanations we should be. However, like so many things in the spiritual realm, this is inverted. Somehow, faith seems to breed insecurity. So many people, Christians especially, recite their creeds and declare their beliefs and then turn around and nervously, no, frantically, swat away every other competing possibility as though to even *look at it* will lead them astray. What frightens them so? Are they worried that exposure to something other than what they believe in will somehow lay bare the revealing truth that perhaps they don't really believe in it at all?

It would appear that this insecurity arises from at least two areas of fear: other religions, and science. We have already dealt with the teachings of other religions with Mosaic Theology. But what of science? Why is science such a threat to faith, particularly in the realm of Christianity? Perhaps it's because science deals with answers and faith with questions. Maybe faith exists because the questions exist. Maybe faith needs the questions because once the questions are answered, faith is no longer required. As science solves more riddles and answers more questions, taking the mysteries out of life and replacing them with cold, hard facts, faith seems to lose its place, shrinking into the background, archaic and forgotten. Perhaps it is this that the faithful fear. Maybe they want some questions left unanswered, some enigmas left undisturbed. Could it be that *not knowing the answer* is what is keeping their faith alive? After all, consider the *New Testament*'s definition of faith: "Now faith is the assurance of things hoped for, the conviction of things not seen" (*Hebrews* 11:1 ESV). "Assurance" sounds like a pretty strong word, but it's the "things hoped for" that betrays the real truth of this definition. Notice that the definition does not read like this: "Now, faith is the assurance of things that we know for a certainty." *Things we hope for* implies uncertainty. If you know how something is going to turn out, hope is irrelevant. Hope only applies when the outcome is uncertain. Perhaps this is why the faithful are threatened by science. Science would take away all the uncertainty, replacing it with inert data and mechanical answers.

Apparently, faith needs this element of uncertainty; otherwise, it ceases to be faith. I suppose that is understandable. If you were entirely certain about something, it would not be faith; it would be fact or at least a fact in your own estimation. Could this be what the champions of the scientific camp find unacceptable about faith? One would assume that a scientist is a scientist precisely because he is possessed by a driving need to *know*, to have the facts, to have access to all the information, leaving no stone unturned, no mystery unsolved, no question unanswered. Perhaps where other people might be emotional or passionate, the scientist is logical, methodical, and academic, preferring palpable certainties to ethereal uncertainties. There is nothing wrong with logical, cerebral people. They are who they are, and the world needs them to be that way. Nevertheless, maybe they just need a small touch of passion, a tiny mustard seed of faith to round them out. Likewise, there is nothing wrong with the emotional and spiritual people. They are who they are, and the world needs them to be that way, too. Perhaps the faithful need just a little bit of logic to temper their otherwise unbridled devotion (because unbridled devotion often leads to fanaticism).

Science thrives on curiosity, the need to *know*. In fact, the English word *science* comes from the Latin word *scientia*, which means *knowledge*. Faith, on the other hand, thrives on uncertainty, the need to *believe*. The very nature of faith requires belief because if something is known, there is no room for speculation (after all, what is faith but a confident form of speculation?). On the other hand, if something is only suspected or supposed, then it's something to be believed or disbelieved. In view of this, faith and science would seem to be at odds: one wants to know for a certainty; the other wants to believe in spite of uncertainty. *Are* they at odds? Perhaps a better question is this: *must* they be at odds, or can they work together? Joshuanism says no, they do not have to be at odds; and yes, they can work together. Joshuanism sees faith and science as two vastly different attitudes, with two vastly different types of people who possess them; yet, Joshuanism maintains that both avenues point to the same God. Or more accurately stated, both avenues *can* point to the same God if one allows that to happen. That is the essence of the Joshuan Fusion.

How do both point to the same God? Suppose a lonely woman longs for a husband. She has been single for so long that part of her is beginning to lose hope that she will ever find the man of her dreams, but no matter how tempted she is to abandon her hope, she refuses to do so. Come hell or high water, she is going to keep on believing that someday her prince will come, as the song says. Therefore, on the one hand, the woman has *faith*. Now, suppose that despite her fierce desire for a husband, the woman does absolutely nothing to help her chances. Suppose she never mingles with society, never goes to those places where men can be found, and never

119

even leaves her house. Now, if this is the case, she can go on clinging to her hope until the end of time, but one thing she will not do is find a husband. If she thinks that God is just going to magically deliver Mr. Perfect to her front door, she has forgotten one crucial truth about how God works: he feeds the birds, but he does not put the seed in their nests. So, what instead should she do? She should add *science* to her faith. In other words, if she really, truly wants a husband, she should, of course, go on clinging to her hope, but at the same time, she should undertake the necessary steps to leave as little room for uncertainty as she can. Remember, the word *science* means *knowledge*. The woman, then, needs to pursue some knowledge. She needs to read books on how to attract men. She needs to study the ways and behaviors of men. She needs to study the ways and behaviors of women who have success in finding men. She needs to investigate the art of romance. In short, she needs to conduct *research*, but she shouldn't stop there. She needs to test her research, measure it against outside reactions. She needs to *experiment*. She needs to go out into society, be around men, try different approaches, and observe the different *results*. She has one goal: a husband. She has two tools at her disposal: faith and science. Both can work together to propel her toward her desired goal.

It is the same with God. Those who pursue God with a heart to know him cannot do so without faith, but does adding science to the mix hurt? It does not have to. Science can enhance faith, and faith can enhance science. One man can look through a telescope and see a cloud of starry gas on the other side of the Universe and say to himself, "See? There is no God. There's only junk out there, the result of some cosmic accident." He may be intelligent enough to know what elements constitute that cloud, how much it weighs, what it's doing, how it got there, and how fast it's moving, and so forth. Nevertheless, despite his vast intelligence, all he sees is a cloud. Another man, who is just as intelligent and knows all the same data, can look through the same telescope, see the same cloud of starry gas, and say to himself, "Ah, see? There *is* a God. Look at that wonder floating around out there. Only God could make something so astonishing." Like everything else, it basically comes down to attitude, perception, and a willingness to remain open. Those who remain open surpass the conflict between faith and science. Those who remain closed remain in the carnage of the conflict.

Take evolution, for instance. There is pretty compelling evidence that evolution, as postulated by Darwin, is indeed the lay of the land. Yet, some people refuse to acknowledge it, preferring to stay rooted only in what their religious faith has to say on the matter, with no room for science. However, there was pretty compelling evidence that the Earth was round, too. Yet, some people hundreds of years ago refused to acknowledge it, opting to remain in the status quo, going on with the comforting notion that what they were taught all their life was indeed true and no change in belief or mindset was necessary. But they were wrong! Likewise, consider the Inquisitors.

They were very close to killing Galileo for spreading the belief that the Earth was not at the center of the Universe. But he was correct! They were wrong! Was it a credit to these Inquisitors that they clung to their faith when it was their faith itself leading them into error? I would say no.

Have we learned nothing from history? Have we still failed to understand that people can keep their faith and still embrace scientific discoveries? Did all 17th century Europeans who chose to agree with Galileo suddenly abandon their faith because of that agreement? Of course not! Those that kept their faith *and* embraced the new ideas of the day merely understood that the believer can do both. We can still do the same thing today, whether the issue is evolution, the Big Bang, the theory of relativity, or something else altogether. Sure, a change in mindset might be required. Discomforting implications might have to be reconciled. Growing pains are, by nature, painful, but each new scientific discovery does not have to undo our faith in God. It only does if we let it.

The Joshuan does *not* let it. Joshuanism sees no conflict between faith and science. The Joshuan sees faith and science as two tools designed for the same goal: knowing God. The Joshuan is not threatened by science, nor does he allow faith to hold him back. Faith that holds you back is not really faith at all; it is fear disguised as faith. Right faith should always propel the believer *toward* the truth, not *away* from it. Any time faith causes you to resist positive, warranted change and enlightened, necessary evolution, your faith is holding you back. Any time faith entices you to clinch your fists and fight against progress for the sake of your own comfort, your faith has betrayed you. Your faith is dead weight at that point. However, if your faith is solid and secure, not easily threatened, not prone to stubborn acts of self-preservation, and strong enough to see you through modifications in scientific thought and awareness, whether big or small, without diminishing or dying, then you have a pure faith, a living faith, a faith that God can use. So which will you choose? Will you let your faith spur you forward, or will you let it hold you back? I am a man of faith, and so I value faith, but I would say that when faith becomes a hindrance rather than an aid, something is clearly wrong.

Remember, you may oppose science, but that does not mean God does. If God created the world and indeed the entire Universe, then he is also responsible for all the scientific properties found therein. If God is the author of science (which he must be if he created all that exists), he must therefore also be the author of each new scientific breakthrough and discovery. Moreover, if he is the author of each new breakthrough and discovery, then humans could never uncover any scientific truth that fails to point to God. As we have observed time and time again in this book, it is a matter of *perception*, as everything is in the realm of God. Everything depends on what you are looking at and the perspective from which you are looking. Some people want to look at science and see something evil, a threat, a virus that infects faith and brings disease to the mind. Others prefer to look at science and see another wonderful confirmation that a remarkably creative and ingenious God exists. If your belief in that God is firm, then nothing science produces can shake it and should only add to it. If your belief in God is fragile, then perhaps science *is* a threat to you because a fragile faith is threatened by almost anything.

Now, I suppose we must address that there have been several instances in the past when scientific discoveries have cast doubt on certain long-standing religious beliefs, even Biblical ones. The age of the created world, for example, has been disputed between the faithful and the scientific. For centuries, Biblical scholars have maintained that through the scriptural texts they have been able to date when the Earth was created. According to their calculations, the events described in the first chapter of Genesis took place no more than 6,000 years ago. The history of humanity, according to this supposition, is therefore relatively young. Yet, discoveries from all quarters of science, such as astronomy, astrophysics, archaeology, anthropology, and geology, have presented compelling evidence that the Universe is billions of years old, the Earth is millions of years old, and Homo sapiens are at least 200,000 years old. So, what are we to do when only one avenue points to a history of 6,000 years, and multiple other avenues, all of which agree with each other, point to something else entirely? Do we lose the power of our faith if we modify what we previously held as true? Maybe some people do, but no one has to, just as no one had to hundreds of years ago when humans were forced to come to terms with the startling truth that the world was not flat.

Consider the creation of humanity. The *Bible* is very specific about how humankind came into being. There was a garden. It housed two special trees, a snake, and two recent creations of God: Adam and Eve. Now, we all know the story about the apple (Was it an apple?), the fig clothes, the fall, the flaming sword, and all the rest. The creation story as described in *Genesis* sounds more like something out of *Gilgamesh* or the *Popol Vuh* than an actual historical account. Nevertheless, the believing faithful have for centuries clung to the story of Adam and Eve with tenacity, refusing to view the story as anything other than solid, indisputable fact. What does science say? Well, it tells quite a different story. Once again, with compelling evidence, science demonstrates how humanity has evolved slowly, over time, the result of a series of mutations and chain reactions, and science has the bones to prove it. The literal bones, I mean. Carbon-dated bones. So, again, what are we to do? If a man believes in God and operates with the kind of love Joshua taught, does it really matter if he decides to view *Genesis* as mythical or allegorical rather than fact? Would the story lose any of its potency? It does not have to. The same truths can be communicated through a mythical tale just as easily as through a factual account. Perhaps that is why Joshua used parables to communicate great truths to his

Jewish audiences. Is it really so shocking to entertain the notion that maybe Moses, or whoever wrote *Genesis*, used parables, too?

A truly *post/Christian* attitude toward these matters would be one that holds certain elements of faith as *indisputable* and certain other elements of faith as *open to alteration*, pending further scientific discovery. Is a belief in God's existence necessary for spiritual or religious faith to continue? Absolutely. Is a belief in the Son of God necessary for Christian or Joshuan faith to continue? Without a doubt. Is a belief in the Holy Spirit (if you are a Christian), or the Soul of Godliness (if you are a Joshuan) necessary for faith to continue? Definitely. Is a belief in the historical accuracy of *Genesis* necessary for faith to continue? No. Why not? Because a *post/Christian* mindset understands that the level of human knowledge as it existed thousands of years ago (when *Genesis* was written) in no way measures up to the level of human knowledge as it exists today. We know so much more than Moses knew. We have explored and exhausted so many scientific mysteries since then. We have progressed. We have evolved to the point where basing our scientific and historical awareness on the mindset of men who wrote scriptural texts thousands of years ago just seems unreasonable. It would be just as ridiculous to reject modern medicine and surgical techniques in favor of how sicknesses were treated in the days of Babylon. No one in their right mind would turn down a 21st century medical procedure, opting instead for some brutal, crude technique popular at the time Ramses II sat on the throne of Egypt. Yet, the same people who would reject ancient medicine would cling to ancient history. The same people who would laugh at the notion of having a tumor removed Babylon-style would base their beliefs in humanity's origins on a text written during that same time period. Does anyone else see a problem here? To me, the problem would seem to be quite apparent. Therefore, a *post/Christian* mindset is one that breaks away from this hypocrisy. A *post/Christian* mindset is one that no longer clings to outdated suppositions, and no longer *needs* to cling to outdated suppositions. A *post/Christian* mindset is one that warmly welcomes an ongoing metamorphosis of knowledge—even *scientific* knowledge.

Recall, if you will, the idea of Scriptural Relegation, which is 1) the hypothesis that scripture might not be completely inerrant; and 2) the willingness to modify scripture where scripture requires modification. It certainly applies here. Any time science indubitably surpasses what scripture has to say about a certain topic, the scripture, not the scientific fact, should be subject to re-evaluation. Of course, not everyone will swallow that idea. But then again, there will be people who cannot swallow anything Joshuanism has to say. *C'est la vie.*

So, the decision, then, is not science *or* faith, it's science *and* faith. Leaning toward one or the other is your choice as long as you choose *both.* Toward which should you lean? Whichever suits the specific way God engineered your personality.

However, in all things remember this: avoid extremes. Seek balance in life inasmuch as you are able.

The Joshuan Creed

In view of everything we have discussed in this section, we can now create a Joshuan creed. Just as being a Christian is to believe something specifically set apart for Christians to believe in, so being a Joshuan is to believe something specifically set apart for Joshuans to believe in as well. Christianity has its creeds. Joshuanism has one, too. As you read the ensuing creed, keep two things in mind: 1) believing *in* something is not that same as what you believe *about* that something (you may believe there is a God, but it's what you believe about God that counts); and 2) the creed itself isn't the object of your faith. The ultimate object of your faith is God. A creed is merely a statement of belief, a tool designed to specify those things you believe about God and those ideas concerning God's interaction with humanity. By itself, the creed is just an assortment of words, completely powerless. However, when you believe the words, when your faith is in the truthfulness of those words, then a powerful dynamic is released in your life. That said, whether or not you choose to believe in the following words is entirely up to you.

This, then, is the Joshuan Creed:

We believe that God exists.

We believe God exists as a Singular Fellowship of three separate yet equal parts: the Father, the Son, and the Soul of Godliness.

We believe that God is eternal, unchanging, all-knowing, all-powerful, and ever-present.

We believe that God created the Universe and initiated all matter, all life, all the physical laws, and all the processes found therein.

We believe that God has no equal.

We believe that God is good and kind, that he is loving and compassionate, and that he is love.

We believe that God is fair and just, that he treats all his creation equally.

We believe that God keeps his word and is therefore trustworthy.

We believe that God is intimately concerned with the lives of each individual human.

We believe that God hears the words of those who pray to him.

Joshuanism

We believe that all matter and all life is subject to God's authority and yet, in spite of this, God has granted free will to humanity.

We believe that God reveals himself to humanity, that this revelation is unfinished, and that as humanity evolves in its capacity to know more of this revelation, God enables humanity to know more.

We believe that God created humanity in his image.

We believe that humanity, thus created, is special.

We believe that humanity, though special, is inherently sinful.

We believe this inherent sinfulness produced the Great Barrier, which separated humanity from God, preventing humanity from knowing God.

We believe God, because of his love, sent his Son to be born as a human with the specific purpose of dismantling this barrier.

We believe the Son of God was thus born of Mary's womb.

We believe the Son of God was named Joshua (Jesus, in Greek).

We believe that Joshua was the promised Messiah as foretold by the Old Testament prophets.

We believe that Joshua's message was primarily a message of love.

We believe that Joshua lived a perfect, sinless life.

We believe that Joshua was executed by crucifixion.

We believe that Joshua's sinless death paid the penalty for our inherent sinfulness.

We believe that Joshua's body was buried in a sealed tomb.

We believe that after three days of death, Joshua rose from the dead, emerging triumphant from that tomb.

We believe that Joshua's death and subsequent resurrection succeeded in dismantling the Great Barrier.

We believe that through faith the Joshuan can enter into union with God, enjoying Absolute Deliverance.

We believe that Joshua now resides with God the Father.

We believe that Joshua will return someday, ushering in the end of this world and the creation of a new world.

We believe Joshua has defeated all forces of evil in the spiritual realm.

We believe that the Soul of Godliness resides within the Joshuan, providing the Joshuan with guidance, counsel, comfort, conviction, and discernment.

We believe that the truth sets us free.

We believe in eternal life.

We believe that to love God and to love humanity are the two greatest commandments and that these two commandments are the summation of all other commandments.

We believe that love therefore is the most important factor in the life and experience of the Joshuan, greater even than faith, hope, morality, and virtue.

We believe that God desires Joshuans to have a healthy mind, body, and spirit.

We believe we can accomplish anything through Joshua.

We subscribe to the Eight Immovables of Joshuanism.

We subscribe to the Ten Tenets of Joshuanism.

We observe the Five Elements (conversation, illumination, meditation, observation, and application), believing them to be necessary tools for spiritual growth.

We believe there need be no conflict between science and faith.

Let us now review the theological material we have discussed thus far.

Joshuanism, at its heart, is a way of thinking and a way of living that reflects 1) a belief in God; 2) a belief in humanity's inability to *get to* God (the Great Barrier) due to sin and imperfection; 3) God's desire and willingness to *come* to humanity (or to *invade* humanity) by being born as a human; 4) that such a human was indeed born, being not only fully human but also fully God; 5) that this human was named Joshua in Hebrew and Jesus in Greek; 6) that this Joshua lived a perfect, sinless life; 7) that Joshua died the death our sins required; thus fulfilling the necessary punishment for that sin; 8) that he rose from the dead on the third day; 9) that all of this work resulted in the Dismantling of the Great Barrier, thereby allowing humanity to have fellowship with God; and 10) that upon entering into this fellowship through faith in Joshua, the believer receives salvation (or, Absolute Deliverance) from God, through God, in God, and for God.

Joshuanism is also a progressive spirituality that seeks to be open-minded where other religions and spiritualties might remain closed-minded. Diversity is encouraged, even celebrated. The wisdom of other religions and cultures is not rejected

Joshuanism

at face value. Elements of Zen are grafted into Joshuanism where necessary (and at the Joshuan's discretion). The inerrancy of the scriptures is brought into question. Science is embraced with enthusiasm and is no longer viewed as a deterrent to faith. Love is elevated above all else, and the Son of God reigns as Lord and Savior, just as he does in Christianity. Remember: Joshuanism does not forsake the Son of God. Joshuanism does not even forsake the name *Jesus*. Joshuanism merely *prefers* to use the name Joshua due to the evident benefit arising from doing so.

We have thus covered all of the particulars of Joshuan theology and belief. I have done my best to take you on a journey of thought, a meander through a new idea filled with new expressions. I've attempted to construct this journey of thought in such a way as to lead you from one junction to another, building an argument along the way for the necessity of this new path I call Joshuanism. Are you starting to see the potential here? The implications? I hope so.

Are you ready to explore how Joshuanism works?

Lock and load...

Michael Vito Tosto

PART FOUR: Joshuan Community

I have a strong feeling that many who were hanging with me through the first two parts of this book might have departed after the third. I realize that much of what I have had to say challenges accepted Christian thought. The best defense I can offer is that Joshuanism *should* challenge Christian thought. If I felt that Christian thought was just fine as it is, I would not have proposed a path beyond it. For too long theology of a decidedly Christian persuasion has held a monopoly on the Son of God (how we look at him, how we follow him, how we see our world in relation to him). There was a time when people could not ask the questions I ask or say the things I say because if they did their loving Christian authorities would burn them at the stake. Thankfully, those days are gone. Today, curious pilgrims like me can open their minds, open their mouths, and give voice to other ideas and new possibilities. As a student of history, I am well aware that challenging the status quo earns a person many enemies and few friends. (As I write this sentence, I am reminded of something John Donne once said, "I am my own executioner."). However, if I accomplish nothing else in my life, I want to at least let people know that Christianity does not hold open the only door to God. If there is only one door to God, then it is God's Son that holds it open, and *anyone* can go through that door no matter where the starting point is and whether the person is a Christian, Joshuan, or something else altogether.

To those who departed after Part three, I bid farewell. To those who are still with me and ready for more, I thank you for your courage. I suspect that if you have not left yet, you are probably going to stick around until the end. Excellent! We ragged few still have quite a journey ahead of us. Shall we plow onward?

Another major area of change proposed by Joshuanism that will cause considerable grumbling among the proponents of the status quo is the Joshuan view of *church* (what the church is, how the church operates, how we "do" church, etc.). This is because Joshuanism undermines the infrastructure of the institution by taking church out of the *corporate setting* and restoring it to the *home setting*. However, before we get in to any of that, let's take a basic look at this thing called *church*.

The Extraction

When you hear the word *church*, what comes to mind? Pews? A cross? A pulpit? Hymnals? Words on a screen? A certain musty smell? Stained glass? A sermon? Coffee and doughnuts in the lobby? A steeple? A nursery? A parking lot? A building? A cathedral?

Whatever it is that comes to mind, it's probably a *something* rather than a *someone*. It's probably a *place* rather than a *people*. But the *New Testament* is quite clear on what the church is. It's not an object, a place, or an institution. It is *the humans themselves* who believe. *You* are the church. *I* am the church. *We* are the church.

Consider the word *church*. In the *New Testament*, it appears 114 times, and in each instance, the Greek word used is *ekklēsia* (ἐκκλησία), which literally means "called out" or "called forth." Therefore, by definition, the word *church* refers to a body of people characterized by a specific trait. What is this trait? They have been called out, set apart, or as we say in Joshuanism, *extracted*. For example, in *Galatians* Chapter 1, when Paul begins his letter by addressing it "to the churches in Galatia," what he is really saying, in Greek is "to the *called out* ones in Galatia." He is not referring to a building, or place, or even an *idea*. He is referring to *a people*.

The actual English language word *church* is derived from the Old English word *cirice*, itself derived from the Germanic word *kirika*, which comes from the Greek *kuriakē* (κυριακή), meaning "of the Lord." This word itself is not found in the *New Testament*. When translating the Greek into English, the word *church* is used in place of the actual correct translation of *ekklēsia*. Even then, the English word *church* traces its roots to a Greek word which still has nothing to do with a building or a place. It just means "of the Lord."

In either case, what we have here in the word *church* is a term that refers to a certain body of people called out *from* something *to* something for a specific purpose. Called out from what? The world and its system. Called to what? Holiness. Godliness. Authentic inner transformation. For what purpose? To demonstrate the power and love of God to the watching multitudes so that they, too, through faith in Joshua, can be made holy. Is that what you think of when you hear the word *church*? Me neither.

Therefore, Joshuanism rejects the idea of church as a place you go on a certain day of the week. Joshuanism rejects the idea that church is a building with offices where people work. It rejects the idea of church as having anything at all to do with a specific action taken at a specific time at a specific place in a specific way. It rejects the idea of church as a locale, an event, or a weekly obligation you scratch off your list. It rejects the idea of church as something you dress up for, behave well at, or suffer through patiently. Moreover, Joshuanism rejects the idea of church as being an institution.

In fact, Joshuanism rejects the word *church*. It's not that the word itself is bad. It's just that today the word means something that is miles away from the original intent. Just as the name Jesus stirs up all kinds of associations, not all of which are good, so, too, is the word *church* accompanied by a host of misconceptions, distorted images, and erroneous connotations.

Therefore, let us leave *church* in the realm of Christianity and focus instead on Joshuanism's alternative: *the Extraction*, which seems to be a much more faithful translation of the word *ekklēsia* (ἐκκλησία).

> [*The Extraction*] – the collective group of believing Joshuans (or, all believers, Joshuan or otherwise) who have been extracted (called out, set apart) *from* the world, declared holy, and *sent back in* to the world to bring the message of Joshua *to* the world.

Where Christians emphasize, "*going to* church," Joshuans emphasize "*being* the called out ones" or "the extracted ones." The geographical location, the physical building, and the act of going there at a set time in a specific way have all been taken out of the equation in Joshuanism. In their place is simply *an identity*. Whereas church is an event one attends, the Extraction is an identity one assumes or participates in, or, one might even say, an identity *bestowed upon* the believer(s). Church is a *what*. The Extraction is a *who*.

This is precisely the way the writers of the *New Testament* use the word *ekklēsia*, by the way. In each of the 114 instances where the word is used, it's never once associated with a building, a locale, or any kind of establishment. It's always used in reference to a people embodying that specific trait of having been set apart. Check this out for yourself. Get a concordance. Isolate each usage of the word church (*ekklēsia*). Time and again, the word represents *who we are* as believers, never a place. Thus, in this respect, Joshuanism once again restores the *original intent*.

The Extraction resembles little or nothing of the Christian church. This does not mean that Joshuans do not gather together, worship together, pray together, or have fellowship with one another. They do. In fact, the coming together of the believers is just as important in Joshuanism as it is in Christianity. It's just that, once again, Joshuans do it differently, with new expressions and a new approach (though in many ways, this new approach is a very old approach, harkening back to the first century).

Tables

Long before the "church building" became a standard fixture in Christianity, the believers simply met anywhere they could. More often than not, they met in someone's *home*. Indeed, the earliest gatherings of believers, as documented in the *New Testament*, were home gatherings. Consider these examples from the NIV:

Greet also the church (*ekklēsia*) that meets at their *house*. (*Romans* 16:5)

Give my greetings to the brothers at Laodicea and to Nympha and the church (*ekklēsia*) in her *house*. (*Colossians* 4:15)

To Apphia our sister, to Archippus our fellow soldier and to the church (*ekklēsia*) that meets in your *home*. (*Philemon* 1:1-2)

There is a certain dynamic captured in the home gathering that is lost at the corporate gathering. What is this dynamic? Intimacy. My question to you, therefore, is this: if you are a Christian and you "worship" at a certain church on a Sunday morning, do you know the names of those you are rubbing elbows with each week? Are you intimately involved in their lives, their struggles, their victories, their sufferings, their daily experiences? Do you know the pastor, preacher, or priest by name? Does he or she know you? Even if the pastor knows you, does the pastor know everyone he or she is ministering to? Probably not, unless it's a very small church. Even if you do know most of the people at your church, how often are you with them? Do you fight their battles? Do you mourn their losses? Do you share in their everyday hardships? Is your daily success or failure wrapped up in theirs? Or are you isolated believers experiencing isolated trials who happen to come together one or two days a week, shake hands, and gloss over the real issues under the surface?

Joshuanism brings the intimacy back by bringing the home dynamic back. Joshuanism forces you into the lives of your fellows and forces them into yours. It insists that you grapple together for daily bread and daily victory. It asks that you work against the isolation that humans in the 21st century cling to so fiercely. Joshuanism throws you together into a shared experience so that you grow together, fall together, get back up together, and learn together. How? By reintroducing the home gathering.

Now, before we move forward in our discussion of home gatherings, we need to address one other crucial item: breaking bread. Joshuanism also seeks to take all of the religion, ritual, and sacramental procedure out of Communion (the Lord's Supper). What do I mean by that? Simply this: when Joshua and the twelve disciples were having the meal that Christians now call "The Last Supper," what exactly was going on there? Were they passing around little wafers and tiny cups of wine that someone had blessed beforehand? Or was it just a meal like any other? The indication seems to be that it was just a meal. They were eating dinner. That's it. Just eating dinner. During this dinner, which otherwise was like every other dinner they had had together (it may have been the Passover feast, but the meal itself was just a meal), Joshua says...what? He says, "every time you eat bread and drink wine, remember me and what I did." In other words, he is saying, "Every time you as believers come together to take a meal (break bread), remember me and the sacrifice I made when

Joshuanism

I gave my body like bread and my blood like wine." This seems to imply an organic, casual act, one void of ceremony. Like so many other aspects of the *original intent*, Christianity has ritualized and religionized[8] that which was supposed to be just another part of everyday life.

Joshuans intend to return the breaking of bread to everyday life. For this reason, the home gatherings of Joshuanism are called *Tables*. Therefore, while Christians go to church on Sunday, Joshuans meet in each other's homes throughout the week, each particular group or gathering being a single Table.

> [*Table*] – 1) a home gathering of Joshuans, derived from the idea of breaking bread together at a table; and 2) a single unit of bonded Joshuans involved in each other's lives.

How often should a Table meet throughout the week? As often as possible but no less than three times in a seven-day period. If that seems excessive, consider that one of the main reasons Joshuanism exists is to offer something different, something unique, something special, something that is real and powerful and dynamic, something that will revolutionize your entire life. Being so involved with your fellows that you meet with them at least three times a week (and hopefully more than that) is the only way to bring into Joshuanism that which seems to have been lost in Christianity and indeed the entire world: *community*. Joshuanism must be a place where you feel a sense of intimate community, of belonging, of being surrounded by people who love you and know you; otherwise, all of this is for naught anyway.

When should Tables meet? Anytime. Sunday morning. Sunday night. Monday night. Saturday afternoon. All day. Whenever. It doesn't even have to be something that is set every week, just as long as you are faithful to meet *regularly*.

What goes on at a Table? Excellent question. There are no hard and fast rules about *how* the following activities should be carried out, but these are the basic elements that should characterize a Table meeting:

1. **Prayer.** It doesn't matter how you do it so long as you do it *regularly*. Each time your Table meets, prayer should be the first and last thing you do together. Prayers should be worshipful and thankful first, intercessory and supplicant second.

2. **Confession.** There is an element of transparency lost among today's believers, and Joshuanism seeks to restore that much-needed component. Joshuans should be in the habit of confessing their sins to one another on a regular basis. This healthy and liberating (see *James* 5:16). Each Table meeting should involve a time of collective *verbal* confession (either to the group or with a *confession partner*). Judgment and guilt should *never* be present; forgiveness, love, and acceptance

---

8   Yes, I made that word up. But it works in this case, does it not?

should *always* be present. Joshuans should remember to thank God often for his forgiveness of the sins they confess.

3. **Encouragement.** Whereas Christians go to church to hear a sermon, Joshuans meet at Tables to receive encouragement. This can take the form of theological or zoêological discussions, the swapping of stories and experiences, or a word of teaching from the Table leader (we will get to the Table leader in a moment). The point is that all Tables should be *interactive* so that even during a word of teaching, questions and discussions abound.

4. **Breaking Bread.** This is the meal aspect, which we have already discussed. Now, not every Table meeting needs to be accompanied by a meal as long as you take a meal together at least once a week. When you *do* take a meal together, the specific remembrance of Joshua's death and resurrection should be observed.

5. **Fellowship.** Tables should be conversational, candid, and personal, a place where camaraderie and friendship are fostered. The people who meet at your Table should be people you go to the movies with, people you have coffee with, people you invite over to watch the World Series, people you welcome into your *oikos*. The specific dynamic of companionship and fellowship that characterize a Table meeting should nurture these friendships.

You will probably notice that *worship* (in the musical sense) is missing from this list. This is not to say you cannot or should not include musical worship in your Table meetings. You can. Worship has always been an essential element of fellowship, and it always will be. Nevertheless, there are two reasons why it is not included in the above list of recommended activities: 1) your specific group might be lacking a musician, and more important, 2) Joshuanism wants to discourage the notions that worship is solely associated with music and that worship is an act discharged only at a certain time. Joshuanism suggests that believers should live *lives of worship* rather than seeing worship as something one begins, performs, and then ends. In other words, worship shouldn't be like the act of taking a shower (something you were not doing before, now you are doing, and when you're finished you'll move on to something else). Joshuans see worship instead as being similar to breathing, something we do constantly by the way we live and the dispositions of our hearts and minds. Does this mean you should not sing together? Of course not. The scriptures encourage us to sing together. At the moment, there are no Joshuan worship songs, but one hopes that will change. However, worship—real worship—does not begin or end with music. Worship is a *lifestyle*.

Joshuanism

At any rate, the point is to be involved in each other's lives intimately and trustingly. Whereas the "church experience" creates an "us and them" dynamic (i.e., the separation between the congregation and those leading the congregation), the Joshuan Tables are meant to do away with all things institutional or theatrical. What do I mean by theatrical? Well, too often the Christian "church experience" feels like a production certain people (like the musicians and the preachers) are *putting on* and certain other people (the congregation, those in the pews or seats) are *taking in*. The act of then passing the money basket seems like a collection of the "entrance fee" to this particular production. The Joshuan Table takes the production factor completely out of the equation and replaces it with conversation and community. Moreover, because of its intimate, personal, interactive atmosphere, the act of merely spectating is eliminated at a Table meeting. There should be a real sense that "we're all in this together."

How large should a Table be? No more than twelve members strong. Why twelve? Because Joshua understood something that we seem to have forgotten today: no one can really know hundreds of humans intimately. This is why he invited only twelve disciples into his confidence and close fellowship. The larger a group is, the greater the gulf between each member. That is why the phenomenon we see in Christianity called "megachurches" appears counterproductive to real change in the lives of those who attend them. The leaders simply cannot know all those whom they are leading, and as a result, hundreds of people get lost in the multitudes, mere nameless faces in the crowd. That is a tragedy. Joshuanism maintains that without intimate, personal knowledge of our fellows, God's work cannot be done in our lives. For this reason, Tables should be limited to twelve members. Anytime a group swells above that number, a new Table should be formed.

What about kids? Bring them. Include them. Joshuanism should be a family effort, where the kids are growing alongside the adults, always learning, always seeing God at work in other people's lives. Remember, there is no right or wrong way to carry out a Table meeting as long as the items on the above list are observed. *How* you observe them should be unique to your group. Some groups will have kids. Some will not. Some Tables will exist on college campuses. Some will exist in the suburbs. Some will exist in the high rises of a downtown metropolis. Some will take place around a campfire. Some will be aimed at the young, some at the old, and some at mixed-age groups. It does not matter.

At the beginning of this book, I promised you a surplus of new expressions. So far in this section, we have talked about the Joshuan Extraction (the collective term for all Joshuans, or all believers, really) and Tables (the individual meetings, or gatherings of those we fellowship with). Now let me introduce you to some new ideas about leadership...

Joshuan Leadership

I once belonged to a medium-sized church that was suddenly doing very well financially. At the start of a new year, a meeting was convened to discuss what to do with the millions of dollars that were unexpectedly starting to pour in (that can apparently happen when your church boasts a proficient worship band). The consensus was almost unanimous: a bigger, better church building was needed. Why? Well, to house a larger congregation, of course. After all, a larger congregation means even more money. More money means an even bigger building in five years, which means an even larger congregation, and so on. What else does a larger congregation imply? A bigger salary for the leaders of the church in question. Now, I was present for that initial meeting. But I was the lone voice against the erection of a bigger church building; otherwise the consensus would have been unanimous. Why did I vote against a new facility? I happened to know that a large contingent of impoverished people lived in our town. I knew that hundreds of people living just blocks away from our church were unable to pay their bills and unable to properly clothe their children. I knew there were thousands of unemployed people in our midst who were going to go to bed hungry that same day while we sat and discussed what to do with our newfound riches. When I raised these facts at the meeting, it was pointed out to me that what these people really needed was Jesus and that a large, successful church in the neighborhood would be just the thing to bring the message of Jesus to them. I humbly suggested that by bringing food, supplies, and finances to those people who apparently needed Jesus, we could bring his message to them with real, tangible relief, a genuine example of love. "We could pay their bills for them," I said. "We could save their homes from foreclosure, feed their children, set their lives right." No one listened. The church built its multi-million-dollar facility, and five years later the poor people of that town were still poor. I'm not sure what it was that the leaders of this church were practicing, but it wasn't Christianity—or perhaps I should say it wasn't that which Joshua intended. I didn't stick around.

No matter what anyone says, the Christian Church is a business. People work there. People are paid there. People make donations there. What is being sold? A service. Good music. Inspirational, motivational speaking. An image. Now, let me ask you this: how much of the money flowing into these churches is being used to clothe the poor? How much of it is being used to feed the hungry? How much of it is being used to house the homeless? How much of it is being used to restore our communities? Doesn't most of the money coming in through the giving of a church's members end up paying the salaries of those in charge? Doesn't most of the money end up paying the rent or mortgage on the building? Doesn't most of the money end up paying to keep the lights on and the sound system working? Is that what Joshua intended? Is that what Peter or Paul intended? Is that what the *New Testament* encourages?

Consider this question: how many millions, if not billions, of dollars a year go toward keeping the Christian churches up and running? How many millions go toward paying the salaries of those running them? What would happen if that money suddenly went into Africa or even the ghettos of America? What would happen if you stopped giving a hundred dollars a week to your church and instead went to the local deli each Sunday, purchased as many sandwiches as a hundred dollars could buy, and spent the rest of the day passing them out to all the homeless people you could find? What would happen to the world if the believers sacrificed the incubating comforts of their swanky churches and turned their finances instead toward those in real need? What would happen if the Vatican suddenly decided to sell all the art, artifacts, and whatever other treasures might be found in its archives and used the billions of dollars that such a sale would generate to once and for all eradicate poverty? After all, didn't the Son of God clearly tell us *not* to store up treasures on Earth? Do you think that will ever happen? Neither do I.

Unfortunately, the Christian Church is a system, a *financial* system, a multi-billion dollar a year system. Can you deny this? If you truly asked yourself where those multiple billions of dollars are going, could you really sleep with a clear conscious? I could not. I'll be honest; I cannot sleep soundly at night knowing that 1) God's believers are collectively moving billions of dollars around in the course of a year; and 2) very little of it is reaching the starving, homeless, hopeless, wretched, desperate, sick, dying, crying people of this world. That alone was a compelling reason why I ultimately had to leave Christianity. I simply could no longer be part of that system. I did not want that kind of blood on my hands. I specifically created Joshuanism to exist outside of that system so that whatever financial resources might be available can be freely directed toward those people who have *real* needs.

Therefore, each and every single person in a position of leadership within Joshuanism should have a day job, just as the apostle Paul was a tentmaker. No one who leads a Table is to be paid for their work. Does this mean Joshuans do not give of their finances? Certainly not. However, as we will see a little later, they give in a *different way*.

Now, there are two levels of leadership within Joshuanism:

1. [Helm] – one who leads a Table. He or she sits at the head, or helm, of the Table. In other words, the Table most likely meets in the Helm's house or apartment.[9] The Helm's job is to steer the spiritual progression of a Table in the right direction. The Helm may give words of teaching or merely facilitate discussions and prayer. A Helm should be a person of recognizable spiritual depth whose character and integrity engender them to a position of leadership.

---

9   Though this does not have to be the case.

2. [Pilot] – one who leads the Helms of any given city. For instance, suppose there are three Joshuan Tables that meet in the city of Scranton. That means there are three Helms in that city. From among those three, one should be elected as the Pilot of the other two Helms. The Pilot's job is to pray with the other Helms and be a spiritual mentor. The Pilot of any given city (who is also the Helm of a Table) meets with the Helms one on one, encouraging them, addressing any needs, and providing guidance. There can be more than one Pilot to a city, depending on how many Tables meet in a given city. Each Pilot should mentor no more than three Helms.

That's it. It doesn't go any higher than that. There is no hierarchy of power within Joshuanism, no supreme leader (like a Pope), and no jockeying for status or positions in the upper echelons. There are no upper echelons. The emphasis is on discipleship, mentorship, guidance, and encouragement.

I often hear people talking about the evils of "organized religion." These people might wonder whether Joshuanism truly offers anything different since it, too, seems to have some organization to it. My answer would be threefold: 1) Joshuanism may be organized, but it isn't really a religion; 2) it may be organized, but the financial element has been eliminated; and 3) when people speak about their disdain for organized religion, it seems what they are really upset with is the way things are *currently organized*. In other words, it might not be that having things *in* order is the problem but that how things are ordered *now* is the problem. Besides, there was never a movement that had any real effect on the world that did not also have some level of order and organization to it. Joshuanism is organized just enough to have a basic structure to it but no more. What is this basic structure? The collective body of Joshuans is called the Extraction. The Extraction meets at home gatherings, twelve members (or less), called Tables. These Tables are led by Helms, who in turn are led by Pilots (who may lead no more than three Helms). That's it. It's as simple as that.

With the financial element and the power-struggle element removed, Joshuanism has absolutely no basis for corruption. Take money and power away from any situation and you'll be hard-pressed to find a way to corrupt that situation. How's that for a breath of fresh air?

Joshuan Forums

Joshuanism does not forsake the dynamic of the corporate gathering; it just favors the home gathering. Nevertheless, corporate gatherings are encouraged. What is discouraged, however, is any kind of corporate setting that is evocative of how the Christian church operates. In other words, there will never be a building on the corner of any street in America with the words "Joshuan Church" on its sign. In

Joshuanism

fact, the words *Joshuan* and *church* are oxymoronic. There will never be a sanctuary or an auditorium with a stage and a pulpit and pews, where people come on a given day to worship and hear a sermon. There will never be a place associated with Joshuanism—a geographical location noted by the outside world as the place where Joshuanism *happens*. Joshuanism is a lifestyle, a mindset, and a community. It's not an institution. The instant it becomes an institution, if it does, it has already lost its relevancy. Let us hope that never happens.

So, what kind of corporate gatherings are we talking about? They should be distinctly Joshuan in nature. They should be events where the exchanging of views and the sharing of resources transpire on a large scale, where genuine fellowship and open communication thrive. They should be venues where learning, celebration, recreation, and creativity blossom. There is only one word that captures all of this. These gatherings could only be called *Forums*; nothing else fits so well. What would these Forums look like? Here are some ideas:

1. **Joshuan Art Fairs.** A given city could promote fairs where local Joshuan artists can come to show or sell their wares. This would be a time not only of artistic sponsorship, but also of fellowship, with Joshuans from various Tables mingling corporately with each other and exchanging artistic ideas.

2. **Joshuan Concerts.** Joshuan musicians could put on shows, in an intimate setting, or a large-scale setting. This would allow them to display their talents and musical message, as well as network with other Joshuan musicians of that city. Granted, this is a form of *production*, but unlike the Christian church, a Joshuan concert would not masquerade as something *other than* a production. These concerts would be advertised as concerts and operated like concerts. There is nothing wrong with production for production's sake, but substituting a dramatic production for real fellowship and then denying it's a production and calling it real fellowship is duplicitous.

3. **Joshuan Theater.** Dramatic plays of a Joshuan nature could be staged by Joshuan actors. Like the art fairs and concerts, these theatrical events would be a time of corporate fellowship, allowing for intermingling and networking, as well as providing quality entertainment.

4. **Joshuan Symposiums.** These would be large-scale meetings specifically initiated to foster dialogue and conversation. Topics could be anything relevant to Joshuanism or the changing world. Each city should hold a symposium at least once a year, open to all Joshuans from that city and anyone else interested in attending. Individual seminars, dis-

cussion groups, interviews, and workshops could be arranged so as to generate a collegiate, intellectual atmosphere.

5. **Joshuan Festivals.** At least once a year all the Joshuans of a given city should come together for mass celebration and mass fellowship. These festivals would consist of all the above-mentioned events, happening at once, on a giant scale. This would be a time of festivity, celebration, communication, artistic expression, dialogue, and learning. Where should this happen? Anywhere. You could rent an arena or some acreage of land. You could assemble in the streets or in a park. It does not matter.

6. **Pilot Conferences.** Once a month, all the Pilots of a given city should come together for the purpose of assessing the needs of their city, the needs of the Joshuans of that city, the direction the Joshuan movement in that city ought to take, and any other problems or concerns relevant at that time. Community events, outreaches, and other corporate gatherings for that city could be planned at these conferences. Helms may choose to have monthly conferences as well, if they so desire.

All of this is open to discussion and modification. These are just loose recommendations designed to get *you* thinking. However, there is no set way any of this has to be done. It can be unique to you, your city, your Table, your region, whatever. Nothing is set in stone. These Forums could be huge. They could also be small and intimate. If your city or town is too small to produce more than a few Tables, you could still do any of the above activities, just on a smaller scale. The great thing about Joshuanism is that there is so much room for you to make *your* expression of this movement unique, personal, and suited to your community.

It would fall to the Pilots of a given city to arrange for all of these events. They would have to assemble financial support from the Joshuans of that city (but since there are no church buildings to maintain, or staff to pay, all kinds of money should be available for such ventures). And Joshuans are encouraged to give.

If you're wondering how much they are encouraged to give or to whom they are encouraged to give, read on...

The Three Cornerstones

Humans have become isolated creatures. They spend most of their time alone, behind windshields and computer screens. Christians are not immune to this increasing isolation. Even when they come together for small groups or *Bible* studies, there is still a very private element to the way they communicate with one another. How many people actually tell the truth about what is really going on in their lives or their minds? How many people really admit how messed up their world is? How many people divulge their needs of the moment? Very few. Why is it only a few? Because no one wants anyone else to know that his life is not the picture perfect scene that it appears to be on the surface.

Christian churches are just as isolated as the people in them. Most of them sequester themselves away from other churches just a few blocks down the street. Why? Because one church does things one way, and another church does things a different way. God forbid they should do the unthinkable and mingle. As we noted in the preceding section, they squabble over semantics and peripheral theological issues to the point that one denomination would never dream of associating with another. Consequently, individual churches become isolated little kingdoms filled with isolated people.

However, this is not the picture painted in the *New Testament*. This is not the *modus operandi* encouraged by the apostles. Consider the historian Luke's interesting description of how Joshua's earliest followers operated:

> All the believers were one in heart and mind. No one claimed that any of his possessions was his own, but they shared everything they had. There were no needy persons among them. For from time to time those who owned lands or houses sold them, brought the money from the sales and put it at the apostles' feet, and it was distributed to anyone as he had need. (*Acts* 4:32, 34-35 NIV)

This account of how the early believers behaved (i.e., sharing each other's lives, each other's problems, and each other's resources) is so far from what we see today that one can hardly believe Luke is writing about Christians. But he is. Now, re-read the above excerpt again and ask yourself what is the one word that sums up the described activities? For me, it is the word *community*. What is community? A group of people assembled around a common purpose, people who are intimately involved in each other's lives. Maybe you are lucky enough to experience that in your particular church, but the truth is that most people do not experience these things at church.

That is exactly what Joshuanism offers. Community. Joshuanism is meant to be a counterattack against isolationism. Joshuanism exists to restore that lost sense of community, of *belonging*, to the human race. How? The Tables. The Table is specifically designed to be interactive, even *invasive*. What do I mean by invasive? I mean that you cannot belong to a Table and regularly meet at a Table without being forced into complete and total transparency. We are supposed to walk in the light. Isn't that what the scriptures tell us? No one can walk in the light and have secrets at the same time.

Therefore, Joshuan community, as experienced at Table meetings and indeed in everyday life (since Joshuans are supposed to be involved in each other's everyday lives), has some very specific characteristics to it. What are these characteristics? They are based on the aforementioned excerpt from *Acts* 4, which is quite clear about how the early believers interacted. Let's explore these characteristics one at a time...

1. **Harmony.** *All the believers were one in heart and mind.* Does this mean they never disagreed? No. Does this mean that they all shared the same opinions? No. Does this mean that people did not have their own preferences? No. What does it mean then? It means that each believer, though different, was aggregated with his or her fellows around the same *purpose*. Being one in heart and mind does not mean they suddenly stopped having individual personalities. It means that even in their differences they found a common ground to stand on. What was that common ground? God. Joshua. Love. They were in harmony on the issues that mattered. They stood together despite whatever marginal differences they might have had. Joshuanism restores this dynamic to fellowship through Diversified Uniformity, as detailed in the previous section.

2. **Sharing.** *No one claimed that any of his possessions was his own, but they shared everything they had.* This is going to be tough for us isolated humans to swallow, but it was evidently a distinctive characteristic of the early believers. Whereas today people love to hold on to what is *theirs*, Joshua and the apostles encouraged everyone to let go. Now, does this mean no one can own anything or keep anything? Of course not. Nothing should ever be so extreme as to become like a law, but the point is that Joshuans are encouraged to share their resources with one another. If your fellows need this or that and it's within your power to give it to them, lend it to them, or secure it for them, you should. Joshuanism should be a place where people can know that others truly care about their needs. It may sound like a cliché, but if the "what's mine is yours" attitude does not permeate Joshuanism, then it is doomed already.

3. **Giving.** *There were no needy persons among them. For from time to time those who owned lands or houses sold them, brought the money from the sales and put it at the apostles' feet, and it was distributed to anyone as he had need.* In the Christian church, people are asked to give their money on a regular basis. Now, there is nothing inherently wrong with that. Further, it's good to show God you trust him by being generous with your money. However, the problem is this: these people

Joshuanism

show up to church, put their check in the plate, and then go back home to their isolated lives never knowing exactly who or what is getting their money. Who *is* getting their money? Most likely, it is the pastor or whatever other form of church leader exists. In most cases, that pastor does not even know all the names of those who are supporting him financially. Now, who is probably *not* getting that money? The homeless guy on the street corner. The starving little girl in Kenya. The starving little girl in Detroit. The single mother who can barely afford to keep the electricity on in her crummy little apartment. The point is that while no one is saying church leaders should not be paid, the early believers distributed money to *anyone as he had need.* In other words, the money went first to those in real need. In Joshuanism, no Helm or Pilot will ever guilt you into giving ten percent of your money to them; first of all, they are not paid for what they do, and second, there is no precedent in the *New Testament* for the regular giving of ten percent. What is encouraged in the *New Testament*, however, is having an attitude of generosity, an attitude of giving. Therefore, Joshuans are encouraged to give *where* and *when* they see a *need* to outsiders, as well as to each other. There is no demand, no regulation, and no expectation. It falls to the individual Joshuan to decide to be generous, where to be generous, when to be generous, and how much to give.

These three characteristics (harmony, sharing, giving) found in Luke's description in *Acts* 4 of how the early believers interacted form the basis of Joshuan community. They are the Three Cornerstones, if you will, of Joshuan interaction. If Joshuans fail to be harmonious with each other or generous with those in need, they will be as ineffective in this world as some Christians have become.

In view of that last sentence, this is probably a good place to make a statement. It may seem as though I look upon my Christian counterparts with contempt or that I think I am better than they are. Believe me, I know myself. I am not better than anyone else. It's just that I have a lot of impatience with Christianity. Sometimes, there is an anger one can feel that isn't fully sinful. Yes, I admit it. I am angry with Christianity. I am angry that I see pastors driving around in BMWs while the homeless guy down the street goes hungry. I am angry when I hear another young girl has been kicked out by her Christian parents because her teenage pregnancy has shamed them. I am angry that I have seen so many dozens of churches split down the middle over issues like musical preferences or dress code. I am angry that a hurting world looks in at what Christianity has to offer and sees only bickering and snobbery. I am angry that people who are drawn to alternative lifestyles are shunned and hated by those who are supposed to be kind and loving. I am angry that mere differences in theological semantics can create bitter, lifelong enemies. I am angry that what was never meant to be *religious* still clings so tightly to its religiousness. Do I think I am better than the Christian? No. I just wish all Christians would get as angry as I do about these things. At times in this book, it may seem as though I am going out of my way to make ugly remarks about all things Christian, as though this book is a cleverly disguised diatribe. I give you my word that this is not my intent. What *is* my intent, however, is to make it abundantly clear why this new route called Joshuanism exists. To do that, I must show *the need* for a new route. In my humble opinion, a new route is long, long overdue.

FAQs about Joshuan Community

So, no leaders within Joshuanism will ever be paid?
Never.

Will there ever be a building specifically built for Joshuans to gather together?
No, never.

What about weddings?
What about them?

Weddings usually happen in churches, don't they?
So they do, but no one says they have to. Joshuan weddings should take place where the Tables take place: in the home. Expensive weddings are counterproductive to true charity, anyway. Save the $30,000 you would have spent on your fancy wedding and give it to the poor.

Then who performs Joshuan weddings?
Anyone licensed or certified to do so.

What about baptisms?
Unlike Christianity, Joshuanism does not mandate or even encourage baptism. If the Joshuan wants to be baptized, that is his or her choice.

Where would these baptisms take place?
Wherever there is water.

Do Helms and Pilots have any authority?
None that is not given to them by those they lead. The Helm of your Table is not "the boss" or "in charge." The Helm's job is merely to facilitate and, where necessary, steer.

There is no supreme leader of the Joshuan Extraction?
Not in human form, no. The only supreme leader is God.

Well, what are you?
Just a guy who writes books.

Is the Joshuan Extraction at odds with the Christian Church?
No. After all, they share common themes, claim the same Savior, and serve the same God. It's certainly true that the Extraction operates in a much different manner than the Christian Church, but the two are not at odds (at least not from the Joshuan side of things).

Are there any conditions or stipulations one must meet in order to be Helm or a Pilot?
Nothing official. However, the person ought to be spiritually mature, possessing a palpable godliness and disposition to lead others.

Do Helms or Pilots need any special training or educative degree?
Absolutely not. Refer to *Acts* 4:13 for a rarely quoted suggestion regarding leaders within the believing community.

Can Helms or Pilots be women?
Certainly.

So Joshuans don't give a tithe to their leaders?
Joshuans give money to those who need it when they need it. If the Helm of your Table has a need, meet it. If a woman you have never met before has a need, meet it. Meet the needs of anyone who has a need when it's in your ability to do so.

You said that Joshuanism exists outside the system. What does that mean?
Simply this: when Joshuans give of their financial resources, they're giving where and when they see a need. This means that not a single dollar is going toward keeping the electricity running in a church building. Not a single dollar is going toward paying the rent or the mortgage on a church building. Not a single dollar is lining the pockets of those who lead. All of that money is freed up to go where it was always supposed to go: to the poor. Sure, Tables may incur some expenses. To break bread together means to have a meal, and to have a meal means someone is paying for food. Likewise, any kind of refreshments, printed literature, or community websites might also require

funds. In comparison to Christian churches, these expenses are trivial. There should also be sufficient resources to fund the aforementioned Joshuan Forums, and those could potentially be pricey. However, as the Forums meet infrequently, the cost should still pale in comparison to the vast amounts of money the Christian Church requires.

So, having discussed how Joshuans gather together *collectively*, let's now explore how Joshuanism is practiced by the *individual*.

PART FIVE: The Practice of Joshuanism

Sometimes, it seems almost like a forgotten book of the *Bible.* You don't hear much these days about the *Old Testament* book of *Ecclesiastes*, written presumably by King Solomon. Among other things, *Ecclesiastes* is an account of how Solomon methodically looked for meaning and purpose within every human endeavor he could think of, sinful or otherwise. He turned his attention to all kinds of pursuits, experimenting with each to see which, if any, would give meaning to his life. He tried sensual delights, like feasting and drinking and partying. He tried sexual pleasure, amassing a horde of wives and concubines, indulging in whatever sexual fantasy he wanted. He tried wealth and financial contentment, filling his treasury and storehouses to overflowing, making himself the ancient equivalent of a billionaire. He then tried spending all that money, buying slaves and flocks of animals and costly commodities. He tried hard work, constructing cities and houses, planting vineyards and gardens, designing parks and pools. He tried wisdom and knowledge, training his mind to be profound and surpassingly intelligent. None of it made him happy. None of it gave him any meaning. In the end, he concluded that all of his pursuits were like a man chasing after the wind. "Meaningless!" He declared, his famous words every bit as poignant today as they were thousands of years ago. "Everything under the sun is meaningless!"

Except, he says, for one thing. The only thing in his entire life that ever truly brought him purpose and meaning, it turns out, was walking with God.

About ten years ago, during the height of my journey through Christianity, I was reading *Ecclesiastes*, and for some reason I decided that I, too, should try all the alternatives that life had to offer before self-assuredly concluding that only the Christian God has the answers. The prospect was an exciting one because those who have been involved in Christianity all their lives, from infancy, have no idea what it's like to be away from Christianity. They have no knowledge of living contrary to those virtues and ideals they hold to so tightly. As a result, they confidently profess that theirs is the only true way while they themselves have never sampled any of the competing alternatives.

Thus, I undertook an investigation similar to the one Solomon attempted. I tested the sensual delights. I checked out the party scene. I explored sexual pleasure. I landed a good job with great pay and built up quite a savings. Then, I quit the job and blew the savings. I rented a posh apartment in the city and filled it with expensive furniture. I pursued knowledge and wisdom, educating myself on all kinds of weighty things from astrophysics to philosophy to existentialism to anatomy. I taught myself music theory and learned to play multiple instruments. I studied art and history and metaphysics, constantly asking questions about life and the Universe and the meaning behind all of this. I tasted some of the other religions as well, chiefly Buddhism. I even tried atheism, just to see what it was like. When none of that made me happy, I tried marijuana. Then, I tried opium. Then I went back to sex and rode that wave for a long time, thinking that the right girl in the right situation would unlock the meaning that everything else seemed to be lacking.

Of course, you know how the story ends. My investigation ended the same way Solomon's did. I discovered the same truth he discovered. So, I came back to the God I had left behind to chase all those other options. The only difference now was that I truly knew that which before I merely suspected; now I knew with certainty that which before I only acknowledged verbally: the only thing that the human being can do in this life that truly brings any lasting meaning, purpose, joy, or peace is to seek God, to know God, and to walk with God.

The Unfolding

In regard to walking with God, a wise man once told me that we grow by inches, not by miles. "Zeal can only take you so far," he said, "but true growth is always subtle." I have never forgotten those words. They have stayed with me. As I have grown a little older and left behind the excited, impulsive youth I once was, I have seen for myself the truth in his wisdom. We always want to become Peters and Pauls the instant we take up the faith. We always think we should be farther along than we are now, and we berate ourselves for failing to be so. The truth is that authentic godliness unfolds over a period of many years, the seasoned result of countless difficulties and traumas, ongoing study, patient reflection, and the slow, gentle passage of time.

That is why Joshuans view walking with God as the *Unfolding*.

> [*The Unfolding*] – 1) the Joshuan expression for walking with God, growing in God, interacting with God, and developing spiritually; and
> 2) the pursuit of godliness, or the ongoing *unfolding* of godliness in the life of the Joshuan.

Why the word *unfolding*? Because this word perfectly captures the true dynamic of what it is to know God. Knowing God is like a drama that, well, unfolds, with each scene or each act leading to the next in the sequence. The word also implies that it is God who unfolds this drama in your life, revealing himself to you in stages, nurturing you along according to his timing, bringing you in step with his design for your personal growth (provided that you're obedient in not only following but also moving at his pace).

Humans are speedy creatures. They love to move faster and faster. They cannot stand it when something gets in their way and slows them down. Every six months, a new phone or computer makes its predecessor obsolete merely by moving data a few milliseconds quicker. Entire cities are planned and constructed around movement, so that their residents can get to where they are going with insane haste. Everything that *can* be done through a drive-through window *is* now done through a drive-through window. When we do have to wait in line, we look for opportunities to butt in front of someone else. How many accidents on the highway are the result of some hothead deciding he simply cannot sit in traffic? Yes, we love our speed. And we want things with God to be the same way. We want instant communication from him, instant results. We want him to deliver what we want, how we want, and most important, *when* we want, but God does not work that way. God has a pace. God has a rhythm. God moves a lot more slowly than we do. That is why to walk with God is to make a concerted effort to *slow down*, not to be carried away. We grow by inches, not by miles. Tattoo that on the inside wall of your brain if you have to. *We grow by inches, not by miles.*

In Joshuanism, the Unfolding is specifically designed to reflect this idea of subtle growth rather than hurried growth. The Joshuan understands that life itself is the training ground for godliness, that there is no destination. How is there no destination? Could you ever reach a stage where you are as godly as God? Could you ever reach a point in your life where you have finished growing, where you know all you need to know, where you have purged all you need to purge? Can you ever get to a place in life where you have fully understood and exhausted every mystery of God? Of course not. No matter how much you grow, no matter how mature or godly you are; there is *always* room for more. That is why godliness is not a destination. If you treat it as such, you will never get there. Godliness is a process, a slow moving, meandering expedition through life that God himself will lead you on if you are willing to submit not only to his leading but also to his stride. I am reminded of something the Buddha said: "A bucket fills one drop at a time." That is the dynamic we are aiming for: one drop at a time. Not a gushing torrent of water. Just a faithful dripping that slowly fills the bucket over time. We are the bucket. Each drop is a forward advancement into God. Each new drop adds to each preceding drop. That is how godliness unfolds, and in Joshuanism, that is what the Unfolding is all about except that this bucket (the human being) can never be completely filled (or, reach the end of godliness).

Like everything else in the spiritual realm, the Unfolding is a mutual cooperation between God and humanity. It's not all God's doing, and it's not all our doing. Moving with God through the Unfolding requires an ongoing symbiotic partnership with God. He may lead, but we have to follow. He may set the pace, but we have to keep it. He may shine the light, but we have to have our eyes open. God initiates the Unfolding, but it only unfolds inasmuch as we give ourselves to it. As soon as a person stops paying attention, the Unfolding stands still. Yet, when one gets one's focus back on God, it picks up right where it left off. I once spent four years on hiatus from God. It may sound strange, but I just needed a break, a breather. I needed to rest my mind and my heart from all the weighty things of God. However, when my hiatus was over and four years had passed, I returned to God and the Unfolding began again, resuming at the exact place where, four years prior, I had pressed pause. That is the nature of the Unfolding. Twenty years could separate one new drop from the last preceding drop, but all the water that has previously trickled into that bucket is still there, waiting for more.

What unfolds in the Unfolding? Godliness. Growth. Spiritual depth. Intimacy with God. Maturity. Wisdom. Knowledge. Revelation. Discernment. Transformation. The spiritual fruit mentioned in *Galatians* 5: love, joy, peace, patience, kindness, goodness, faithfulness, gentleness, and self-control. The Unfolding is the personal process by which individual Joshuans evolves how, where, and when God desires them to evolve, in the specific, unique way he has designed for them to evolve.

What is godliness? How would you define it? I would define it this way:

> [*Godliness*] – the achieved objective of becoming *like* God through: 1) the putting off of the *old* self; 2) being *transformed* through the *renewal of the mind*; and 3) putting on the *new* self, which conforms to God rather than to the ways of the world.[10]

What is the old self? The old self is what you were, how you lived, and why you lived that way prior to salvation. The old self is that part of you that grew and developed while you were still spiritually dead. Because you were spiritually dead during this development, you grew in such a way as to reflect the ways of the world rather than the ways of God. The old self is that part of you that lived in sin, preferred sin, and was enslaved to sin. Salvation does not magically make this old self disappear. Well, it disappears in *theory* but not in *practicality*. You still have to unlearn the old self's ways and inclinations. You still have to undo all the mental and emotional damage the old self inflicted upon you. You still have to make a daily effort to combat the old self, its priorities, its temptations, its propensities, etc. *That* is how you *put off* the old self. Godliness, though, is more than just putting off the old self; it's also putting on the new self. The new self is that part of you that is now spiritually alive. The

---

10   See *Romans* 12:2, *Ephesians* 4:22-23, and *Colossians* 3:9-10.

new self is that aspect of your nature that is now in God. The new self might have been created at the moment of salvation, but that does not mean you automatically wear the new self without effort. You have to put the new self on, every day, through the *renewal of your mind* and through intentional activities specifically designed for this purpose (which we will get to in just a minute).

Now, at this point, we need to discuss the third member of the Singular Fellowship (which, if you recall, is the Joshuan expression for the Christian doctrine of the Trinity). Just as Jesus gets a new name in Joshuanism, so, too, does the Holy Spirit. Why? For the same reasons we have discussed several times in this book: associations, stigmas, baggage, connotations. As soon as you hear the word *Holy Spirit*, you are immediately transported to the Christian realm, where decidedly Christian expressions and implications reign supreme. Joshuanism is an attempt to move away from those expressions and implications. So, just as we have revamped our terminology for Christ (replacing it with Deliverer), The Church (replacing it with The Extraction), the geographic church (replacing it with home gatherings called Tables). the Trinity (replacing it with the Singular Fellowship), and, of course, Jesus (using the name Joshua instead), we are also going to give the Holy Spirit a new expression that still should accurately reflect what we believe the Holy Spirit is role is. What is this new expression? *The Soul of Godliness.*

> [*The Soul of Godliness*] – 1) the third person of the Singular Fellowship (who Christians call the Holy Spirit); 2) that aspect of God which resides within the believer, providing guidance, counsel, comfort, conviction, and discernment; and 3) that aspect of God responsible for the Unfolding in the life of the believer.

Is this really such a drastic change? I don't think so. *Godliness* is another word for *holy*. *Soul* is another word for *spirit*. Nonetheless, by effecting a change of name, we liberate the person *behind* the name from so much human infection, as the name Joshua does for Jesus. Therefore, just as Christianity maintains that the Holy Spirit is responsible for the personal, godly growth of the Christian, so, too, does Joshuanism maintain that the Soul of Godliness is responsible for the Unfolding in the life of the Joshuan. How does this happen? The Soul of Godliness invades the heart, soul, and mind of the Joshuan at the moment of salvation and takes up residence within. At that point, the Joshuan begins to be moved and nudged along by the promptings of the Soul of Godliness, guided and steered through the unique course God has set apart for that particular Joshuan. The Soul of Godliness sets the pace, and the Joshuan must keep it. Never forget this paradoxical truth: God initiates the Unfolding, but whether or not it actually unfolds is entirely up to you.

How do we carry out our part of the Unfolding? By practicing the Five Elements.

The Five Elements

As I noted previously, the first question people usually ask me about Joshuanism is this: "What do Joshuans believe?" The second question is almost always: "How does one practice Joshuanism?" That question is an excellent one. I think you will find the answer quite interesting.

Like Christianity, Joshuanism has a private aspect and a public aspect. The public aspect of Christianity is, of course, going to church. The private aspect is prayer and *Bible* study. The public aspect of Joshuanism is the Table, the home gathering. The private element of Joshuanism is practice of the Five Elements.

> [*The Five Elements*] – 1) the private, personal aspect of Joshuanism; 2) a manifold selection of disciplines that the Joshuan practices in order to do their part in carrying out the Unfolding in their life.

An element is the basic building block of an object, an idea, or an equation. The elements of any one thing form its substance. The substance of the Unfolding, the substance of the Joshuan's life, is made up of elements the same way the water that drips into a bucket is made up of elements. What elements make water? Hydrogen and oxygen. You could call those the Two Elements of Water. You could call oxygen and carbon dioxide the Two Elements of Breathing. So what are the Five Elements of the Unfolding?

1. Conversation
2. Illumination
3. Meditation
4. Observation
5. Application

These Five Elements are those intentional activities specifically designed for the pursuit of godliness I mentioned earlier. Let's investigate each Element individually.

1. Conversation (The First Element)

This is what you might think of as prayer, except in Joshuanism, it is so much more. The act of praying, by its very nature, is something you *do*. It has a beginning, a duration, and an end. At one point, you are not praying. Then, you pray. Then, you are done, and the prayer is over. Practiced in this way, the prayer is a bit like a phone call. You're going about your day, doing the things you need to do to get through your day, focused on this and on that, and then, at a specific time (usually in the morning, or in the evening, or before a meal), it's prayer time. In other words, you are picking up the phone and dialing God. The call lasts for a while, and then you hang up and return to your regularly scheduled life. Sometimes, you need to make an emergency phone call. You know, trouble is brewing, the hammer falls, the dam breaks, and misfortune comes crashing into your life like a flood. In these moments, there is nothing to do but dial 911, except in this case it's God on the other end. Maybe on these occasions you actually get down on your knees, shed a few tears, and make some bargains with God. "I'll do (fill in the blank) if you get me out of this jam, God!" You know what I mean. Now, if this is how you want to live, that is entirely up to you, but this is *not* walking with God. This is just having God on speed dial when you need him, or merely when it's the set time to make the daily call.

Walking with God ought to be like having God on a headset, an open call that never begins and never ends. At any moment in the day, you can talk to him. You go about your work, doing your human stuff, but as you do, your focus is only partly on what you are doing. The other part is continuously on God. As the apostle Paul says in *Colossians* 3:2, "Focus the attention of your mind on God and his stuff, not on this world and its stuff." This is excellent advice, because for the Unfolding to truly unfold in your life, you need to be in an ongoing, constant *conversation* with God. You should treat him as though he is right next to you at all times (which he always is) and as though you can tell him anything and everything from the minutiae of daily life to the deep secrets of your heart (which you can). Isn't this what Paul instructed the believers to do? "Pray without ceasing" (*1 Thessalonians* 5:17 ESV). In a conversation like this, there is no wrap up with a hasty "in your name we pray, amen." This kind of prayer resumes the moment you wake in the morning, and it goes dormant when you fall asleep at night (unless, of course, your mind is so focused on God that you keep talking to him in your dreams).

> [*Conversation*] – 1) the first of the Five Elements; 2) the Joshuan expression for ongoing, constant *communion* with God; 3) the art of sharing every detail of life with God, and 4) the art of *hearing* from God.

The reason this is the first of the Five Elements is not that it's the most important. Each Element is equal to the others in importance. Conversation is first because without this Element firmly in practice, the Joshuan will have little success in carrying out the other four. A human heart that is not trained to operate in continuous dialogue with God is a heart that is not fully committed to the Unfolding and is therefore a heart not fully disposed toward God. If you cannot teach yourself to enter into an ongoing conversation with an unseen God, you are going to have little success in living for him.

It's important to remember that there is no right or wrong thing to say when you're talking to God. Unfortunately, *prayer* is too often associated with that which is *religious*. As a result, we often believe the act of praying ought to be reverential, formal, and courteous, as though if we fail to pray *correctly* God will not only ignore us but also send his wrath upon us. This is foolishness. The *Bible* says God is love, not anger. Nor is God waiting for you to make the slightest mistake so he can do that which you always suspected he truly wanted to do all along: send you to hell. God is patient, kind, and understanding. Talk to him as though you believe this. Pour your heart out to him. Do not worry about whether you're praying "correctly." The only "incorrect" prayer is one that is not genuine.

Now, conversation also involves *hearing from* God in this same ongoing, constant manner. You might say, "Well, if I am doing all the talking, how can I do any listening?" It doesn't work that way with God. God can read your mind just as easily as he can plant a thought in it. God does not need you to shut up before he can speak to you. Human conversation is that way, but godly conversation is not (there *is* a time for "being still;" we will get to that in a minute). Godly conversation is like the queues and tendrils the Na'vi possess in the film *Avatar*. Remember how they flew those giant dragon-bird-cat creatures? The tendrils of their queue interlocked with the tendrils of the creature's queue, creating a bond of communication between both entities. It's the same with conversation; except in this case it's your heart, soul, and mind joining with God's for mystical connection.

That is how God speaks, by the way. Contrary to what some may claim, God does not speak audibly anymore. He speaks through the scriptures, through life experiences, through the wisdom of other humans, and also by just *dropping thoughts and impressions into your heart or mind*. Sometimes, you can just sense that God is saying something. You do not hear anything, at least not with your ears, but you sense it. You hear it with the heart. Something within you records an impression from God, and it's delivered to your brain in such a way that you have no doubt that he has spoken to you. It's mystical and supernatural when it happens and could never fully be explained with words.

Joshuanism maintains that God still speaks to the human being today, and that the way the Joshuan hears from him is the same way the Joshuan talks to him: unbroken, unending *conversation*. Without talking *to* God and hearing *from* God, nothing godly will ever truly unfold in your life.

Steps to cultivating *conversation* in your life:

- *Begin seeing prayer as a spiritual form of breathing.* What happens when you stop breathing? You die. What happens when you cease ongoing conversation with God? The Unfolding stops. Therefore, as your body constantly breathes in and out, so also should your spirit constantly breathe in (hearing from God) and breathe out (talking to God).

- *Work at this kind of conversation.* At first, if it's foreign to you, it may not take hold right away. Rather than feeling bad about that, keep training yourself to get into the habit of this ongoing dialogue with God. In time, it will become natural. In time, you will do it with little or no effort, almost involuntarily.

- *Ask God to speak to you.* No one who has a sincere desire to hear from God will fail to do so. Often, the question is not whether or not God is speaking to you but whether or not you are listening. Listening to God is more than just being still in his presence; it's having a heart and a mind trained to hear and thoroughly disposed toward open communication with him even when the situations of your life prevent you from finding enough time to sit and be still.

- *Practice the other four Elements.* Each Element feeds off the others and yet strengthens the others. The more you practice one, the easier it is to practice another. As you begin practicing the other four Elements, you will be endowed with all kinds of fodder for conversation with God.

2. Illumination (The Second Element)

The word *illumination* is an interesting one. It implies the existence of a light source and an area affected by that light. Seen in this way, the idea of illumination has two components: 1) a source, and 2) a repository. For instance, if you were to illuminate your den for the purpose of writing a letter, you would turn on a lamp (the source), which would then fill the room (the repository) with light. The source is the place from which the light emanates, and the repository is the place where the light is stored, or its destination.

As the Second Element of the Unfolding, illumination uses these same two components, except that in this case, instead of light, the transmission is knowledge, information, revelation, and understanding, and *we* are the repository—our minds, our hearts, that place within us where we not only know something factually but also intuitively. The source? Books. Texts. Scriptures. The written accounts made by all those who have gone before us and who recorded their spiritual and transcendent pilgrimages with ink and paper. In other words, illumination in Joshuanism has to do with *reading* or *study*. At the same time, it's more than just reading. It's also storing up the knowledge gleaned from reading within one's inner sanctum. It's the arming of one's self with profound understanding. It's the process by which the data received through study takes on transformative power within. Illumination is therefore quite mystical.

So, while the First Element (conversation) has to do with communicating *with* God, the Second Element (illumination) has to do with attaining knowledge *of* God and godly matters.

[*Illumination*] – 1) the second of the Five Elements; 2) the Joshuan expression for ongoing, and consistent educative *study*; and 3) the act of methodically shedding light within through the disciplined attainment of *knowledge.*

Let's talk a moment about knowledge. Christianity values knowledge, but it seems as though, to the Christian, knowledge takes a back seat to faith. In fact, if given the choice, the Christian will err on the side of faith in the face of bad knowledge. Joshuanism, on the other hand, sees knowledge as equal to faith in importance. In the realm of Christianity, the hard questions are too often casually evaded with a shrug of the shoulders and remark like, "God's ways are above our ways. We choose to believe such and such even though we don't understand it." Joshuanism maintains that "understanding it" is as essential as "believing it." Sincere faith ought to sincerely seek good information and right knowledge. Remember, it is the truth that sets you free, according to Joshua. While we know that the truth is more than just an idea in this case (it is a person, and that person is the Son of God), we also know that knowledge is related to truth. Nothing untrue has truth in it, and nothing that is factually incorrect or logically impossible is true.[11] In other words, part of seeking the *truth* is seeking good or right *knowledge.* Accepting something by faith without a rational probing of that which you are accepting does not impress God. The followers of Jim Jones blindly accepted something by faith that resulted in the mass suicide of 914 people in 1978. Putting your faith in something without fully understanding it to the best of your mental capacity is actually quite dangerous.

Therefore, while many Christians keep on keeping on, holding on to things that make absolutely no sense and doing it under the banner of faith, Joshuans believe that God wants humans to have good information and accurate knowledge undergirding their faith. Joshuans prefer to believe that God desires us to ask the hard questions and that he also desires us continually to seek better answers to those questions.

Now, let's investigate the benefits of knowledge:

1. **Knowledge feeds you.** Ingesting knowledge is like ingesting food for nourishment and sustenance. Remember how Joshua responded to the Liar (the Joshuan word for Satan) when he was tempted to turn stones into bread? "Man does not live by bread alone," he said, "but by every word that comes from the mouth of God." Storing up theological and zoêological knowledge within is what sustains the believer during seasons of spiritual famine (which *will* come). The Unfolding requires nourishment if it is to go on progressing. The more you

---

11 Some would say the resurrection of Joshua was logically impossible, but that's only when we measure this feat against our own ability as humans. Measured against God's ability, the resurrection is quite logically conceivable.

know, the more you understand. The more you understand, the better situated you are to respond positively to God's movements in your life. The better you respond to God's movements, the more he will trust you with further Unfolding (we talk so often about trusting God, but it's an interesting thought to consider whether or not *he* trusts *you*).

2. **Knowledge encourages you.** Feeding good knowledge into the mind is like applying healing medicine to those parts of you that ache for truth. We all ache for truth; even the staunchest of atheists. We all ponder the deep questions even if we never voice them. We all stare at the night sky and consider the stars and wonder what is out there, what the purpose of all this is, what truly matters in life, and so on. By continually digesting good information about God and life and the things that matter, we begin to fill in the blanks. As this happens, we also begin to get a sense of the larger picture, our place in it, and how God's ways fit together in our life. This has the effect of endowing us with a certain peaceful security (although I am not convinced the ache will ever fully subside in this life).

3. **Knowledge illuminates you.** In other words, it *sheds light* on the dark places that live inside your heart and mind. Having God reside within you after salvation does not mean that all the dark, unspiritual, sinful, human qualities you hold inside are instantly undone. You may have thought that was the case, but it's not. These things are undone over time, through the ongoing Unfolding. Part of this gradual undoing of the darkness within occurs as you illuminate your mind and heart with godly knowledge. That is why it is the *duty* of all Joshuans to commit themselves to study. The ultimate goal of the Unfolding, and indeed one of the definitive purposes for every human life, is to *attain godliness*. Without godly knowledge, godly living is impossible.

Therefore, study plays an important role in the Unfolding of God in the life of the Joshuan. The metaphor might seem silly, but the Joshuan sees himself as a barn. Studying scriptural and spiritual texts is like storing up seed within that barn. In other words, through the methodical, consistent, and introspective study of written material designed to engender the mind and heart toward greater understanding and revelation (whether it's scripture, or some other form of spiritual writing), the Joshuan builds up a powerful supply of illuminative knowledge within.

Steps to cultivating illumination in your life:

- *Set aside daily time for study.* There is no denying that to truly experience the Unfolding in your life requires extreme commitment. For the

21st century human being, finding time in the day for quiet, contemplative study will not always be easy. However, it's an absolute must if you are serious about pushing forward in the Unfolding.

- *Decide what texts to study.* There is a wealth of theological and spiritual material available in the world. Granted, at this point there is not a lot of Joshuan reading material out there. In fact, other than this book, there is no Joshuan reading material out there (though *the Joshuan Pages* version of the *New Testament* will be out in a few years). Further, I intend on writing many more books about Joshuanism. Who knows, maybe others will take the torch and carry this farther than I. Anything is possible.

- *Be methodical about it.* Now, not everyone has a methodical personality. Nevertheless, the Joshuan should get into the habit of having some sort of order to his study. In other words, make a schedule. Choose a theme. Be disciplined in your approach. Discipline eventually gives way to habit. The word *habit* is not a dirty word, you know. It's just that there are many dirty habits out there, but cultivating good habits in your life can be rewarding. Study should be organized and habitual.

- *Hone your spiritual filter.* The closer believers are to God, the better equipped they are to separate the good information from the bad. Remember, illumination is only profitable if the knowledge is right, good, and true. Once you get into the practice of feeding yourself good knowledge, you will be that much more able to recognize other good knowledge when you encounter it.

3. Meditation (The Third Element)

A major key to unlocking godliness is *meditation.*

We have touched briefly on the Zen aspect of meditation, but there is the Biblical form of meditation to consider as well. Most people think of meditation as a practice unique to the East, but the *Bible* mentions meditation several times, primarily in the *Old Testament*. In each case, the context seems to be pointing toward 1) a silent, profound reflection of spiritual matters; 2) the contemplative evaluation of a particular verse of scripture, or a particular word of that verse; 3) the searching of one's heart and the probing of one's mind in the presence of God; and 4) the act of "being still" before God with an expectant yet patient attitude of heart (see *Psalm 46*:10). The common themes, therefore, would seem to be *stillness, silence,* and *solitude.*

On the surface, it would seem that meditation is at odds with conversation. Remember, however, that conversation is never one sided. Suppose you are sitting in a café with a good friend, sipping chai and reclining comfortably in leather armchairs. If, from the moment you show up until the moment you go home, you do all the talking, never pausing for a response, never asking your friend her opinion on the matters you have been babbling about, is what transpired at the café actually a conversation? No. It was one person chatting and the other person listening. Conversation is a mutual exchange of communication, a two-way street. If you said what you wanted and then silently listened while your friend responded, you are still in conversation with your friend even though you yourself are not speaking at the moment. The conversation is not broken when you stop talking and your friend starts talking. An ongoing, constant conversation can continue even when you have fallen silent. Why? Because it's where the focus of your heart and mind are that counts. There are times when you want to pour your heart out to God. There are other times when you want to just sit still and silently allow his presence to heal and restore your mind. Thus, meditation in the Biblical sense is the counterpart to conversation (one might even call it *silent conversation*). They work hand in glove. This is why I said that each of the Five Elements feeds off the others while at the same time strengthening the others.

Now, let's review the particulars of Zen meditation. Zen, if you recall, has to do with the Now, suggesting that time is an illusion, that the past and the future do not actually exist, and that all you ever have is the present. Accordingly, meditation is the act of bringing one's self into the present (or, into the Now) by observing the thinker and therefore becoming fully conscious. The point of this is to attain enlightenment, which is the absence of suffering (refer to the section titled "Zen Joshuanism" for more information). In this sense, Zen meditation differs greatly from Biblical meditation. Where Biblical meditation is the contemplative reflection of one thing or another (thus requiring *thought*), Zen meditation is the act of trying *not* to contemplate, *not* to reflect, *not* to think, but to rather observe the thinker and try to remove one's self from the illusion of time.

Joshuan meditation is a joining of both Biblical meditation and Zen meditation. That is, the Joshuan must set aside time in his or her day for *both* forms (unless, of course, the Joshuan in question chooses not to be involved with Zen; which, according to Diversified Uniformity, is his or her option).

> [*Meditation*] – 1) the third of the Five Elements; 2) a discipline practiced by the Joshuan which employs *silence, solitude*, and *stillness*; 3) the *quieting* of one's heart and mind in the presence of God (silent conversation); 4) the contemplation of spiritual matters and the reflection of scripture; and 5) the act of *observing the thinker* and entering into the Now.

In order for the Unfolding to truly take place in the life of the Joshuan, he or she must get into the *habit* of practicing the Five Elements every day. Making time for meditation can therefore be a challenge. Oftentimes, life can be such that finding sufficient silence or solitude is next to impossible. For some people, such as those who live alone and have plenty of free time, Joshuan meditation will easily become a natural part of everyday life. For others, those who have demanding jobs, live with a large family, or simply have a difficult time finding a suitable time and place, this will be a struggle. However, remember this: meditation does not have to go on for hours. It should not be hurried either, but sometimes, on certain days, finding even just a few moments to practice your unique form of meditation will be of benefit. Sure, meditation does more for the Joshuan who can find ample time to practice it, but practicing it a little is better than not at all.

What does meditation actually do for you? The rewards are plenty. As I said before, humans are speedy. They flit from one activity to the next, from one task to the other. The one who makes a concerted effort to find time in the course of a day for meditation will discover the many benefits of seeking silence and stillness amidst an otherwise mad world. In time, they will come to love and treasure their moments of meditative solitude. Quiet reflection often yields nuggets of wisdom in your life that those who fail to meditate often miss. Moreover, there is a mystical, transformative dynamic released in one's life after patiently learning to be still in the presence of God with a calmed heart and mind. To silently search your own soul in the presence of God is like taking the lid off a box of treasure and revealing the secret contents therein to all those present (you and God). When secrets are shared, intimacy is established. Without intimacy with God, no one will ever experience a true Unfolding. Finally, those who lean toward the Zen side of things will derive much benefit from learning to move past the illusion of time and reside increasingly more in the Now. Consider that to be fully present is to also be fully alert. The more alert a person is, the better positioned he or she is are to truly sense the presence of the invisible God.

Steps to cultivating *meditation* in your life:

- *Make the decision to do so.* Meditation is one of those things that will never get off the ground until you make an immovable, determined decision to do what it takes to make it happen.

- *Set aside the time.* Inasmuch as is possible, the Joshuan should meditate at least twice a day, preferably at set times (because this will enhance the habitualness of the act). There is no time limit on how long you should meditate; you should wrap up only when you sense your business is finished.

- *Find a place.* Meditation should be done where the Joshuan can be completely alone and completely silent (no phones or computers). It's

best to set aside a regular, established locale; a place you come to identify as "the meditation site."
- *Choose which form suits you.* You may lean toward the Biblical form of meditation, or you may lean toward the Zen form.[12] Find the one that suits you best and go with it. Or, if you are open to both, practice one form in the morning and one form in the evening.
- *Do it.* Having the intent and actually carrying it out are not the same, and only one truly benefits you. Make it so that the Third Element is as natural to you as waking and sleeping.

4. Observation (The Fourth Element)

I am a man who has little to boast about, but one thing I know I am very good at is observing. I was not born that way. It is not in my nature, or at least it did not used to be. I suppose it is now but only because I have taught and forced myself to be that way. I understood a long time ago that the man who makes sense out of life (as much as any man can) is the man who doesn't just watch but also *sees*, who doesn't just hear but also *listens*, who doesn't just know but also *understands*. After years of training and practice, I believe I can claim that I have become much more observant than my DNA originally designed me to be. I see nearly everything. I miss almost nothing. I remember those things I need to remember. I document every twist and turn of my journey. I pay attention to even the slightest of details in life, knowing that the spiritual realm is significantly more relevant than some people want to acknowledge—in fact, it's life or death. The human race is fighting a war, or didn't you know? Who is the enemy? Take your pick. We are fighting depression and despair, hopelessness and emotional isolation, extreme evil and mounting apathy. We are fighting against lies, accusations, temptations, and worries, most of which originate in our own minds. We are fighting the Liar. We are fighting each other. We are fighting ourselves. We are fighting bitter disappointments that keep stacking up, one on top of the other, until we are so weighed down by them that we finally put a gun in our mouth. We are fighting poverty, disease, famine, sometimes even the very elements of the Earth themselves. Yes, my friends, we are at war, and it does not do to shut your eyes or close your ears. The man who is still standing when the smoke clears is not necessarily the man who has made himself *brave* but the man who has made himself *observant*. Why? Because, in war, being armed with good intel is everything.

That is what the Fourth Element is about. Training the mind to be alert and observant and developing a *journalistic* approach to the Unfolding.

---

12 Consult Eckhart Tolle's work *The Power of Now* for a thorough investigation of Zen meditation.

Humans often overlook God's movements in their lives because they are either not paying attention or they don't know what to look for. In some cases, they don't even recognize that God has done this or that, answered some prayer, or laid out a route for them to follow because they have little or no experience in identifying God's characteristic fingerprints. Thus, observation, the Fourth Element, is learning to pay attention, to recognize God's leading, and to begin identifying when and where God has intervened in your life. As I said, there is also a journalistic aspect to observation. This means you begin documenting the Unfolding, recording spiritual breakthroughs and key moments of insight, illumination, intervention, and evolution. In other words, you keep a *journal*.

> [*Observation*] – 1) the fourth of the Five Elements; 2) the Joshuan expression for developing an attentive, observant nature; 3) remaining watchful of how God works; and 4) documenting the Unfolding.

It probably was not done on purpose, but humans have set up a 21st century lifestyle that affords little or no time and mental energy for observation. We are a busy race. We wake up, go here, go there, see this person and that person, sit through umpteen meetings, race home, watch this or that show, work out, and then go to bed so we can do the same thing tomorrow. In all of this urgency and haste, the human being seems to pay ever less attention to what goes on in the spiritual realm. By this, I mean that we fail to notice the subtle nuances that are God's trademark style. The Unfolding is not a 3D film with intense action and astounding special effects designed to keep your attention even when the story falls flat. The Unfolding is a slow, delicate drip, remember? If you do not take the time to stop and watch the drizzle, you will miss it. For this reason, it can be said the Unfolding is in conflict with the current standards of human activity (perhaps that is why the world today seems to be the most depressed it has ever been).

Observation in Joshuanism is a disciplined effort to force yourself to pay attention to that slow drip, to watch the Unfolding, to remain alert and focused, to observe how and where and when God says something, does something, illuminates a certain path, or releases some kind of power in your life. By taking the time to chronicle these moments and document this journey, you establish a written record that can, at any time, be reviewed and studied for the purpose of encouragement and education. What do I mean by education? Well, if you have preserved a written, personal history of the way God tends to interact with you and the particular patterns he tends to use, then by revisiting certain entries you thus educate yourself on God's ways—his particular ways in your life. By training yourself to recognize God's movements, recording God's movements, and then going back and reviewing God's movements, you become a powerful veteran of what are called "his mysterious

Joshuanism

ways." After all, there is a reason the words "journey" and "journal" share the same root word.

When you think about it, perhaps the word "journey" best captures the nature of the Unfolding. To be a Joshuan is to be on a journey, a forward moving expedition, a sojourn, a pilgrimage, a quest for some worthy goal. What is the worthy goal? Well, there are many worthy goals: godliness, enlightenment, transcendence, spiritual maturity, balance, greater evolution, and intimacy with God. As the Joshuan journeys toward these goals, he or she ought to develop an observant, attentive nature, watching for distractions, remaining alert for bumps in the road and dangerous obstructions, learning to *understand* the road, to be familiar with its nuances and configurations, documenting the pilgrimage, the progress of the pilgrim, and the patterns of the guide: God.

Writing does not come naturally to everyone. Fortunately, your journals do not need to win the Pulitzer Prize. They should merely offer a written record of the Unfolding in your life. Even scientists agree that there is some kind of power released in the brain when a fact or a truth is written down. The act of writing something out strengthens its hold in your mind. By getting into the habit of documenting everything and anything God does, how he does it, why he did it, how you responded, etc., you essentially become an expert in those matters. Suppose you spent a year documenting the movements and behaviors of your spouse. First of all, you would have to cultivate a watchful eye, right? You would have to become observant if you want to have any data to document. As you watched and learned, you would probably become aware of patterns, of your spouse's strengths and weaknesses, of his or her peculiar little idiosyncrasies and quirks, the attributes of his or her character, and so forth. After a year of documenting and reviewing this data, who on Earth would have a better understanding of your spouse than you? This is the idea behind a journalistic, observant approach to the Unfolding. Joshuans ought to be experts in identifying God's ways.

Remember *Colossians* 3:2? We reviewed it during our discussion of the First Element, conversation. It's also relevant to our discussion of observation: "Focus the attention of your mind on God and his stuff, not on this world and its stuff." In other words, make an effort amidst the tumultuous noise and whirlwind of human life in the 21st century to be attentive to the spiritual realm. No one who fails to train their mind to recognize the behavior, pace, style, and patterns of God will ever experience the Unfolding. That is just the way it is.

Steps to cultivating *observation* in your life:

- *Learn to quiet your mind.* The mind is a noisy place. The clutter of ceaseless thoughts often distracts the human from recognizing the subtleties of the Unfolding. By training yourself to calm and quiet your mind, you make room for observation, which would otherwise be impossible.

- *Be watchful.* Stay alert. Be observant. Keep your eyes and ears open. Learn the road and the nature of its terrain. Discern what happens and how it happens. Discern *why* it happens. Pay attention to what God does. Miss nothing. Notice everything. Become a habitual observer.

- *Record your observations.* Make an effort to keep a journal. Get into the habit of documenting everything that happens, everything that unfolds, no matter how big or how small and insignificant. Construct a lifelong account of God's activity in your life.

- *Review the journal often.* Recording the data is not enough. You have to go back and study it; watching for patterns, identifying key characteristics of how God has dealt with you. By doing so, you create your own unique scriptures, applicable to you and you alone, which exist for your encouragement, edification, meditation, and illumination (remember, each of the Five Elements feeds off the others and strengthens the others).

5. Application (The Fifth and Final Element)

Suppose a man owns a piece of land. On this land grow hundreds of tall trees. Suppose also that the man possesses every kind of carpentry tool imaginable. Not only does he own all these tools, but he also knows how to use them, how to wield them in such a way as to construct sturdy, sound structures. Now, suppose also that this man knows a hard winter is coming. He knows ahead of time that inclement weather is nigh and that, if left to the harsh winter conditions, he will perish. If, at this point, the man fails to build himself a house, what can be said for his fate except that he sealed it himself? He has the land, he has the trees, he has the tools, and he has the skill. He has every resource and instrument at his disposal to save himself except for one: the determination to do it. He was faced with a decision: apply the available resources and all his skill toward survival, or die. By failing to build the house, which he had the power to do, he chose death.

That is the nature of the Fifth Element. Application in Joshuanism has to do with *using* what we have learned, *exhausting* the resources at our disposal, *applying* the implements we possess to the Unfolding. It's not enough to gather the data. It's not enough to record the data. It's not even enough to review the data. You have to *use* the data. You have to put into practice those things you heard from God, gleaned through study, realized through meditation, and discerned through observation, so that they are not wasted in your life. Remember, God may initiate the Unfolding, but you play a part in it as well, perhaps a bigger part than you realize. What is

God's job in the Unfolding? To lead you. To speak to you. To touch you. To move you. To connect with you. To illuminate you. To strengthen you. To teach you. To encourage you. To *unfold* himself in your life. To draw near to you as you draw near to him. What is your job in the Unfolding? To follow. To listen. To hear. To receive. To respond. To understand. To seek and ask and expect an answer. To draw near. To watch. To pay attention. To study. To contemplate. To pour out your heart to him. To be honest with him, since he knows everything, anyway. When it comes to your job in the Unfolding, perhaps more urgent than all of those things is this: to put into practice every resource, every implement, every nugget of wisdom, every insight, every discovered pattern, every skill, every shred of illuminated knowledge, and every revelation so that you have done everything you can to the utmost of your ability to realize the ultimate goal of the Unfolding, which is godliness.

Walking with God is a partnership. It's not all you, but it's not all God, either. It's both of you working together: one leading, the other following; one imparting knowledge, the other applying that knowledge to spiritual evolution. That is the meaning of application: taking it upon yourself to build the house you have the means to build, the tools to build, the skill to build, and the need to build. Then, when the storm comes, you have a safe haven. God may have supplied the land and the trees, but he leaves it to you to cut those trees down and fashion a house. Remember, God feeds the birds, but he does not put the seed in their nests. The birds have to do their part. They have to apply themselves to finding sustenance. *That* is the nature of application.

> [*Application*] – 1) the last of the Five Elements; 2) the Joshuan expression for putting into practice everything assembled through the observance of the previous four Elements; and 3) being *intentional* about godliness inasmuch as you can.

I love the word *intentional*. I always have. It reminds me that I am not some puppet whose strings God pulls. I share a role alongside him in the Unfolding. During my Christian years, I sometimes did feel like a puppet. I often encountered this proverb in Christian circles: "Let go, and let God." In other words, "Throw up your hands and expect God to do it all." That is not the attitude of the *New Testament*, and it's certainly not the attitude of Joshuanism. The Joshuan does not sit on the side of the road, waiting for God to make all the good stuff happen and keep all the bad stuff away. The Joshuan understands that while only God is God and only God can do God-like things, the human being plays a part in the Unfolding and shares in the work of God. What did Paul tell the Philippians? "Work out your own salvation," he says (*Philippians* 2:12 ESV). The Joshuan recognizes that God has invited the human being into the process. Consequently, application is being *intentional* to leave God's job to God and focus on your own, carrying out your part in the story, and being faithful to use every means at your disposal to release God's Unfolding in your life. We grow by inches, not by miles, but even when God invites you to move even an inch, it's your job to comply.

There are no steps for application. All that can be said is that everything you learn, observe, receive, discover, and decipher must be put into daily, habitual practice. You must apply that which you possess. Build your house!

Now, let's review the Five Elements of the Unfolding:

1. *The First Element: Conversation.* Ongoing, constant dialogue with God (talking *and* listening).

2. *The Second Element: Illumination.* The disciplined pursuit of knowledge through study.

3. *The Third Element: Meditation.* The act of seeking contemplative silence and solitude in the presence of God, or bringing yourself into the Now by watching the thinker.

4. *The Fourth Element: Observation.* Training yourself to be alert and observant of how God works and the journalistic documentation of those things thus observed.

5. *The Fifth Element: Application.* Putting into practice those things discerned through the conversation, learned through illumination, comprehended or attained through meditation, and detected through observation.

Now, make sure to keep in mind one important piece of advice: do not try to implement all five Elements at once. No one can do that. Spirituality is not a crash course. The Unfolding is meant to be a slow drip, right? Treat it as such. The ideal course of action would be to choose one Element and work on it for three to six months, while setting the other four aside. This will enable you to strengthen your practice of that particular Element. Once you have made that Element habitual, move on to another one, and then another one until you have mastered all five. Remember, God is a very patient person. He is never in a hurry. Neither should you be.

You might ask, "I thought you said all the Elements work together and draw from each other and that in order to practice one we need to practice the others? How then can you now say to focus on just one at a time?" I'm saying focus on one at a time *in the beginning* while you're getting used to Joshuanism's approach. Not all of the Elements will come easily at first. Some might feel foreign, and some might seem weighty and difficult to the untrained pilgrim. Trying to master all five at once is therefore a recipe for disaster and discouragement. Yes, the ideal situation would be masterfully practicing all five on a daily basis, but no one becomes a "master" overnight. Begin slowly. Begin carefully. Take your time. Build your strength. Hone your habits. We grow by inches, not by miles. A bucket fills one drop at a time. Never, ever forget that.

One more thing before we move on: if you come from a decidedly Christian background, you may have observed that one item in particular seems to be noticeably missing from the Five Elements. Indeed, "the Missing Element," as it were, is so entrenched within Christian thought that it can hardly fail to be conspicuous in its absence. I am talking, of course, about sin. For reasons that I do not think I will ever quite understand, Christians seem to be obsessed with sin. They love to bathe both in the forgiveness of their sins and the guilt of their sins. On the one hand, Christians never tire of proclaiming unending gratitude for the great pardon the Son of God's death purchased for them. On the other hand, they wallow in their ongoing sinfulness, taking some sort of strange joy in the self-punishment and self-loathing that guilt inevitably brings, as though clinging to guilt will pay for what was supposed to be freely given in the first place. Moreover, because of his obsession with sin and guilt and the dark psychology associated with both, the Christian forsakes other worthier endeavors and weighs himself down with an impossible endeavor. What is this impossible endeavor? To stop sinning, of course. This endeavor is problematic for two reasons. First, only part of him truly wants to conquer the sin he professes to be plagued by; another part of him does not. Somewhere, deep within his psyche, he knows that to lose that sin and the familiar aches that come and go with it is to lose a piece of his identity and the comfort that comes with that identity. The same principle is applied to those people who are mentally unable to find happiness. Why can't they find it? Because as soon as one problem is solved, their mind frantically searches for a new one or invents one when a suitable replacement is not apparent. Why do humans do this? Because sadness is easier to control than happiness. Sadness requires very little of us. Happiness takes effort. It's the same with sin. A sin that plagues you is, by definition, a sin you are familiar with. Rarely do humans willingly forsake that which is familiar to them because familiarity brings comfort. The truth is that the man or woman who is afflicted by ongoing sinfulness is actually drawing a form of comfort from the affliction. That's problem number one. Problem number two with the endeavor to stop sinning is this: it's just not possible. You are never going to attain total sinlessness in this life. Never. What happens if you tell a child not to play with matches? The first chance the child gets he will play with matches. What happens when you throw all your effort toward ceasing to sin? You are just going to sin all the more. Why? Because your focus is on sin! You are so attentive to sinfulness that you cannot escape it. You are defeated before you even begin.

Does this mean that Joshuanism condones sin in the life of the Joshuan? Certainly not! However, perhaps the Joshuan knows a secret that the Christian does not. Perhaps the Joshuan understands that to attempt sinlessness is to attempt the impossible. Perhaps the Joshuan has come to recognize that by observing the Five

Elements in a disciplined, ongoing manner (meaning that the Unfolding is releasing cumulative godliness in one's life); the avoidance of willful sinfulness becomes a natural by-product. In other words, by taking the focus off of the endeavor to stop sinning (which is a negative) and putting it on the pursuit of godliness (which is a positive), the Joshuan accomplishes both, over time.

That is why the Five Elements contain no hint of the battle to conquer sin. That battle is unconquerable when the battle itself is your focus. The Five Elements have been thus designed to reflect this dynamic. Practice the Five Elements passionately, faithfully, and sincerely, and you will see sin's hold over your behavior diminish on its own. Pursue the Unfolding in your life, and you will notice yourself being drawn to sinfulness less and less.

The Joshuan Way

I was sitting in Barnes & Noble the other day, pouring over several books, researching the history of Christian theology. I was jotting down some notes when he came. So engrossed was I in my work that I did not notice him standing over my shoulder, amiably surveying the litter of theological books strewn across the table.

"Interesting reading," he said.

I looked up and met friendly eyes, but the middle-aged face around them was foreign. I did not know this stranger, but that has never before stopped me from conversing affably with my fellow man. "Agreed," I answered, putting my pen down and taking a swig of tea.

"I had to study books like that at school," he said.

"Oh? Which school was that?"

"Covenant Seminary. Here in St. Louis."

"Ah," I said. I knew Covenant Seminary. Several years ago (in another life, it seems), I applied for admission there and was denied for lack of funding. In hindsight, that was probably for the best.

"May I?" He inquired, pointing to the other chair at my table.

"Please," I said.

So he sat. We shook hands and exchanged names. I won't tell you his real name (as it turns out, the man was somewhat well known in St. Louis), but for the purpose of this account, let's call him Stew. Why Stew? Well, I thought the man bore an astonishing resemblance to Jimmy Stewart.

Stew was smiling warmly at me, apparently pleased to see a younger man knee-deep in theological books—*Christian* theological books.

"So, a seminary degree, huh?" I asked.

Stew nodded and went on tell me how he had obtained his degree several years ago and afterward had gone on to pastor three Christian churches. I listened patiently to his story about how the church he was pastoring now was in a fit over the recent firing of the youth minister. I smiled and gave him my full attention, all the while thanking God I was quit of the whole church scene.

Stew's sincerity was obvious. I could tell after only a few minutes of conversation that here sat a man who truly believed in what he was doing and who felt his faith deeply. A man of God, that much was clear. Nevertheless, I wondered what Stew would say about the book I was writing. I was actually in the process of making the decision to avoid the matter altogether when Stew said, "So, what's with the research?"

I was not going to lie to the man. He had asked me a direct question, and there was nothing for it except to give him a direct answer. "I am writing a book," said I. "I am taking notes at the moment on certain topics relevant to my subject matter."

He beamed, suddenly quite interested. "That's great!" He answered. "What about?"

I groaned inwardly. *Here it comes*, I thought. But I knew I had to be ready for this. This was not the first time this battle had been fought, and God knows it will not be the last. The moment I first sat down to pen this book I understood that my road would be a hard one. *You asked for this*, I said to myself. *Stand stout for what you believe.* That last thought strengthened me, and my mouth spoke, "Joshuanism."

Stew blinked and sat silent for a moment, confusion apparent on his face. "Joshuanism?" He said at length, uncertainty in the pronunciation of the word. "What is that?"

"It is a new spirituality, a path beyond Christianity," I replied. Part of me was wishing I were in some other Barnes & Noble in some other country on some other planet at that moment, but the other part of me glad to give voice to that which I believe in so strongly. I had no wish to offend Stew or to enter into some kind of battle of theological wits. I merely wanted to answer his questions truthfully.

"A path beyond Christianity? How come I've never heard of it?"

"Well, because I kind of designed it, and until the book I am writing gets published, if it gets published, only a handful of people on the planet have heard of it."

"*You* designed it?" Stew probed, all the friendliness gone, all the warmth in his eyes suddenly absent. The countenance of his face seemed to morph before my eyes, and this kindly older gentleman, who only moments ago seemed like such a sweet man of God, began to eye me with gross disgust as though I were a spider that needed killing. "What are you talking about?"

I sighed, gathered my resolve, and plunged in. I told him everything. I left nothing out. Stew listened quietly, still eyeing me scornfully; his face otherwise betraying no hint of whether he found my explanation offensive or not. I was wrapping up my summary when he finally held a hand up, silencing me in mid-sentence.

"There's something you fail to understand," Stew said.

"What's that?"

"The point of all of this."

"The point of all of this? The point of Christianity, you mean?"

"Precisely. You've missed the point completely."

I had still been making an effort to remain friendly even if he was not. However, my next response was a bit harsh: "The point? Do please enlighten me."

"The point," said Stew, "is to make the world see that there is no alternative to Christianity."

"That's the point?"

"Oh yes. The point and the mission. If Christianity accomplishes nothing else, it must at least succeed in making the rest of the world Christian. So, what you're doing is wrong because you are working against that mission."

We talked for another half hour. Well, Stew did most of the talking. I just politely listened. He felt he was doing me a great favor by pointing out several errors in my endeavor. The kindness returned to his demeanor but only because he thought he was winning me over. I have learned not to argue in these situations; it benefits no one. Plenty of people love getting into debates, but I am not one of them. For one thing, I articulate my thoughts much better through the written rather than the spoken word. The main reason I dislike debating, though, is that the objective is to prove yourself *right* and your opponent *wrong* as though the debate is some sort of verbal jousting match. I have no patience for jousting and no interest in vanquishing my foe. I would rather put my energy into not having foes. Nor am I so insecure that I must prove myself right at the expense of others. I am not concerned with being right. I am concerned with being a kind and loving peacemaker. Besides, I would rather be wrong and possess a loving soul than be right and possess a pompous soul. Nevertheless, I believe within my heart of hearts that I am not wrong, that God stands behind Joshuanism, that God himself planted the idea for it within me. At any rate, I chose not to be drawn into much more discussion with Stew. I had stated the answers to the questions he asked, but that was it.

I do find it interesting, though; that a Christian pastor pontificated to me for a little under an hour about the merits of Christianity but never once mentioned anything about Jesus. To him, the point of all this was the thing called Christianity—not the person upon whom the Christian religion is based but the religion itself. When talking about "what the point of all this is," Stew never said a word about the Son of God, love, or salvation. "Make the world Christian" was the banner under which he marched. Let me say right here and now that my goal is not to make the world Joshuan. I do hope Joshuanism catches on, that it takes root and changes some lives. I believe it has the ability to do that. I really do. Nevertheless, my mission is not to make the world Joshuan. If I were going to try to make the world anything, I'd make the world *loving*, no matter who believed in what, because contrary to what Stew thought and confidently proclaimed, the "point of all of this" is still today what it has always been since day one: love. I have said it before and I will say it again. I will go on saying it until I die or someone kills me. The point of all of this is love. Joshua knew that. He spoke adamantly about it. "The only thing you need to do to carry out all God asks," he said, "is to love. Love God, as totally and as fiercely and as passionately as you can. And love every single human being you encounter, be they friend or foe." (No one says you have to *like* everybody, but you do have to love everybody.)

It is astounding to me how often this is disregarded. Sometimes I just cannot understand it. When I read the *New Testament*, it jumps out at me with neon signs and blaring horns. "LOVE!" The text seems to be screaming. "LOVE! THIS IS ABOUT LOVE!" Nevertheless, for some reason people prefer to rally their causes around everything else in the *New Testament* as long as it's *not* love. Who has truly missed the point, Stew or I? It's not about who's right and who's wrong, whose way is better and whose way is worse, whose theology is sound and whose isn't, or who steps wayward toes out of line and who keeps a spotless image. The world cares about that stuff. The Pharisees cared about that stuff. The staunchest of fundamentalists care about that stuff. The Christian seems to care about that stuff, but that stuff is *not* what Joshua cared about. Did Joshua want people to continue living in sin? Of course not. Did Joshua want people to accept bad theology? Never. Did Joshua want people to be armed with good and right information? Obviously. Yet, all these desires took a back seat to his most deep-seated desire: that human beings would be creatures of love, instruments of love, beacons of love, agents of love, advocates of love, and bearers of love. *Real* love, by the way. Not some cheap imitation. Not some clever, verbal outmaneuvering disguised as love. Not some conditional love. Not some love contingent on knowing the right answers. Rather, love that looks *beyond* right and wrong. Transcendent love. Transformative love. Authentic love. The kind of love that "covers a multitude of sins" (*1 Peter* 4:8 ESV).

If you were to ask a Christian *why* he or she is a Christian, you would probably get a wide range of varying answers. "I wanted my sins forgiven," one might say, or "I wanted my life to have meaning." Still another may say, "It seemed right to me," or "Nothing else made sense," or "I had a religious awakening." Some might even say things like, "It is how I was raised," or "It is all I've ever known." The more zealous ones would most likely say something like this: "I am a Christian because God predestined me to be one," or "I am a Christian because God called me; I heard his voice and responded," or "Because the revelation of Jesus Christ overtook me and I was compelled to believe." The point is that there are all sorts of answers to the question, which means there are all sorts of reasons why Christians are Christians. Some of them passionately believe in the path they have chosen. Others could not care less and only claim Christianity because their parents did or because that is just what a good American does. Some Christians take their faith very seriously; they look forward to going to church, seek opportunities to serve, study their *Bibles* regularly, and do their best to live in a godly manner. Other Christians are only Christians in the same way they might be German, Irish, French, Republican, or Democrat. It's an adjective, one of the many they claim. If they are filling out a form, they check the "Christian" box under the *religion* section. They probably go to church on Christmas and Easter or for weddings and funerals, but there is nothing about their life or lifestyle that anyone would recognize as Biblical or godly. Then there are those Christians who fall somewhere in between these two extremes.

Now, consider this question: how would you define *the Christian way?* What do I mean by "Christian way?" Only this: that specific manner of living; that fixed assumption of how the Christian is supposed to operate and expected to behave; that recognizable mindset, attitude, or intention that, when you hear of it, you immediately identify it as being, well, the Christian way. So, how would you answer that question? How would you define the Christian way? Or better yet, how would Christians define the Christian way? Again, it would depend on whom you spoke to. Some would say the Christian way is to achieve spotless morality. Others would say the Christian way is to do the work of God (when you ask what the work of God is, you would again get all kinds of answers). To some, the Christian way means practicing Biblical principles. To others, it means "making the world Christian," (as Stew made clear to me). To still others, it means having a relationship with God, going to church, or being a good, well-behaved, compliant, straitlaced, proponent of the status quo. What saddens me beyond expression is that I truly believe few Christians would ever mention the word "love." Some would. Some are spot on when it comes to what the Christian way is *supposed* to be, but the sad truth is that many are not.

Therefore, let us iron out here and now what *the Joshuan way* is. Let us make a proclamation that is fixed and universal and absolutely *not* open for negotiation. Let us answer the question even before it is asked and leave no room for doubt. Let us crush any opposing idea that might vie for the special, singular honor of that which will forever be remembered as the words we used to answer the question. Would that I could carve the words in stone like Moses' two tablets! Or tattoo them inside the brains of every human being alive! I shall have to resign myself, however, to penning them in the pages of a book. What is the Joshuan way, that specific manner of living, that fixed assumption of how the Joshuan is supposed to operate and expected to behave, that recognizable mindset, attitude, or intention that, when you hear of it, you immediately identify it as being conspicuously *Joshuan*?

You know the answer already.

It...is...LOVE!

> [*The Joshuan Way*] – 1) the defining characteristic of what it means to be a Joshuan; 2) the reason a Joshuan *is* a Joshuan; and 3) the determination of the Joshuan to carry out, above all else, the two greatest commandments: to love God and to love humanity.

In other words, the Joshuan way is the way of love. Why is a Joshuan a Joshuan? To be loving for the sake of love because of love. All other endeavors, intentions, objectives, and desires, worthy though they may be, fall in line *behind* love. This must be the case, or else Joshuanism is dead before it is born. As I said earlier in this book, the last thing the world needs is another arm of a crumbling institution. The world needs love, as clichéd as that sounds. And clichéd or not, the truth is the truth. Love is the greatest prescription for the human race, the cure for all evils. If even half the population of the world's believers were suddenly to decide that *being right* was no longer the main objective, that *making the world Christian* was no longer the main objective, that *spotless behavior* (every "i" dotted and every "t" crossed) was no longer the main objective, that *winning verbal wrestling matches* was no longer the main objective, that *following stolid rituals* was no longer the main objective, that *faithfully attending church* was no longer the main objective, and that being an instrument of real, genuine *love* was the main objective, what would happen to human life on the planet Earth? What would the world look like?

Perhaps at this point we should define love. Again, ask ten people what love is, and you are bound to get ten responses. I once heard a Christian pastor say that blasting his opponents with a clever, crippling argument and harsh, condescending words was the best way he knew how to love someone. I asked this man how the statement he just made reflected anything having to do with love. He quoted *Ephesians* 4:15, which has the apostle Paul instructing the believers at Ephesus to "speak the truth in love." The "truth," according to this particular pastor, was synonymous with *his* opinions, *his* interpretations, and *his* estimations of what is right and what is faulty. Speaking *his version of the truth* "in love" meant pointing out to his opponents how *wrong they were*. What could be more loving, he reasoned, than to get someone who is wrong to see just how wrong they are? After all, even if you do it with harsh words in an offensive manner, it will save them in the end, right? Wrong! He took the scripture, "Speak the truth in love" and altered it to sound like this: "Defeat your foe with the right answers at all costs, for to do so will help them in the end, making you a loving person in spite of your methods." I feel safe in asserting that this is *not* what Paul had in mind when he wrote those words.

With ideas like this floating around the believing community, it's no wonder that outsiders see hypocrites where the believers themselves see only obedient followers of the one and only right opinion.

What, then, is love? Perhaps a better question is this: what is love in the realm of Joshuanism? In order to answer that question, let's return to a previous question: *Why is a Christian a Christian?* You would get a wide array of answers to that question if you asked a roomful of Christians. *Verbal* answers, that is. Yet, would there be a common theme found among the truest answers of their deepest hearts? People do not always answer questions truthfully (not that you need me to point that out for you). Further, sometimes people answer with only half of the truth, concealing the other half. As we noted, some Christians would answer one way, and others would answer another way. Nevertheless, I am convinced that if you could somehow peer into the deepest chambers of their hearts, whatever their verbal answers were, you would see this one lurking underneath: *I want to get into heaven.*

Are you surprised? Why? We have been laying all kinds of honest cards on the table in this book, haven't we? Let's just state the truth we all know and see it for what it is: if you are a Christian, the real reason you bear that name and practice that religion (however passionately or apathetically you practice it) is that you fear death, or, better put, you fear what happens after death, or even better put, you fear hell. Isn't that what this is really all about? Isn't that what this whole saga has always been about? You are a Christian, doing Christian things, believing Christian beliefs, and behaving in a Christian manner because, if truth be told, you are afraid your eternal fate would be all too grim should you choose to do and live and believe and behave otherwise. Isn't this really the heart of the matter? Search your heart now. Be honest. True, some of you might search your hearts and find that the fear of hell *is not* the real reason you are a Christian. My hat is off to you if that is the case. Many of you, though, might search your hearts and discover, to your own discomfort, that the fear of hell *is* your main motivating factor.

First, let me say this: fear should never, ever, ever be a motivating factor when it comes to matters of the heart, the soul, or spiritual faith. In fact, I am not convinced fear should ever be a motivating factor period. Even more important than that is this: if Christianity, at its heart, is really just an endeavor to make sure we get into heaven, then we have an enormous problem right from the start.

Consider the question itself. *How do I get into heaven?* Notice anything interesting about it? The only party present in the question is *you.* Two other parties are conspicuously absent. They also happen to be the same two parties mentioned in what Joshua said were the two greatest commandments. Who are the two missing parties? God and your neighbor (your neighbor is not just the dude that lives next door to you; it's *everybody*). So, what we have here in the Christian religion is this: 1) an institution that is supposed to be based on the Son of God; 2) an institution that is therefore supposed to be characterized by what the Son of God said was the main point (love); and 3) an institution whose followers follow it because they're worried about their own skin, a clear disregard of items 1 and 2. Worrying about how "I" get into heaven is me-focused. In other words, "I am doing this for myself. I am a Christian because it benefits *me*." So, I ask you, *is* this love? To let either fear or selfishness be the primary motivating factor for all the "Christian" things we do, is that love? If I am a Christian not because I want to bring love to the world but because I am frightened of what will happen to me when I die if I am *not* a Christian, how can I possibly come even remotely close to carrying out the two greatest commandments?

Joshuanism

I said all of that to say this: love in the realm of Joshuanism has certain characteristics, and number one among those characteristics is *altruism*. The Joshuan must adopt an attitude of selflessness and incessant generosity. The Joshuan should molt the me-focus and take up the you-focus or people-focus. Joshuan love is about people, people who are not *you*. Is this not the very demonstration Joshua himself carried out? No doubt, part of him did not want to go to the cross. He must have known exactly what that course held in store: the scourging, the nails, the humiliation, the terrible and excruciating inability to get a full breath of air, the slow, agonizing death by asphyxiation. Remember, Joshua was just as much a human being as he was God. The human side of him must have been absolutely terrified, but the part of him that was God had a job to do. What was this job? To demonstrate true love to the world. Thus, Joshua laid down his own life. For our sins, yes, but we get so focused on what his death *accomplished* for us that we forget what his death *showed* us, what it demonstrated *to* us. This was the ultimate example of laying down the me-focus and taking up the you-focus, as though these statements were being echoed into eternity for all the world to hear: *at my own expense will I pay your fee; to my own demise will I meet your needs; to my own sorrow will I purchase your joy; with the end of my own comfort will I secure yours; by harm to myself will I see you to safety; with my own life will I redeem yours...*

That is love. *That* is the Joshuan way.

The Joshuan is not a Joshuan because he is worried about hell. The Joshuan does not think about hell. The Joshuan does not afford the afterlife much thought. Sure, the Joshuan believes in an afterlife, but the Joshuan knows that the afterlife is meant to be lived *after* life. Life, on the other hand, is *now*. There are people who need love *today*. The Joshuan, therefore, refuses to think or behave in terms of his own destiny. The Joshuan refuses to be motivated by anything other than the needs, concerns, and pains of those around him.

The Joshuan way is the way of love. Love for God. Love for humanity. If the Joshuan does not have love, then everything about Joshuanism (Tables, Zen Joshuanism, Mosaic Theology, the Unfolding, practicing the Five Elements) means absolutely nothing.

Remember, much of the world is going to oppose Joshuanism. They will say it is evil. I ask you, can love and evil sleep in the same bed? What did Joshua say would be the one defining characteristic that would show the world who his true followers are? He did not say *faith*. He did not say *good behavior*. He did not say *having the right answers*. He did not say *being clever*. He did not say the *ability to win debates*.

He said *love*. All you need is love. Love is all you need.

Joshuan Love

Joshuan love has some very distinctive characteristics, the first of which is altruism. What of the others? Consider this list of seven attributes which must distinguish Joshuan love (though this list is not exhaustive):

1. **Joshuan love is Altruistic.** The word comes from the Latin *altrui*, which means "somebody else." The Oxford Dictionary defines altruism as "unselfish concern for the needs and well-being of other people." In other words, altruism is simply putting other people ahead of yourself. Is that not the very nature of love? Flip through *1 Corinthians* 13 and read Paul's description of true love. What is he talking about if not altruism? Moreover, wasn't the work of Joshua the most definitive example of altruism the world has ever seen? Not only is this so, but also he commanded his followers to behave as he did. "The world will know you by your love," Joshua told his disciples. He also told them that his followers would do even greater works than he did (*John* 14:12). Make no mistake about it, my friends. The Son of God and altruism belong in the same sentence, the same breath, and the same thought. That is why followers of Joshua—*true* followers of Joshua—must be as altruistic as the Savior they profess. They should express love not only with impressive words but also with tangible deeds, denying themselves for the benefit of "somebody else," even a stranger. The Joshuan way begins with altruism.

2. **Joshuan love is Indiscriminate.** Joshuan love must be accepting of those who think differently, believe differently, and live differently. There must never once be a moment where anyone in the entire world can ever use the words *Joshuanism* and *judgmental* accusatorily in the same sentence. Joshuan love must prevail where sin prevails, even more so. Love, if you recall, covers over a multitude of sins. God meets people exactly where they are, just as he met you exactly where you were. You must do the same. No doubt you have often heard this expression within Christianity: "hate the sin, love the sinner." However, even by hating the sin, are you not sitting in judgment on your brother or sister? Didn't Joshua specifically tell us not to judge, lest *we* be judged? Therefore, "hate the sin, love the sinner," is a dysfunctional statement. Let me propose a better one: "Love the human, no matter what they do or don't do—just as God does with you." Joshuan love never sets conditions on those who are eligible to receive our love because *everyone* is eligible at *any time.* The instant you set a condi-

tion for your brother or sister to meet before you will love them you have condemned yourself. You are worried about the speck in their eye when you have a plank in yours. So practice humility, tolerance, acceptance, patience, and understanding. Do this, and you will be a powerful conveyor of authentic love.

3. **Joshuan love is Liberal.** Do not let yourself get upset until you read what I mean by "liberal." Your politics can be conservative, your traditions can be conservative, your theology can be conservative, but your love *must* be liberal. What does this mean? It means that when it comes to love, you must be open-minded, flexible, and progressive in your thinking. In practical terms, this means that love cannot and should not be fettered with backward customs, or stifled by fundamentalist expectations. The Joshuan must love even when the circumstances are uncomfortable, even when to do so requires one to violate one's otherwise conservative principles. Love must rise to the occasion. Love must put aside its own preferences and inclinations and be extremely broadminded toward every human recipient, regardless of who they are, where they come from, or how much they may have wronged us. "Love your enemies," Joshua said. What could be more liberal than choosing to love those who hate you?

4. **Joshuan love is Conciliatory.** "Blessed are the peacemakers," Joshua said. Yet, for almost 1,000 years, his followers have been among the world's most aggressive warmongers. Joshua's brother, James, says that those who sow peace reap a harvest of godliness (*James* 3:18). In other words, love is meant to be *conciliatory*, a peacemaking agent. Joshuans must be peacemakers. Remember the story Joshua told the disciples about offering gifts to God? "If you have a gift for God," he said, "don't give it until you've made peace with everyone you've been in conflict with" (*Matthew* 5:23-24). What he is really saying is that you cannot pretend to be right with God (who is unseen) if you are not right with other people (whom you can see). This does not mean you will never have disagreements, even heated ones. Such is life. Disagreements will come. Nevertheless, Joshuan love should be intentionally assuaging, mollifying, pacifying, and soothing. Moreover, if you are truly practicing indiscriminate altruism, it should be easy to let the affronts of others roll off your chest. Now, total peace is not in your control. You cannot get inside the heart and mind of your enemies and make them love you, forgive you, or come to peaceful terms with you. However, all *you* can do to foster peace you should do. Resolve your conflicts to the

best of your ability even if the resolution is one-sided. Love that fails to do so was never true love to begin with.

5. **Joshuan love is a Decision.** If you wait for *feelings* of love to overtake you and make you into some stunning display of noble selflessness, you will be waiting for the rest of your life. The truth of the matter is that even the most profound of heartfelt pilgrims do not always feel like being loving. To be a human is to *want* to be selfish. No one can escape the black hole of human nature; it sucks you in every time. That is why Joshuan love is not a love that waits for feelings to move it along. It does not wait for the bearer to experience some kind of mystical or transcendental emotion. Love is an *action*; it is, therefore, something one *decides* to do. Getting out of bed when the alarm sounds at 6:00 a.m. is an action that few of us ever feel like carrying out, but because it's an action, we have the power to decide to do it every time, even though we want nothing more than to slither back under the sheets and ignore the rest of the world. Love is like that. Love is something that you resolve to do. You make the decision, and you carry it out. Sometimes, you may feel it. Other times, you won't. However, the Joshuan is faithful to do it in either situation. You may not *want* to cancel your golf game and spend that time bringing supplies to an impoverished single mother. You may want more than anything in the world to just go and play your game of golf, but love is a decision we make. I must *decide* to be altruistic. I must decide that a destitute single mother (*somebody else*) is more important than a game of golf (which benefits *me*). We may not *feel* that way; but we make the decision, nonetheless. It is that decision that sets us apart from those who chose golf (or whatever their selfish desire was). To be a Joshuan is to choose love. Every time.

6. **Joshuan love is Adaptive.** Let's discuss a seldom-quoted nugget from the apostle Paul, found in *1 Corinthians* 9:22: "I become all things to all people." What do you make of this curious statement? While you are thinking about that, think about this: when was the last time you saw a Christian temporarily discard who they are and "become" something that is better positioned to love those who are different from them? Or better put, when was the last time you saw a Christian put aside their own preferences, opinions, inclinations, and set ways for the specific purpose of being welcoming, accepting, and warmly engaging to those people who might have differing or even opposing preferences, opinions, inclinations, and set ways? Most people would

rather die than forsake who they are for the benefit of someone else, especially if that someone reflects stark, discomforting differences. Yet, that is not what Paul did, and that is not what Joshuans should do either. Joshuan love should be *adaptive.* The Joshuan should not expect or even wait for others to come to their level or comfort zone. The Joshuan should, instead, be intentional about adapting to the levels and comfort zones of whomever they are with at the time. True love requires some kind of *proximity*. By that, I mean you cannot love those you refuse to connect with, link with, or be near. You may not be able to *relate* to every difference someone has, but that should never stop you from establishing a *relationship* with him or her, based on altruistic love. Love that is adaptive is a love that says, "Don't climb over to me; I'll climb over to you," or "I won't wait for you to move over to me; I'll move over to you." Meet people where *they* are, not where you are. Adapt. Become the chameleon. Become all things to all people. Remember, the heart of love is the denying of one's self.

7. **Joshuan love is Practical.** Remember the story about the two men who happen upon a homeless mother? One is a Christian; one is not. The Christian man hands the woman a tract and says, "I'll pray for you." The other man sees to her practical needs. Which response reflected true love? Joshuan love is a practical love, a love that identifies the real need and does everything it can to meet that need in a practical, tangible way. There is nothing wrong with telling someone you will pray for him, but why stop there when you have a pocket full of money? When your home is on fire, why pray when you can get a hose? Now, am I trying to cheapen prayer? Not at all! But why stop at mere words when decisive action makes the need for the prayer obsolete? If you were diagnosed with cancer, I bet you would not stop at prayer. You would be on your butt in the doctor's office faster than a speeding arrow, but then again, cancer is something that is happening to *you*. It's easy to be practical when it's our own safety or comfort being threatened, but when it's someone else's safety or comfort being threatened, it's always, "Oh, here's a pamphlet, and I'll be sure to remember you in my prayers." No, sir. Not good enough. Am I saying prayer does not work? No. It does work. I have seen it work. Nevertheless, why should I pray for a bowl of soup to feed a starving man when I can just go and buy him a bowl of soup? Pray for the things that absolutely require prayer. With everything else, however, if it's in your power to act, get off your knees and act. Offer practical, tangible love. Anything else is just empty air.

I am convinced I could spend the rest of my life writing books about love and never run out of things to say. We have other things to discuss, however, and so we must move on. Before you read further, though, honestly assess yourself. Ask yourself if any of these seven characteristics reflect your interactions with other people. Do you put others ahead of you? Do you accept everyone, meeting them where they are? Do you sow peace where you can? Do you do everything in your ability to resolve conflicts? Do you decide to love others even when your feelings desire the opposite? These are the things that bring the smile to the face of God. These are the things that save us, my friends. Faith may launch Absolute Deliverance in our lives, but love sustains it. Faith is like the key that starts the car. Love is the fuel that makes it move.

So far, this discussion of Joshuan love has been primarily focused on the *second* greatest commandment (love your neighbor as yourself). Now let's talk about the *first* (love God with all your heart, with all your soul, with all your mind, and with all your strength). Let's combine *heart* and *soul* under the theme of "the Soul." Let's also interpret *strength* to mean "the Body." And the *mind* is, well, "the Mind."

Therefore, we love God through three channels, or with three instruments, if you prefer:

1. The Mind
2. The Body
3. The Soul

A perfect trinity, reflecting the Singular Fellowship. God has a *mind* (the Father). God also has a *body* (Joshua, or Jesus in Christianity), and God has a *soul* (The Soul of Godliness, or the Holy Spirit in Christianity). Remember what the apostle says in *1 John* 4:8? "God *is* love." It is only natural that love should reflect who God is because God *is* love and love *is* God.

Perhaps we should talk about each instrument separately…

The Mind

The mind is a dangerous landscape. It's probably the most dysfunctional, destructive element in the life of the human being. I read recently that suicide has replaced heart disease and cancer as the number one killer in America. What this really means is that the mind is killing people a lot faster than anything else in the body is. Small wonder, when you think about it. The mind is where life happens. Biological life may teem through your body as a result of blood and tissue and organs, but the mind is where your life is *lived*. That is why the battle always takes place in the mind. When life comes at you, when fate comes at you, when bad luck comes at

Joshuanism

you, or when the Liar[13] comes at you, where does the battle take place? In the mind. Always in the mind. Cancer could be killing your body, but whether or not you are really living—truly living each moment, regardless of your situation—depends on what is going on in your mind.

How do you love something with your mind, especially when the mind is such a despicable place? How do we love God with these malfunctioning minds of ours? The answer is simple. You love God by *undoing* the malfunction. One of my favorite verses in the entire *New Testament* is *Romans* 12:2, which says, "experience transformation by refurbishing the condition of your mind." In other words, you love God by *conditioning* your mind. This means you clean up the mind. You repair the dysfunctional parts. You make a disciplined effort to gain control of your own mind. How does this translate into loving God? By conditioning and healing the mind, you make it a place God can use. You would not give your spouse a bag of garbage on Christmas, would you? Then, why give God a diseased mind? Give God a healthy, ordered, functional mind that he can invade it freely and use it to his purpose. Give God a conditioned, fit mind so his communication and intimacy with you can be enhanced. That is how you love God with your mind. To love God with your mind is to yield your mind to his transformative influences.

So, how does one condition one's mind? Personally, I am convinced that the practice of Zen goes a long way in reversing much of the malfunction, rendering the mind more fertile for love. Not everyone will embrace Zen, however. Nevertheless, even those who decline to practice Zen can still diligently condition their minds.

How? The secret is *truth*. Truth is the only weapon that has any real power for repairing the mind. Remember what Joshua said about truth? "The truth will set you free." This is especially the case when it comes to the battle of the mind. Why? Because when the battle of the mind takes place the weapon used against you is the *lie*. The lie is the weapon that destroys the mind. The truth is the weapon that destroys the lie and protects the mind.

What do I mean by the lie? I could it explain it you, or you could find out for yourself. Do this: put the book down and find a notebook and pen. Sit silently for the next half hour and write down all the thoughts that go through your mind. Do not assess them, do not judge them, do not interpret them, and do not listen to them. Just document them, and then come back.

Finished? Good. Now, look at your list. How many of the thoughts were accusatory? How many of the thoughts were self-deprecating? How many of the thoughts were offensive attacks designed to shatter your confidence and obliterate your inner peace? How many of the thoughts were designed to trick you into believing horrible things about yourself or about God? How many thoughts were designed to induce worry where worry did not previously exist? How did your mind lie to you? Did it

---

13   The Joshuan expression for Satan.

tell you that you are unattractive? That you are worthless? That you are doomed? That you are stupid? That you will never make it? That there is no hope? That you will never be loved? That you never have been loved? That you are evil? That you are lost? That you are too far from where you need to be to even try getting there?

Lies! All lies!

You are being lied to. Zen would say it is your mind itself lying to you. Christianity would say it is Satan (the Liar) lying to you. In reality, the *origin* of the lie makes little difference. The fact of the matter is that you are being lied to one way or another. The more you believe the lie, the more dysfunctional your mind is. The more dysfunctional your mind is, the more depressed you are. It is hard to love God when you are depressed, and I have news for you: God is not going to take your depression away. That is your job. Absolute Deliverance means you no longer *have* to be depressed, but only you can decided not to be. Yet, where to begin? Begin with the lie, and disarm the lie with the truth.

As you begin to regularly document these accusatory and destructive statements that repeatedly replay in your mind, you may begin to notice a pattern. You may begin to see what your particular weakness is. For me, it is hopelessness. When the lie comes, it usually attacks my hope. For my lovely wife, it is has to do with appearance and self-worth. When the lie comes at her, it usually attacks her confidence. The point is that as you begin to identify how the lie usually comes at you, you will be better able to have the truth ready and at your disposal. For instance, suppose I begin to notice that this thought repeats itself in my mind too often to be mere coincidence: *there is no one out there who gives a damn.* Now, first of all, I must identify that this is a lie. Second, I must recognize that because the thought comes at me frequently, this is probably a particular weak area in my mind and whatever or whoever is lying to me knows this and uses the lie as a weapon against me.

If I were to decide to believe the lie (which only empowers the lie), my life would be characterized by a defeatist attitude and a hopeless outlook. Then, the depression starts. The more depressed I am, the slimmer my chances of loving God are. However, if I choose not to believe the lie and instead disarm it with the truth, the lie loses its power, and I win the battle for my mind. How would I disarm that lie with the truth? I would counter it with this statement: *there is someone out there who gives a damn, and that someone is God.* The more I repeat the truth, the more I condition my mind to believe that truth naturally. That is why whenever I detect that a certain lie is gaining control in my mind, I immediately write the lie down. Then, I immediately write the truth underneath it. Now I am armed and ready for battle.

It is not easy. You do not always win every battle, at least, not at first. Over time, however, you get stronger, deftly combating lies the instant you detect them. Remember, the truth will set you free. Free to what? Free to love God. Love God with your mind by conditioning your mind to be healthy place.

The Body

How do you love God with your body? By using it as an instrument of love. By offering the body that God gave you back to him for his use and his purposes. What that means in practical terms is this: being healthy, being holy, and being available (or accessible).

1. **Being Healthy.** Your body is God's gift to you. Therefore, how you treat it says a lot about your gratitude. If your spouse gave you a diamond for your birthday, would you throw it in the bottom of your drawer underneath piles of junk or leave it sitting on the front porch overnight? No. You would guard it. Cherish it. Treat it like the precious object it is. You must do the same with your body. No one is saying you have to win marathons or become some chiseled bodybuilder. Nor is anyone saying you have to become a vegetarian (which I could never do) or be the Jenny Craig spokesperson. What I am saying, though, is that your body is a gift and, according to the *New Testament*, a sanctuary (*1 Corinthians* 6:19). You should therefore keep it healthy and fit. You do not have to be fanatical about it. You do not even have to be enthused about it. But you do have to do it. The Joshuan loves God with his body by preserving his body as the sanctuary the *New Testament* says it is.

2. **Being Holy.** Your body is an instrument. With this instrument, you can do evil, or you can do good. By choosing to use it for good, you express your love for God. Consider what the apostle Paul says in *Romans* 12:1, "God is good and merciful. Therefore, I invite you who are believers to generously donate your living bodies to this God; and make sure your donation is suitable for his godly purposes. This is how you worship the God you say you believe in." In other words, you cannot brazenly and willfully use your body for sin and then expect that God will want to use your body for himself. And how does God use your body? By moving within you to do this or that, thus carrying out his plans. If you are going to give yourself (and your body) to God, give him something good. The Joshuan keeps his body clean and holy. That is the true heart of worship.

3. **Being Available.** Your body is a vessel. It carries God's love wherever you go if you are faithful to allow it do so. Loving God with your body means making it available for his work. What is the work of God? Loving everybody else. If you make yourself and your body available for the needs and problems of others, you are therefore using your

body for God. In truth, this is why God gave you your body to begin with. He wants you to make it available to him, to be a vessel, a messenger, a beacon, and a tool. Live in such a way as to make your body an implement in the hand of God. God will use all those tools available to him, but he seldom uses those tools that are not available to him (in other words, God will never "rape" you, by which I mean, he will not force himself upon you). Make yourself available, therefore, and do it with a smiling heart. *That* is how you love God with your body. The Joshuan's daily job is to submit his body upon waking in the morning, saying. "God, this day I offer my body to you and make it available. Use it as you will."

The Soul

The soul is a tricky concept. We don't always know exactly what it is we are talking about when we mention "the soul." For the purposes of this discussion, I have inserted "the heart" in there as well, only adding to the perplexing nature of these ideas. So, let's talk about what "the soul" and "the heart" actually mean.

How many times in your life have you made or heard someone make a statement like this: "Well, I wanted to, but my *heart* wasn't in it." Or perhaps something like this: "I thought about it, but after a while I knew in my *heart* it wasn't right for me." We talk about our "heart" all the time, and we when do, we are not referring to the fist-sized organ in our chests that pumps blood through our bodies. So, what *are* we talking about? Some people call it their "soul," others just call it their "gut." Some might even say something like, "I knew the truth *deep down*." Whatever words are being used, the point is that they are all interchangeable, specifying that place within where the *essence of your life resides.* Right? Whether we speak about it as our "heart" or our "soul," what we are really talking about is some sort of internal treasure chest or spiritual cavern where our deepest fears, longings, regrets, dreams, secrets, and doubts all slither about underneath our conscious minds. We are in the land of the ethereal even talking about it. You could not see this place on an X-ray or an MRI. Surgeons could not open you up and remove this internal treasure chest. It coexists both in us and somewhere in the spiritual realm. People who seem to be leading particularly dead or cold lives are spoken of as "not having a heart." What is really being said about these people is that it appears the spiritual cavern within them is either empty or nonexistent. The heart (or the soul) is a very zoêological concept because it is here in this treasure chest or cavern that spiritual life (*zoê*) resides. When the Soul of Godliness enters the human being at the moment of salvation, this is where it sets up shop.

So, how do we love God with our soul? How do we love God with something that can barely be adequately defined? Well, consider that it's with your heart and soul that you love your spouse or significant other. It's with your heart and soul that you love your parents or children, dog or cat. After all, a heart is the universal symbol for love. No one actually thinks that love originates and is nurtured in the physical, biological human organ known as the *cor humanum* (the Latin word for the human heart). The heart is the symbol for love because everyone knows and understands that love radiates from the inner sanctum, that spiritual cavern we have been discussing. Just as a planet has a gravitational pull, so, too, does a heart or soul have an unseen, mystical force springing from it: love.

Therefore, you love God with your heart or soul by, well, adoring him. In other words, you are enthusiastic about him. You are excited to know him. You are passionate about your belief in him. You admire him. You worship him completely. He is your everything, the first among all your, what? Your *loves*. To love God with your heart or soul means that you have moved beyond the logical conclusions of the mind, the resolute decisions of faith, and dry theological observations, and now *feel* something for God that originates and exudes outward from the inner place where the essence of your life is found. To love God with your heart or soul means you actually love him the way you love anyone dear and important to you. Your love has therefore evolved beyond a mere *decision* and has entered the realm of *passion*.

This kind of love does not always happen overnight. For some people, it does. They have these rich, powerful spiritual awakenings and are suddenly somehow struck with love-lightning for God. For most of us, though, learning to love God is a lot like that slow drip of the Unfolding. It grows with subtlety over time. That's okay. God has no problem with things that move slowly. He does not mind a love that evolves gradually, strengthening and deepening as you come to know him better and better over a period of, well, an entire life.

This is the Joshuan way. Whether it happens instantly, or slowly, over the course of time, the Joshuan's deepest desire is to move from cognitive love (the kind of love that results from *choice*) deeply into transcendent love (the kind of love that results from *passion*).

Still with me? Still shaking your head? Or are you starting to think that maybe I am on to something here? Either way, we have discussed a great many things in this book thus far. If I have succeeded in saying nothing else, I hope I have at least made this much abundantly clear: Joshuanism is about love. Period.

Michael Vito Tosto

Regarding the Joshuan

I was nine years old when I entered the land of Christianity. I was thirty years old when I walked away from it. My time as a Christian endowed me with precious gifts, ones that I will never lose nor forget. Among these are a hunger for God, a passion for theology, an awareness of the matters of the heart, a social consciousness that allows me to see people beyond their appearance, an attitude designed for encouragement, and a wealth of Biblical understanding. These gifts served me well during my years as a Christian. And yet...and yet there was something missing the whole time. I did not feel it at first. I was probably too young to feel it. However, as time went on and my Christian walk took both root and shape, I began to sense that something was not quite right. I was at a loss to say what it was. On the surface, everything seemed fine. I struggled with certain sins for a while; much like other Christians do, but the nagging impression that something was amiss seemed to reside deeper than my weaknesses and temptations. I suspected so primarily because that nagging feeling was present even during the days of my most triumphant victories and mountaintop experiences. Sometimes, I was able to ignore it. Other times, I did not want to ignore it; I wanted to know what was wrong. I prayed about it. I talked to several pastors and church leaders, asking them for wisdom and guidance in trying to figure out what the problem was. I didn't figure it out, though, until a few years after I had left Christianity.

I was sitting in my car one day, waiting for a green light, when out of nowhere a strange thought struck me. It was a question, really. I had the distinct impression that someone had purposely planted that question firmly into my psyche. I also had the distinct impression that someone was God. I have probably asked God a million questions during my lifetime, but this was the first time I ever felt as if God was asking me a question. The question was this: *was my Son a Christian?* I just sat there silently, without answering, reflecting on the question. Then, another question came just as suddenly as the first: *what about me? Am I a Christian?* Again, I just sat wordlessly, pondering these two strange questions. If it *was* God speaking, and I was almost certain that it was, then he was asking me whether or not Joshua was a Christian (I was still calling him Jesus in those days) and whether or not he, God the Father himself, was a Christian. Now, to you this might be a no-brainer, regardless of your answer, but for me the implications were astounding. I had already left Christianity at this point for many reasons. Nevertheless, I was not sure where to go next. I had basically shelved any and all Christian behaviors, but I still prayed, still contemplated God. Then, these two questions came out of nowhere.

What *about* those questions, anyway? Is God a Christian? Was Joshua? Is there any instance in *Matthew, Mark, Luke,* or *John* where the Son of God even mentions the word *Christian*? Is there any instance where Joshua does anything even remotely resembling Christian behavior? Does he ever talk about Christian creeds? Does he ever talk about church attendance or membership? Does he ever say a word about worship music, praying the rosary, or dressing up in your Sunday best? Does he ever even utter a single word about starting a religion called Christianity? Personally, I am convinced Joshua wanted nothing at all to do with religion. It's not that religion is necessarily bad, but religion is *humanity's* architecture. God existed before humans were around to dream up religions about him, and he will exist long after the last humans have finally fallen into extinction (if and when they do). That is what many of today's believers seem to forget. They forget that their clever theological equations and impressive tomes of doctrinal arguments do not predate God. Moreover, the word *Christian* (an adjective originally used to describe people in the first century who worshipped the Son of God) had not even been invented at the time Joshua rose from the dead.

Was Joshua a Christian? I would say no.

What about God the Father? As we noted, he predates the Christian religion. He predates all religions. He predates humanity. He predates the Earth and even the Universe itself. If Christianity is a human religion, how could one possibly regard God himself as a Christian since he existed long before the first human ever drew breath? In my opinion, no one could call God a Christian. That is how I answered those two questions that day in the car. After only a few moments of quiet meditation, I said aloud, "No, you're not a Christian, God. And neither was your Son."

When I was telling my wife about this instance, she said this: "Well, if you have an entity (God) and humans who worship that entity (believers), it stands to reason that only the humans would carry the name used by the believers; Christians in this case. No one would expect God to be on the same level as the humans; therefore, *no one* would think of God as a Christian."

"But they do," I told her. "They may not admit it, but most Christians think Jesus is just like them. They assume God thinks the way they do. The Lutherans think God is just as Lutheran as they are, the Baptists think Jesus is just as Baptist as they are, and on and on it goes. God is removed from our human identifications, yes; but try telling that to most believers."

As for myself, I labored under that misconception for years. I might not have ever been able to put it in those exact words, but I thought God matched the current manifestation of the Christian religion. I never questioned it. I never once considered whether or not the current manifestation of the Christian religion matched God. Until that day in the car.

As soon as I had answered the first two questions, the third and final question came: *If I am not a Christian, and my Son was not a Christian, who says you need to be?*

As I pondered that third question, everything finally came together, and my eyes were opened. I knew instantly that what I felt was missing all those years was not something absent inside of me. What was missing was any correlation between what I was doing as a Christian and what I witnessed in the *New Testament*.

Let me explain. On the one hand I knew that Joshua (again, I was still calling him Jesus at that point) had said that if anyone wanted to follow him, that person must deny himself. Yet, I never denied myself as a Christian, nor had I ever met a single Christian who did. I knew that Joshua had said that anyone who would save his own life would lose it, and he who would lose his own life would save it. Yet, as a Christian I never gave a thought to anything other than self-preservation (when push came to shove, at least), and neither did anyone else. I knew that Joshua had said that no one should judge another person. Yet, I judged everyone, and everyone I knew judged everyone. I knew that Joshua had said a person ought to love his enemies, but I stood right alongside everyone else in my church on the night of September 11, 2001 and prayed for vengeance against the terrorists. I never gave a damn about my enemies, nor did any of my fellows. I knew that Joshua had said that his followers ought to forgive every person who has wronged them without fail, unconditionally, but I held grudges. My pastor held grudges (I know because I heard him speak of them). I knew that Joshua had said, "Do not store up treasures on Earth, instead store up treasures in heaven." Yet, I lived and died by the size of my wallet, seldom exhibiting anything in the way of generosity. I had never met a Christian who did not worship money, who did not store up treasures on Earth in the form of a nice, fat savings account. I knew that Joshua had said that the world would know his true followers by their love. Yet, I rarely did anything loving. I rarely *saw* anything loving. Moreover, I cannot point to one single time in the history of my Christian experience where I ever heard even one word from the pulpit about loving my neighbors. In fact, I heard precious little about love at all. The major themes were always sin, sin, and more sin.

Am I trying to blacken Christianity? No. Believe me, no. I am just trying to paint an accurate picture of a poignant truth: a person can go their whole life doing all kinds of Christian things and still never once do anything that resembles what Joshua did, what Joshua said, or what Joshua taught. If you disagree, I suggest you take a look at *Matthew* 7:21-23.

Therefore, consider this question in your own life: are you doing Christian things, or are you doing God's things? There *is* a difference.

That was what dawned on me that day in the car, waiting for the green light. For years, I had thought something was missing inside of *me*, but I suddenly understood that I had been mistaken the entire time. Something *was* missing, but it was missing from Christianity, not from me. Rather, it was missing from that which Christianity has *become*. I suddenly knew that the nagging feeling that had plagued me for years must have been the prodding of God. He had been nudging me toward a realization

Joshuanism

that the religion I was practicing had little to do with what he actually wanted from me.

That was when I knew it was okay for me to be something other than a Christian, but it took a few more years until I imagined Joshuanism. I have been a Joshuan ever since, and I have never looked back.

Now, we have talked a lot about what Joshuanism is, how it's practiced, and the nature of its beliefs. We have gone into great detail about the many theological departures that distinguish Joshuanism from Christianity. We have also explored, to some degree, the characteristics of those who practice Joshuanism: the Joshuans. Now, I would like to explore those characteristics even more.

Remember the definition of a Joshuan?

> [*Joshuan*] – 1) a human who, by faith, has met God, now lives *in God*, and now has God living *in them*; 2) someone who has left their old life and old self, has been transformed, is *being* transformed, and is putting on a new self; 3) a person who resembles a Christian in many ways, but in other ways is a completely new conception; 4) a person who believes it is *through* the Son of God (*Joshua* to Joshuans; *Jesus* to Christians) that one is connected to the Son's Father; that is, God; 5) a person who is free (internally), alive (eternally), forgiven (completely), and absolutely delivered in a way that only those who have faith in the Son of God can be; 6) a person who behaves and operates based on what Joshua did and how he did it; and 7) someone who expresses all of these wonderful things through a life *reflective* of the one responsible for all of it: Joshua.

You will notice that this definition has seven parts. Let's address each part separately...

1. **A Joshuan is a human who, by faith, has met God, now *lives in God*, and now has God living *in them*.** In other words, the Joshuan is spiritually alive. At the moment of salvation, the Joshuan enters God, and God enters the Joshuan. Christianity calls this being "born again." Regardless of the terminology, the point is that prior to Absolute Deliverance, the believer was physically alive but spiritually dead. Now, after having entered this Absolute Deliverance *through faith* in Joshua, the Joshuan is both physically alive *and* spiritually alive; and he will go on being spiritually alive even when his physical body dies. To be a Joshuan is to be spiritually alive; and to be spiritually alive is to *know* God, to be *in* God, and to have God *in you*.

2. **A Joshuan is a human who has left his or her old life and old self, has been transformed, is *being* transformed, and is putting on a**

new self. This is reflective of scriptures like *Romans* 12:2, *Ephesians* 4:22-24, and *Colossians* 3:9-10. Joshuanism suggests there are two parts to salvation: 1) that which happens instantly, and 2) that which happens slowly, over time (remember the slow drip of the Unfolding?). The instant part is that which occurs at the moment of salvation. In other words, the instant a human being becomes a Joshuan through faith; certain elements of salvation immediately transpire (forgiveness, redemption, reconciliation, spiritual life, the invasion of the Soul of Godliness—basically, everything Absolute Deliverance implies). However, the other part of salvation does not happen instantly. It happens slowly, over time. This is the Unfolding, the Joshuan's daily practice of the Five Elements, which serve to engender godliness (putting off the old self, being transformed, and putting on the new self).

3. **A Joshuan is a human who resembles a Christian in many ways but in other ways is a completely new conception.** Christians and Joshuans have similarities. They believe in the same God. They worship the Son of God. They read the *Bible*, pray, seek to carry out God's will, etc. Nevertheless, they are also quite different. Christians view the Son of God as Jesus. Joshuans view him as Joshua. Christians go to church. Joshuans attend Tables. Christians battle sin. Joshuans pursue godliness, knowing that to do so will cause sin to diminish on its own. Christians emphasize faith. Joshuans emphasize love. Christians read Christian *Bibles*. Joshuans read *The Joshuan Pages*. In the eyes of those who are neither Christian nor Joshuan, the Joshuan should be noticeably distinguishable from the Christian, and vice versa.

4. **A Joshuan is a human who believes it is *through* the Son of God (*Joshua* to Joshuans; *Jesus* to Christians) that one is connected to the Son's Father; that is, God.** Like Christians, Joshuans believe salvation is exclusive to the Son of God. Unlike Christians, Joshuans believe anyone can have faith in the Son of God and in so doing receive salvation from God; whether they do it through the Christian route, the Joshuan route, or some other route altogether. Think about it in these terms: The Universalists would say, "All roads lead to God." Christians would say, "All Christian roads lead to God." The Joshuan says, "Any road traveled with the Son leads to the Father." Therefore, Joshuanism does not forsake the exclusivity of salvation through the Son of God, but it does maintain that the Son of God travels more than one road.

5. **A Joshuan is a human who is free (internally), alive (eternally), forgiven (completely) and absolutely delivered in a way that only those who have faith in the Son of God can be.** We have already touched on forgiveness and spiritual life, but what about freedom? Joshuanism maintains that part of Absolute Deliverance, part of being alive in God, is being free. Remember Joshua's words in *John* 8? "Once your mind has access to the truth, the truth will set you free. And when the Son of God sets someone free, they are *completely* free." The Joshuan is therefore free. Free *from* what? Anything. Everything. Sin. Depression. Addictions. Expectations. Guilt. Spiritual darkness. Obligations. Whatever was binding the Joshuan binds him no longer. What was oppressing the Joshuan oppresses him no longer. The Joshuan is free to be himself. The Joshuan is free to enjoy life. The Joshuan is free to take pleasure in each day. The Joshuan is free to follow his heart, follow his dreams, and shape his destiny.

6. **A Joshuan is a human who behaves and operates based on what Joshua did and how he did it.** Joshuans do not do Christian things. They do Joshuan things. What are Joshuan things? Whatever Joshua did. Joshuans model their daily lifestyles and mindsets after what they read in the *New Testament*. In other words, the Joshuan denies himself (altruism). The Joshuan takes up his cross (is willing to suffer for God). The Joshuan refuses to judge another human being. The Joshuan handles confrontation with authentic meekness (meekness is *not* weakness, by the way). The Joshuan refuses to hate his enemies. The Joshuan refuses to love money. The Joshuan endeavors to do his godly deeds without flourish and fanfare. The Joshuan refuses to hold grudges. The Joshuan forgives habitually. The Joshuan lives to serve, not be served. The Joshuan lives to love. The Joshuan endeavors to bathe everything he says and everything he does in absolute love. Anything else the *New Testament*s says Joshua did, that, too, is what the Joshuan does.

7. **A Joshuan is a human who expresses all of these wonderful things through a life *reflective* of the one responsible for all of it: Joshua.** This means that the Joshuan's life is a testimony to the Son of God. Everything the Joshuan does and the way he does those things should ultimately point toward Joshua in an irresistible way. While Christians go out into the world trying to make other Christians through convincing rhetoric, the Joshuan allows his conduct to lead others to God. The Joshuan forces Joshuanism on no one. The Joshuan does not even

force the Son of God on anyone. The Joshuan simply believes that by living and behaving in a manner reflective of what Joshua actually did and how Joshua actually lived, the unbeliever will see through actions what rhetoric could never express.

Therefore, based on everything we have discussed in the previous sections about what Joshuanism is, and everything we have just now observed about who the Joshuan is, let us now construct a picture of one of these believers who operates not under the title of Christian but under the title of Joshuan:

1. **The Joshuan is free of the stigmas associated with the name *Jesus*.** Joshuans are Joshuans precisely because they view Jesus Christ as Joshua the Deliverer. While Christians take their name from the word *Christ*, Joshuans take their name from the word *Joshua*. This makes Joshuans and Christians two distinctly different types of believers (for more reasons than just this one, but without this initial reason none of the other reasons would exist). By viewing the Son of God as Joshua instead of Jesus, the Joshuan opens his heart and mind to new perceptions of the Son of God, free of all the baggage associated with the name *Jesus*.

2. **The Joshuan embodies traits that would be considered *post/Christian*.** While Christians exhibit Christian traits, Joshuans exhibit *post/Christian* traits. In other words, Joshuan traits are similar to Christian traits, but represent enough differences to fall under the category of that which is *post/Christian* (i.e., progressive and considerably evolved). Examples of these traits include significant changes in certain theological views (such as Scriptural Relegation and Mosaic Theology), the optional inclusion of Zen in the Joshuan's daily life, the attendance of Joshuan Tables rather than Christian churches, and the practice of the Five Elements (which, in their Joshuan form, exist nowhere in Christianity).

3. **The Joshuan is nonreligious.** The Joshuan may be spiritual, the Joshuan may be philosophical, the Joshuan may be methodical in his approach to godliness, but the Joshuan is *not* religious. The Joshuan could not be religious, because Joshuanism is not a religion, no more than marriage is a religion. Marriage is something people do, and an identity they assume. It is the same for the Joshuan. Joshuanism is a way of thinking, a way of believing, and a way of living—or an *identity* one *assumes* rather than a *religion* one *practices* (there *are* practices associated with Joshuanism, but there are also practices associated with the Boy Scouts; yet, neither one is a religion). Joshuanism has

no liturgies, no sacraments, no ceremonies, and no worship services. Some will want to see Joshuanism as a religion, but it was neither designed nor intended to be so.

4. **The Joshuan cultivates *post/Christian* thought.** If you recall, *post/Christian* thought is merely a mindset designed to continually question what we know about God. The Joshuan does this regularly, constantly re-evaluating God's revelation to humanity, constantly pushing forward toward greater disclosure and understanding. The Joshuan seeks to know as much of God as humanity can at any given point, believing that as humanity evolves, so, too, does humanity's capacity to know God.

5. **The Joshuan's goal is *love*.** The Joshuan's main objective in life is to be an instrument of true love. While other people question the meaning of life and their specific purpose on this planet, the Joshuan fills in that blank with one singular answer: to be loving. All other goals bow down to that one primary goal.

6. **The Joshuan is *intentional* about the goal of godliness.** Joshuanism provides several implements specifically designed to aid the Joshuan in his pursuit of godliness, such as the Five Elements, the Joshuan Table, the Circadian Effort (which we will talk about later), the Joshuan way, and even Zen Joshuanism (should the Joshuan choose to avail himself of this device). But without an intentional, daily effort to use these implements, Joshuanism will not profit anyone. The Joshuan therefore *is* intentional about using these implements, taking the pursuit of godliness *extremely seriously* in his personal life. Otherwise, why bother being a Joshuan?

7. **The Joshuan does not require total agreement with his fellows.** Through Diversified Uniformity, the Joshuan understands that though we are different we are also the same. While Christians maintain their separations (e.g., Baptists do not go to Lutheran churches, and Catholics do not go to Baptist churches), Joshuans come together celebrating their differences. If one particular Joshuan Table is made up of former Christians, it does not matter whether each member came from a different quarter of Christianity. Nor does it matter if two members of a Joshuan Table practice Zen and the other ten do not. Joshuanism does not require complete agreement between each Joshuan. The Joshuan values and encourages diversity and prefers being *loving* to being *right*.

8. **The Joshuan is not threatened by other religions.** The Joshuan may or may not embrace certain aspects of other religions, spiritualties, or philosophies—provided those aspects do not 1) blatantly contradict the Son of God; or 2) hinder love, damage faith, or incite sin. While Joshuanism does maintain the exclusivity of salvation through the Son of God, it does not contend that the Son of God works only through either Christianity or Joshuanism. As we noted previously, Joshuanism maintains that the Son of God travels more than one road.

9. **The Joshuan is intimately involved in the lives of his fellows, and they are intimately involved in his.** While Christianity continues with the corporate church system, Joshuanism favors home gatherings called Tables (led by Helms, who are in turn led by Pilots). The intention of the home gathering is to foster authentic community, genuine fellowship, intimate friendship, and solid bonds of love between the members of each Table. The Joshuan knows his fellows, confesses his sins to them, hears their sins, meets their needs, shares his needs with them, mourns with them, rejoices with them, suffers with them, and pursues godliness alongside of them.

10. **The Joshuan is *meditative*.** Meditation is one of the Five Elements, but the Joshuan should do more than just practice meditation: the Joshuan should develop a meditative attitude, lifestyle, and stride. Nothing should be done, decided, acted upon, or accepted in the life of the Joshuan that has not first been bathed in hours of quiet, contemplative meditation. As a *noun*, meditation refers to a practice. As a *verb*, meditation refers to the act of observing that practice. But as an *adjective*, the word "meditative" implies a thoughtful, reflective, introspective, and profoundly *measured* approach to daily life. Even if it is not part of his natural personality, the Joshuan pursues a meditative mentality.

11. **The Joshuan is acutely *observant*.** Again, observation is one of the Five Elements, and again, the Joshuan should train himself to be observant as part of his daily approach to living. There is a time for determined observation as a performed activity, but the Joshuan endeavors to be observant as a *way of life*, rarely failing to see, hear, notice, and understand *everything* that is happening around him, why it's happening, how it's happening, and what it means. The Joshuan lives life with his eyes and ears open at all times, keenly alert and deliberately attentive to the way life transpires—constantly watching, constantly listening.

12. **The Joshuan values both *passion* and *logic*.** While some people prefer to live only from their minds and others prefer to live only from the hearts, the Joshuan prefers to balance both. The Joshuan does not write off emotions, passions, and sensitivities for the sake of cold logic, nor does he write off logic, knowledge, and rational understanding for the sake of unbridled emotion. As in all things, the Joshuan pursues balance. He draws from the heart *and* the mind, the better to render him a *complete* human being.

13. **The Joshuan paradoxically embodies both extreme *intensity* and extreme *insouciance*.** On the one hand, the Joshuan is intense about his faith and his daily Joshuan spirituality. He takes the Five Elements, Table attendance, and the pursuit of godliness extremely seriously. On the other hand, the Joshuan is casual, laid-back, and insouciant. He allows himself to be plagued by nothing (not even guilt, fear, worry, stress, anxiety, ambition, or regrets). The Joshuan is calm, cool, and collected. He paradoxically molds his intensity together with his insouciance to create a strange hybrid human being, one who is casually intense and passionately calm, nonchalantly driven and zealously relaxed.

14. **The Joshuan *embraces* science.** While Christianity wages a war against science, Joshuanism declares an eternal peace treaty. Not only that, Joshuanism maintains that no such war was ever necessary. Therefore, the Joshuan warmly embraces science, training himself to be encouraged by progressive scientific discoveries rather than discouraged by them. Because the Joshuan believes God engineered both the Earth and the Universe that contains it, nothing in the realm of science can ultimately disprove God's existence (if seen from the right perspective). Adjustments and modifications in knowledge and accepted worldviews might be required as science answers more questions, but the Joshuan is not deterred by this. The Joshuan holds faith in one hand and science in the other and willingly marches forward into a new age of spirituality and understanding.

I hope that you are beginning to get a sense of what the Joshuan is, what the Joshuan looks like, how the Joshuan behaves, and what matters to the Joshuan. I hope also that you are beginning to see just how the Joshuan differs from the Christian. The differences should be palpable. Does this mean the Joshuan is better than the Christian? Not at all. Does this mean the Joshuan *thinks* he is better than the Christian? Certainly not. Nevertheless, the Joshuan does endeavor to be *different* from the Christian if for no other reason than the simple fact that Christians are Christians, Joshuans are Joshuans, and they are not the same.

Who are the Christians? Go to a church this Sunday, and see for yourself. Who are the Joshuans? Only this: intensely authentic people. Honest people. Caring people. Easy-going people. Peaceful people. Forgiving people. Generous people. Unselfish people. Transformed people. Godly people. Tolerant people. Open-minded people. Meek people. Gentle people. Humble people. Encouraging people. Free people. Faithful people. Loving people. People who are spiritually alive. People who know God. People who are in tune with the needs of others. People who worship the Son of God, but are nothing redolent of that which is Christian.

These are the things the Joshuan is *not*: judgmental, confrontational, pretentious, insincere, dishonest, selfish, bitter, unforgiving, immoral, discriminatory, prideful, closed-minded, unfaithful, enslaved, spiritually dead, ignorant of God and his ways, and oblivious to the needs to others.

The Joshuan exists first and foremost for God. Next, the Joshuan exists for everyone else. His own cares, concerns, and needs come *third*. Always. There is no other way. *That* is who the Joshuan is.

The Daily Life of the Joshuan

What does a day in the life of a Joshuan look like? Like Christians, Joshuans can be found in every strata of society and in any geographical place. You do not have to be an American to be a Joshuan, and you do not have to be a success professionally. However, wherever the Joshuan is found, be it the streets of Philadelphia, the heart of the Himalayas, the mansions of Beverly Hills, or the slums of a ghetto, there are certain things that characterize the Joshuan in such a way as to engender a mild variety of uniformity among those who practice Joshuanism. Now, this is different from Diversified Uniformity, the idea that though we are different we are the same. Diversified Uniformity has to do with belief systems, theological inclinations, and the various expressions diverse Joshuans bring to the table. However, regarding the *daily life* of the Joshuan, there are things that transcend racial, regional, theological, and cultural barriers. In this sense, Joshuanism does possess a certain sense of uniformity in that the things Joshuans do each day, regardless of where they live or what differences they bring to the table, are essentially the same everywhere. This is simply because to do anything else would render the believer *something other than* a Joshuan. To be a Joshuan is to go about daily life in a unique, distinctive, *Joshuan* way.

Let's explore these definitively Joshuan daily endeavors (some of which we have discussed already and some of which are being presented here for the first time):

1. **The practice of the Five Elements.** Through daily practice of conversation, illumination, meditation, observation, and application, the Joshuan pursues the Unfolding. Life is such that fitting all five in everyday without fail can be a challenge; but the Joshuan makes the attempt. Without regularity and consistency in the execution of the Five Elements, the Joshuan cannot hope to achieve godliness or in any way reflect characteristics evocative of Joshua. Joshuans can live in London, Ecuador, or Denver, but wherever they are, they should make every effort to undertake the Five Elements on a daily basis.

2. **Table communication.** Humans lead busy lives, and Joshuans are no exception. However, one hopes that as godliness increases in the life of any believer, so, too, does the propensity to slow down and live in a more relaxed manner. At any rate, Joshuans must find time in their day to communicate or socialize with the other members of their Table. Why? Because the whole point of the Joshuan approach to community is to be involved in each other's lives. Whether it's in person, over the phone, through texting, or via the Internet, it does not matter; the Joshuan should be in daily contact with his fellows.

3. **Confession.** At least once in each day, the Joshuan should make an effort to commune with God in a confessional way (nighttime would make the most sense for this activity, after the day is done and when the Joshuan is in a position to reflect on the day's events, but anytime is fine provided that this happens once a day). What this basically means is that while the Joshuan does not concentrate too much on battling sin (since he understands pursuing godliness will do that for him), he also realizes that he is going to sin. Why? Just by virtue of being in the world, you are apt to get dirty. Making a daily effort to confess your sins before God will keep your conscience clear and your eyes open to those sins, sinful predispositions, and temptations that are unique to you.

4. **The Circadian Effort.** Circadian is just a fancy word for "daily." The Circadian Effort refers to the Joshuan's daily determination to "do something loving." Granted, the Joshuan should be in the habit of not just doing loving things but *being love* habitually. However, the pace of life isn't always conducive to that which is ideal. Further, being in the habit of expressing Joshuan love, even to strangers, might not come naturally to everyone at first. Therefore, the Circadian Effort is the Joshuan's resolve to do at least one loving deed in the course of a day. It can be anything from the writing of a check, to a simple word of

encouragement, to helping someone move, to just lending your ear. It does not matter what it is as long as you do one loving deed a day (preferably more as time goes on). Practice makes perfect, as the saying goes.

5. **Inventory.** Each night before going to sleep, the Joshuan should take an inventory of his day's achievements. Did he carry out the Five Elements? Did he communicate with his Table? Did he do at least one loving deed? Did he journal the day's progress? Also, there are two questions all Joshuans should ask themselves every night before going to sleep: "What did God teach me today?" and "How did I use that knowledge?" Answering those questions in journal form would provide the maximum benefit to the Joshuan, but this is not required. At any rate, by taking a daily inventory, the Joshuan learns to be accountable to God and to himself (one hopes he learns to be accountable to his fellows, as well).

The daily life of the Joshuan is therefore characterized by intentional, methodical, and ongoing behaviors that are distinctly *Joshuan* in nature. Without these daily habits and activities, the believer in question may be something not entirely Christian, but he is definitely not a Joshuan. To be a Joshuan is more than just believing this or believing that. To be a Joshuan is to practice specific *Joshuan* things as a result of that belief. The Joshuan is a very *spiritual* person for to undertake daily activities and cultivate daily habits that are explicitly designed for the attainment of godliness and intimacy with God is the very definition of *spirituality*.

Now, one more thing that bears mentioning has to do with the *will of God*. If you have spent much time in the Christian realm, then you have no doubt heard this term. Christians beset themselves with all kinds of anxiety over the will of God, constantly trying to discern and decipher what the will of God is. In this matter, the Joshuan again differs considerably from the Christian. While the Christian labors to determine the will of God, the Joshuan observes that the *New Testament* has already unequivocally stated what the will of God is. The Joshuan knows that the will of God is the same for you as it is for me, and that it's the same for everyone who would worship the Son of God. What is the will of God? The *New Testament* is quite clear:

1. Love God
2. Love humanity
3. Be generous
4. Be holy
5. Be humble

6. Be honest
7. Be forgiving
8. Pursue godliness
9. Resist temptation
10. Live honorably
11. Cultivate integrity
12. Deny yourself
13. Keep the faith
14. Do not lose hope
15. Guard your heart
16. Protect your body
17. Free your mind

Chase these behaviors in your life and you will be carrying out the will of God, regardless of whether you are a Christian or a Joshuan. If God has a *specific will* for your personal life (i.e., to move to Montana, go back to school, or whatever it might possibly be), he will be faithful to reveal it to you only when and if you are faithful to put all your effort into accomplishing the above-mentioned items. If God cannot trust you to carry out those aspects of his will that he has already made perfectly clear, he is probably not going to be forthcoming with his specific will for your life. Therefore, concentrate less on what may or may not be God's specific plan for your life, and concentrate more on those things he has already asked of you, trusting that as you do so, he will reveal his specific will in his way and in his time.

Becoming a Joshuan (Choosing Joshuanism)

Now, if you have followed me this far, perhaps you have seen for yourself the sense in some of the things I have been saying. Perhaps you see that Joshuanism is not the evil heresy many people are going to say it is. Perhaps you perceive within Joshuanism a new and exciting way to express your faith, an intriguing and appealing alternative to the Christian road you have been walking for so long. Perhaps you have no experience whatsoever with Christianity and have still been able to identify with what I have said in such a way as to evoke within you a desire to try Joshuanism. Or maybe you have been thinking these same things all along and are pleased that someone finally put a voice to them in an ordered, decisive way. Whatever the case, if you have come this far and want to keep going and if somehow I have managed to convince you of your particular need for that which Joshuanism offers, then you might be wondering exactly how to make this transition. Perhaps you are wondering how to become a Joshuan.

I shall tell you. If you are coming to Joshuanism from Christianity, then you need to do the following:

1. Switch from Christian terminology to Joshuan terminology (i.e., from Jesus to Joshua, from the Holy Spirit to the Soul of Godliness, etc.);
2. Ask yourself if you can accept the Eight Immovables of Joshuanism (refer to the section titled "Diversified Uniformity"), and if you can, accept them;
3. Announce to God your transfer from the realm of Christianity into the realm of Joshuanism;
4. Leave your Christian church, and seek out a Joshuan Table (information on how to do so can be found in the epilogue);
5. Begin moving away from the Christian *New Testament* and toward the Joshuan *New Testament* by downloading *The Joshuan Pages* from Joshuanism.com. (Individual books of the NT are available there as they are completed.),
6. Begin thinking of yourself as a Joshuan, begin calling yourself a Joshuan, and begin describing yourself as a Joshuan; and
7. Begin practicing the Five Elements, pursuing the Unfolding, observing the daily habits of a Joshuan, and pursuing godliness in a distinctly Joshuan manner

There is no special prayer or ceremony required; just an instantaneous decision. One moment you were a Christian, the next you are a Joshuan; but the same Son of God remains your Savior.

If you are coming to Joshuanism from somewhere outside of Christianity, then you need to do the following:

1. Read *The Joshuan Pages*. Some books are currently available on Joshuanism.com. Others are still awaiting completion. Begin immersing yourself in the *New Testament*;
2. Ask yourself whether or not you understand what becoming a Joshuan means;
3. Ask yourself if you can accept the Eight Immovables of Joshuanism (refer to the section titled "Diversified Uniformity"); if you feel you can accept them, do so;

4. Tell God you believe in him and his Son, and ask God to grant you Absolute Deliverance through his Son;
5. Believe that you have thus received this Absolute Deliverance;
6. Seek out a Joshuan Table (information on how to do so can be found in the epilogue);
7. Begin thinking of yourself as a Joshuan, begin calling yourself a Joshuan, and begin describing yourself as a Joshuan; and
8. Begin practicing the Five Elements, experiencing the Unfolding, observing the daily habits of a Joshuan, and pursuing godliness in a distinctly Joshuan manner

And that's it. Welcome to Joshuanism. My sincerest hope is that you find love here.

We are almost finished with our discussion. Only one thing remains. I have taken an entire book to describe a movement that technically does not exist—at least not yet. As my work continues, yours begins. Joshuanism will exist in the world only inasmuch as *you* make it happen. Therefore, in the epilogue you will find instructions on how to join with others in igniting what I hope history will one day remember as the Joshuan Revolution.

Michael Vito Tosto

EPILOGUE: The Joshuan Revolution

Well, my friends, we have been on quite a journey together. We started out in the realm of Christianity and finished in the realm of Joshuanism, asking questions along the way, answering them, and forging new ideas as we plowed forward. I hope that reading this book has been an adventure for you. Writing it has certainly been an adventure for me. To be quite honest, when I sat down to pen this work, I wasn't exactly sure which direction to take. I knew what I wanted to say but not necessarily how to say it. I have had Joshuanism in my head for years, though I spoke of it to no one in all that time. When I finally decided to flesh it all out on paper, I was armed only with the desire to make a statement. What that statement would look like was still shrouded in uncertainty at the onset of this project. Once I started working, however, I found that the statement was taking shape all on its own. At times, it felt like all of this was just hovering in the air above me, already formed and ordered, just waiting for me to pull it down and transfer it to paper. In many ways, it feels like I have been on a journey of my own, not so much taking Joshuanism anywhere but rather allowing it to take me. Each new leg of the journey seemed to unfold with or without my help, as though I was just along for the ride. In some cases, I was just as astonished as you probably were at some of the things I was saying. Yet, as I typed, it all just made so much sense. The more I wrote, the more I wanted to write. Before long, I had a book on my hands.

Even now, I have no idea how it will fare. Will it sell? Will it be loved? Will it be rounded up and burned Nazi-style? I am sure some people will hate every word. Other people will welcome it with open arms. I guess like anything in life, it's all a matter of perspective, opinion, and whose hearts and minds are open. One thing that has given me strength in the writing of this book is that I know I am not responsible for the pre-existing condition of my readers' hearts and minds. Whatever my readers bring to this book will have a direct effect on what they take from it. That is their business. The human being who has closed his mind to the possibility of change and hardened his heart to new ideas was never high on the list of people I hoped to speak to, anyway. The unfortunate thing about a closed mind and a hardened heart is that they usually stay that way. I have written instead for those people whose hearts and minds long for something different, something new, something evocative, something removed from the status quo. I have written for those people who have exhausted all the answers currently available and have found that too many troubling questions still linger. I have written for those who have tried to stay within the set course of Christianity and found that they just could not do it, not because of some defect within them but because of a defect within Christianity itself.

I certainly have not written this book as an attempt to get rich. For one thing, I am not entirely sure I would even want to be rich. For another thing, I find it highly unlikely that this book will be *that* popular. I wrote this book with a heart to see certain things changed in the world. However, as a student of history, I know that change rarely has a green light. The world may change on the surface, but underneath it is still mostly the same old terrible place it has always been. Still, those of us who have a heart to change things should make every effort to do so even if the situation looks bleak. Then, perhaps, we can go to our graves knowing we tried. Am I saying I think Joshuanism has no power? Absolutely not. Am I saying I think this book will fall short and change nothing? No. I think this book will change the world for some people. Better put, it will change *their* world. Will it radically alter the lay of the land in every corner of the Earth? Probably not. It took Christianity 2,000 years to become the world's largest religion. Nevertheless, it began as a handful of bumbling fishermen and their wives. Joshuanism (which is not intended to be a religion) may indeed take root and drastically change the spiritual consciousness of this world, but will it happen in my lifetime? I am certainly not holding my breath.

Don't get me wrong. I sincerely believe that God's hand was present during the writing of this book. Moreover, I sincerely hope that the message of Joshuanism will spread in a positive way. I believe that Joshuanism has the ability to do that. I believe that Joshuanism can aid just as many people in the pursuit of God as Christianity can. In fact, I believe Joshuanism will succeed in the coming ages where Christianity might not. This is not to say that I think Joshuanism is better than Christianity. Nevertheless, I do think Christianity is a sinking ship. Joshuanism, on the other hand, has been specifically designed to be relevant to the changing world and the long road ahead. Humanity is facing a tough journey. No one knows exactly what kind of world will be carved out when the dust of this profound age of change settles, if it ever does. But whatever the world ends up being, Joshuanism has been designed to survive the dust storm and evolve alongside everything else. I do believe Joshuanism will accomplish the goal for which it was created. It's just that I do not expect this to happen overnight.

I have not had many conversations about Joshuanism yet. In fact, I have gone to great lengths *not* to discuss it unless I absolutely had to. When I do have conversations about it, I, observant fellow that I am, take care to notice patterns in the way people respond. One particular pattern, or theme, if you will, that I have noticed in the way people respond to Joshuanism is that they weigh its value against who I am. In other words, they seem to care more about the messenger than the message. They look at me and see a man who, in most ways, looks like they do. They see a man who, on the surface, should have absolutely no qualifications to propose any spiritual alternatives. Yes, I went to college, but my degree was in history, not religion or theology. Therefore, they look at me and see someone who probably should not be questioning the status quo. They seem to think it's pretentious. And you know what? I completely agree! That is why I want to make this abundantly clear, right here, right now, so that no one can possibly mistake my intentions: I do not seek glory for myself. I would prefer that people focus on Joshuanism and forget about me. I would prefer that they would allow the message of Joshuanism to do that which it was intended to do and allow me to just fade back into the shadows. Sure, I intend to keep writing books on this subject if I can. However, I am not a leader of movements. I am not a figurehead. I am not someone who wants attention. The fact of the matter is that I want as little attention as possible. I am an introvert. I was not always that way, but I am now. At any rate, I know I will have to speak publicly and give lectures if this book is to have any chance of catching on. I will do that, but my sincerest hope is that the world will see my message (and through that message, God) and fail to see me. In fact, let me just request this right now: do not look at me. Do not worry about me. Do not pay the human being named Michael Vito Tosto any mind. Forget about me. I am just a guy. I snore and burp and fret about paying bills just as much as you do. I have been arrested. I have been intoxicated. I have been high. I have cheated on tests and ran red lights. I do all the same things you do. I have skeletons in the closet just like everybody else. I feel terrible about the bad things I've done. I really do. But we all do bad things. I am nobody special. Joshuanism, however, *is* special because it's an exciting new road to God. I did not create Joshuanism to advance myself. Nor do I intend on being the one who spreads this movement. That is your job.

Let's talk about movements for a moment. Consider this question: did Joshua actually start Christianity? Was Joshua out and about in the streets of Jerusalem pushing a new movement? He was certainly out and about in the streets, but whether or not he was starting a movement is debatable. Personally, I would say no, Joshua was not starting a movement. It seems to me that Joshua was giving people the right tools, endowing them with the proper knowledge, and drawing for them a correct map of the road ahead, but nothing he did in any of the four Gospels seems to indicate Joshua cared about starting a *movement*. That agenda seems to be absent from his activities in the *New Testament*. In fact, Joshua seems to go out of his way to *not* be seen as the leader of a movement. In most cases, after healing someone or performing some kind of miracle, Joshua instructed those present not to say anything. "Don't talk about this," he told them. Of course, they did. They talked about it, and when the crowds got wind of what Joshua was able to do, they swarmed around him, rallying behind his cause, urging him to…what? Start a movement. What did Joshua do in each case? You can read about it for yourself in any of the four Gospels. He wiggled away from their grasp, withdrew from their midst, and sought solitude on some mountainside. No, my friends, the movement that began in the first century (which later became what we now know as Christianity) was not started by Joshua. He gave humanity the tools, and then he ascended into heaven, leaving his followers to decide for themselves what they would do with the tools he gave them. Would *they* start a movement in his absence? That was the decision they faced, and they chose to do just that. The Christian movement was not started by Joshua. It was his followers he left behind who did this.

Granted, I am not Joshua. I am not the Son of God. I am just a guy, as I said before. But the situation is the same. I am a messenger and I have spoken my message. Now I ask you, "What is your response?"

You see, I view my job primarily as an architect. However, without the construction worker, what would the architect have? He can spend his entire life designing the world's greatest buildings, but if no one ever builds them, what difference does it make? Designing a wall and knowing how to *build* that wall are two different things. Consider the making of a movie. Writing a script is one thing. Shooting a film is another. What does it matter if I pen an amazing screenplay, teeming with Oscar-winning dialogue and innovative plot devices if I cannot direct? If I do not have cameras, sets, actors, and a budget to create a movie, all I have is a useless assemblage of words on paper. That is why the erection of a building or the making of a movie requires a team. It takes more than one person to make a mark on the world. It takes a collection of different people, each with his or her skill set, working together toward a common goal.

That is what it will take to make Joshuanism a force in the world. Christianity started as a very small movement. The men and women who believed in it bore it on their backs as they went out into the world. They carried it on their tongues and demonstrated it with their hands. In time, the movement grew. That is how movements work. They *spread*. Like wildfire, in some cases. In other cases, they spread like the motion of the moon in the sky, barely perceptible. Whether or not Joshuanism spreads and the rate at which it spreads depends entirely on you. I have given you the blueprints. I have given you the script. The question is, will you take the tools in hand and build this thing? Will you shoot the film so the world will be able to see it?

Consider what Joshuanism could mean to the world. Think about the scope of spiritual health that could characterize communities where Joshuanism thrives. After all, what does Joshuanism advocate? Love. Altruism. The peaceful removal of discord and conflict. Acceptance. The pursuit of authentic godliness. Progressive attitudes. Mental wellbeing. Emotional health. Genuine community. Dynamic fellowship. Scientific evolution. Fresh perceptions. Tangible help for the poor. Think about the potential these things have. If you became an agent of these ideals in the world, you would cease to be part of the problem and would instead be part of the solution. You could go to sleep at night knowing that in your tiny little part of the Universe you've done all you can do to carry out the two greatest commandments. You could rest your head knowing that you lent your life toward a worthy purpose. Few people succeed in actually changing the world, but those who at least try can face death with a smile. Joshuanism offers you the chance to try. Joshuanism offers you the opportunity to be an agent of tangible love and palpable peace in the world. Joshuanism draws you down a road that cannot possibly fail to lead you to God (provided you practice Joshuanism the way it was designed to be practiced). Further, those who truly find God always end up having a positive effect on the world around them. Why? Because if God is love, as the *New Testament* claims he is, then to find God is to find love—and love is the most outwardly expressive force in the Universe. Even gravity bows down before it. Find God, and you will find love. Find love, and you will become an instrument of positive change whether you try to or not. That is what Joshuanism offers you. That is what the Son of God offers you.

That is the choice you have here, really. Your choice is not necessarily Joshuanism or Christianity; your choice is whether or not to be about the things the Son of God was about. The choice you face is this: Do I want to keep my riches or give them away? Do I want to save my life, or do I want to lose it? Do I want to deny myself, or do I want to glorify myself? Do I want to walk the hard road or the easy road? Do I want to be a part of the problem or a part of the solution? Do I want to be an agent of love or of hate? Do I want to walk in the light or in the darkness? Do I want to pursue worldliness, or do I want to pursue godliness? Is my treasure on Earth, or is it in heaven? Will I be an instrument of good or evil, peace or discord? Remember what Joshua said about the path that leads to death and the path that leads to life? He said wide is the path that leads to death, and many travel it, but narrow is the path that leads to life, and only a few find it. So, which is it going to be? Are you going to be among the many or the few?

When I consider that Joshuanism *is* about the same things the Son of God was about, it becomes difficult for me to understand the opposition I have already faced. Yet, perhaps it shouldn't be that hard to understand after all. Humanity has been opposing the Son of God for centuries. And upon further reflection, I suppose it makes sense that Joshuanism would be a hard pill for some to swallow. Many people are married to the name "Jesus," and I know that the thought of switching over to the name "Joshua" is difficult for some to accept. I understand. It *is* difficult to accept. At first. In time, however, those who try it might find the benefits so outweigh the difficulties that the switch is more than worth it. But to call Joshuanism *evil*...this I do not understand. How can anything that truly endeavors to seek God and genuinely attempts to spread peace in the world be seen as evil? I have said it at least a hundred times in this book: Joshuanism is about love. How can love be evil? How can anything loving be equated with that which is evil? How can that which is evil have any place alongside that which is loving? If God is love, then love is God. Is God evil? Of course not. Therefore, if God is not evil, love cannot possibly be evil, either. Love, my friends, is the foundation everything else in Joshuanism stands on. Opposing Joshuanism is the same as opposing love, and opposing love is the same as opposing God.

I learned a long time ago that opposing God accomplishes very little. It's like a road trip. You have a destination, but if you park your car on the side of the road and refuse to drive, who are you really hurting but yourself? Your refusal to drive does not affect the destination. The destination is the same whether you reach it or not. Other cars that pass you are not deterred by your refusal. The drivers of those cars are going to reach the same destination with or without your help. The only thing you have succeeded in halting is your own progress. Walking with God is the same way. Oppose God, and all you really end up doing is sitting sullenly on the side of the road while life continues to march forward all around you. You are certainly not holding God back by opposing him. If God is behind Joshuanism (and I believe that he is), then you're not going to hold it back by opposing it, either, no more than the enemies of Christianity have succeeded in impeding it in the last 2,000 years.

If you decide Joshuanism is not the road for you, so be it. Go your way, my friend, and go in peace. You have made no enemies here. Do what you will, think what you will, and go where you will; I wish you Godspeed. Whether or not you love the Joshuan will not change the fact that the Joshuan is going to love you, no matter what you choose. If that makes you angry, there is nothing anyone here can say about it. It's an interesting world indeed when someone will hate you just for loving them, but it happens. I have seen it. Could anything be sadder than that?

If, however, you have decided that Joshuanism *is* the road for you, welcome aboard. From this point on, consider yourself a Joshuan. Consider yourself part of the cure, not the disease. Consider yourself part of a fledgling new community of believers struggling to establish their presence in the world. Count yourself among a group of allies whose sigil is not a cross but rather open arms; whose banner is not power but rather love; whose objective is not linguistic superiority or religious authority but rather humility and godliness; whose God is not angry and vengeful but rather patient and kind. Consider yourself among Joshuanism's founding fathers and mothers, the forerunners of all that could transpire if you make it transpire. Consider the destiny of Joshuanism to be in your hands. Consider yourself charged with the purpose of starting a movement. Count yourself among those whom history will look back on and identify as the earliest advocates of the Joshuan Revolution. Who knows, you could end up being to Joshuanism what the apostle Paul was to Christianity.

What do I mean by the Joshuan Revolution? Come on, you know. You know what a revolution is. You know what is being implied here. You know what is required. You know the road ahead. You've known it all along. The question is, can you walk this road? And if you can, will you?

That said, I suppose a brief exploration into the idea of a revolution is in order. What is the root of the word *revolution?* It's *revolve.* What does revolve mean? It means to turn, to circle around, to change position, to rotate. Perhaps that is all Joshuanism is. Perhaps if you took Christianity and rotated it this way or that, the end result would be Joshuanism. The Joshuan Revolution would therefore be nothing more than a simple shift in perception. Isn't that what I have been saying all along?

If you took the "r" away from the world *revolve*, you would be left with the word *evolve.* If you took the "r" away from the word *revolution*, you would be left with the word *evolution*. When you think about it, when has there ever been a significant revolution that did not also require significant evolution in the minds and lives of those involved? A revolution is considered a revolution precisely because it ushers in fierce, drastic change. A revolution always comes against the status quo. More often than not, history has shown that when revolution came, it either came at just the right time or was woefully overdue. Revolutions rarely come when no one is ready for them because human nature prevents people from rallying around causes they do not really believe in or see a desperate need for. Humans, in other words, are lazy, but they can be spurred into action. Oppress a people long enough, and you will drive them to kill you. Hold back needed change long enough, and eventually that change will storm upon you like a tidal wave, washing you away. King Louis XVI of France found that out the hard way.

Let's consider what is needed to pull off a successful revolution. First, you need a cause. We have a cause: Joshuanism. Second, you need numbers. A few rebels aren't going to overthrow anything. This means you need allies, and lots of them. Do we have numbers? Not yet. This book will go a long way toward creating some, and so can you. When you have a cause you believe in, what do you do? You spread it. You preach it. You stand in the streets and declare it; then you wait and see who shows up to join your cause. In that respect, we have some work ahead of us. Third, you need some weapons because once you have the numbers you have to arm them. We have weapons. Not guns or swords or tanks or bombs, no. Our weapons are our words. Our implements are our deeds. As the pen is mightier than the sword, so, too, is an action mightier than an intention. We fight this revolution with actions. We wield words. We show the world our love and explain to them our faith. Little by little, as more humans become Joshuans, we will gain ground. It will not be easy. Change never is.

If you have traveled with me this long and have even gone so far as to assume the identity of Joshuan for yourself, then I ask you this: is Joshuanism worth fighting for?

Is love?

Any movement that advocates love is a movement worth fighting for.

As far as I can tell, the best place to start a movement is right where you are, and the best time to start a revolution is *now*. Once you know a revolution is necessary, the moment is already at hand. If you have read this book with a heart to make all these concepts a reality in your world, then I am relying on you. Your number has been called, my friend. Step up!

The first thing you need to do is join a Joshuan Table. The only problem is that there will not be any Joshuan Tables unless you create them. So, create them! Wherever you live, be it downtown Manhattan or on a farm in the middle of Kansas, your job is to seek out and find other Joshuans. There will not be many, at least not at first. As I said, we do not have the numbers. Yet. More than likely, the few Joshuans you find out there will be people who, like you, read this book and got on board. Join with me in spreading the word. Help me expose Joshuanism to the world. As you do so, assign yourselves into groups that meet in someone's home. Decide who will be the Helm. Begin meeting. Begin experiencing the Unfolding together. Begin helping one another, bearing each other's burdens. Get involved in each other's lives. Break bread together. Form lasting bonds of love and friendship with these people. *Be* the Extraction. When you do all of these things, you have created a Table. If you live in Paducah, Kentucky, you have thus brought Joshuanism to Paducah. You should not worry about whether there are any Joshuan Tables in Seattle, Tucson, or Boston. It's up to those cities to create their own Tables. All you can do is create and sustain your own right there in Paducah, assigning Helms and Pilots where necessary, spreading the word, and carrying out the Five Elements in your own life.

In so doing, you can start the movement in your own city. While you are starting the movement in your own city, perhaps other Joshuans will be starting similar movements in their cities. In time, some cities will grow to have more than one Table. The larger cities may even have several. Whether there are twenty Tables in a city or only one, a Table should have no more than twelve members (including the Helm). As soon as your numbers swell beyond twelve, form a new Table. Stay connected, of course, to your neighboring Table. Maintain a solid network of communication. You may even want to erect some sort of forum, like a website or newsletter in your city, for the purpose of passing on information and providing contact names and numbers for those new Joshuans who might be seeking a Table to join.

It will take time. Years, in fact. The going will be slow. That's okay. Joshuanism does not have to grow with fanfare. A quiet, slow progression is just as effective as a loud, rapid progression. Maybe even more so. One must assume that which is built quickly is built unsoundly. A sturdy structure ought to take time to rise; it bodes well for its future survival. Remember, the Unfolding of godliness in the life of the believer is a slow drip, like a trickle of water. There is no reason why a godly movement

Joshuanism

should not be the same. God never hurries. He always takes his time. If Joshuanism is to reflect God, it, too, should never hurry; it, too, should take its time. A redwood is not born an imposing, giant tree. It's born a twiggy little spurt out of the soil. A redwood becomes imposing only after years and years of subtle growth and the slow, strengthening passage of time, with durable roots firmly sunk deep into the ground. My vision for Joshuanism is for it to someday be like a spiritual redwood among humanity. This book is merely the sowing of seeds. I have planted them. You will water them. God will give them growth. In time. In season. We must trust God to do his part while at the same time being faithful to do our own part. I will be faithful to keep up my end of the work (writing about these matters—my next assignment is to work on *The Joshuan Pages*) as you keep up your end of the work (creating Tables in your community).

Because we humans love to see our tasks in list form (so that we may cross off each item as we complete it), I shall lay out your road ahead in this fashion:

1. *Decide whether Joshuanism is for you.* Re-read this book if necessary. Think about these matters. Discuss them with your fellows. There is no need to make a hasty decision. Search your heart. Talk to God. Discover what is right for you. If you come to the conclusion that the Joshuan road is the road you wish to walk, by all means, begin walking.

2. *Locate other Joshuans.* Again, there will not be many at first. But even two Joshuans make a Table. Scout your city or town. Send word that you are a Joshuan seeking other Joshuans. Make your presence known. Find others who are just as eager as you to get this started. Band together. Keep spreading the word.

3. *Organize yourselves.* Separate into Tables of twelve (assuming you can find that many in your city). Establish which homes to meet in and when. Agree on a schedule that works for your group. Decide on a theme to study or a topic to discuss. Identify the needs of your community, and begin looking for ways to meet those needs.

4. *Choose your leaders.* Whoever ends up becoming the Helm of your Table is entirely up to you, but one thing is absolutely necessary: the Helm must be unanimously agreed upon. The Helm does not have to be the owner of the house where you meet. It might be better if this was the case, but it's not necessary. When the time is right, select Pilots.

5. *Grow together.* Share your experiences when you gather together. Confess your sins. Encourage one another. Discuss the many mysterious

ways the Unfolding transpires in your lives. Pray for each other. Hang out together. The people in your Table should be among your closest of friends, like a second family.

6. *Gather corporately throughout the year.* Refer to the section titled "Joshuan Forums" for a thorough list of ideas on how to initiate larger Joshuan gatherings in your city. The events will no doubt attract considerable attention for the movement, which will serve to advance it.

7. *Spread the word.* Never force Joshuanism on anyone. Never give people an ultimatum. Never threaten them with hell or any kind of punishment if they fail to see what you see, but do spread the word. Gently. Lovingly. Passionately. Lend people your copy of this book, or purchase one for them. Start a discussion group to learn the thoughts of others, how they responded to this material. Pass the message along.

Meanwhile, I will travel where and when I can, speaking about Joshuanism and bringing the message to anyone who will listen, and I will keep writing books until there is absolutely no more to be said. So, there you have it. You have your work, and I have mine. It's nice to have a purpose, don't you agree?

Now, a few more things bear mentioning…

If you are coming to Joshuanism from Christianity, I can only assume what the transition must be like for you. I suspect it will not be an easy one. I also know that *if* you are coming to Joshuanism, it also means you are *leaving* Christianity. Further, you would not be doing that unless you were convinced of the need to do so. In view of that, I was going to say this: "Check your Christian expectations, inclinations, and sensibilities at the door." However, that would be wrong. Why? Because if Joshuanism can draw from other religions, such as Buddhism, surely it can draw from contemporary Christianity as well. Indeed, it would be antithetical to the inclusive personality I hope Joshuanism portrays if I were to ask that. In fact, if I had asked it, I would have been as guilty as my friend Joe was when he told me that we should "keep our separations." Therefore, I would not ask you to lay down your Christian baggage before entering Joshuanism. That said, I would be remiss not to point out that by bringing into Joshuanism those Christian qualities that caused you to seek a new direction in the first place, you are thus bringing with you that which you wanted to get away from. Not only is this so, but you are therefore also infecting that which you are entering. So, what you should leave, and what should you bring? The answer is the same here as it is with any other religion, philosophy, or ideology (according to Mosaic Theology): if it's counterproductive to love, damaging to faith, or indicative of immorality, leave it. To that I would also add this: if it provokes judgment, hypocrisy, exclusion, division, hatred, or in any other way retards the progress of Joshuanism, leave it. Agreed?

I do not say these things to offend Christianity. Christianity is still a healthy place for those who have made it work for them. And yes, there are Christians out there for whom Christianity works and works well. Nevertheless, it would be a lie to say that there are not also those Christians out there who just cannot make it work because, for them, the lines no longer match up. Maybe some of the lines in Joshuanism do not match up either. After all, that which is designed by humans is sure to be flawed. Perhaps, though, Joshuanism is just different enough to offer those disillusioned people something new and effective. Maybe, for them, Joshuanism will work where Christianity has failed.

If you are coming to Joshuanism with no prior exposure to anything religious, spiritual, or philosophical, then you are in a rare and agreeable position indeed. You have a fresh canvas on which to paint, with nothing to stay your hand or encumber your strokes. You will undoubtedly come with baggage because to be a human is to get hurt. To have flesh is to be scarred. However, sometimes I suspect that religious baggage is worse than any other kind. Somehow, it affects the psyche in ways that transcend mere mental, emotional, or even physical pain. Somehow, the religious guilt is the worst of all. I guess the added ingredients of God and the afterlife have something to do with it. If you come to Joshuanism with no prior religious experience, you come with an advantage. You can look at the blank sheet of paper and compose anything you want. Would that we were all so lucky.

Nevertheless, whether you come to Joshuanism from Christianity, Buddhism, Islam, Judaism, atheism, or whatever else you could possibly fill the blank with; one thing you must come with is sincerity. If you are not one hundred percent certain you want to come, wait until you are. Come with your whole heart, with your arms wide open, with your mind ready to grapple with new expressions and startling ideas. Come seeking the truth. Come seeking love. Come seeking life. Come seeking God. Bring with you all the unique traits that make you the diverse piece of the puzzle you are. Bring with you all those wonderful things that make you *human*. We need them. I need them. I cannot do this on my own. Truth be told, neither can you. We need one another. We need each other's strengths. We even need each other's weaknesses. After all, the more colors there are, the more magnificent the tapestry is.

Closing Remarks

I once heard a story about a man who fought a giant. There was no way the man should have won. The giant dwarfed him by almost half, and the man was hardly armed for battle. The only weapon he had was a single rock. The giant had a large, menacing sword. Yet, the man felled the giant with his rock. Why? Because his aim was true, his hand was steady, his courage was fierce, and his faith was strong. God was with him and no doubt guided the rock. Maybe God even blew on the rock a little. The giant fell dead, his size worthless in the end. No one thought the giant would lose. Everyone thought the giant would win. Maybe even some small part inside the man's own mind doubted the outcome. Maybe part of the man expected the giant to win as well (after all, true faith is never without true doubt—remember that), but he flung his rock all the same and down went the giant.

I feel a bit like that man, going up against a giant. Who is the giant? It's not Christianity. No, the giant in this case is merely the status quo, the accepted conventions of our time, the same old same old, Christian or otherwise. The giant is that ironic tendency human beings have that leads them to resist change, even violently if they have to. Why is that ironic? Well, nothing good ever happened to humanity that did not come with change. Yet, we fight change every chance we get. I am just as guilty as everyone else is; I have witnessed myself fighting change in my own life when it threatened my comfort or my sense of security. We all do it. Even the most liberal and progressive among us do it. For all of its innovations and radical evolution, the human race is still basically a very conservative bunch.

Like the man in the story (David was his name), I am not armed with much. When it comes time to sling my rock, such as it is, I wonder about my aim. I wonder about my courage. Will my hands shake? Will my faith fail me? Will I slay the giant as the other guy did?

I guess what I am really asking is this: Will Joshuanism advance? I hope so. Otherwise, I have spent the last three months writing a book for naught. Worse than that is the prospect of all the many people out there wishing and hoping for a path beyond the status quo who will never have the chance to try Joshuanism if it is never brought to them. We are the only ones who can bring it to them.

Can we change the world? Time will tell. *Tempus est in nostra parte.*

APPENDIX

LIST OF TERMS

(in alphabetical order)

[Absolute Deliverance] – The Joshuan expression for salvation, implying that to "be saved" is to experience not just forgiveness of sin and eternal life but also absolute, indubitable, immutable, interminable *deliverance* through faith from every possible aspect of *spiritual* oppression, captivity, defect, unrest, desolation, meaninglessness, and human dysfunction.

[Application] – 1) the last of the Five Elements; 2) the Joshuan expression for putting into practice everything assembled through the observance of the previous four Elements; and 3) being *intentional* about godliness inasmuch as you can.

[The Circadian Effort] – Circadian is just a fancy word for "daily." The Circadian Effort refers to the Joshuan's resolve to do at least one loving deed in the course of a day. It can be anything from the writing of a check to a simple word of encouragement to helping someone move to just lending your ear. It does not matter what it is so long as you do one loving deed a day (preferably more as time goes on).

[Conversation] – 1) the first of the Five Elements; 2) the Joshuan expression for ongoing, constant *communion* with God; 3) the art of sharing every detail of life with God, and 4) the art of *hearing* from God.

[The Dismantling] – the result of Joshua's work on Earth; that by his life, death, and resurrection, the Great Barrier was dismantled, allowing for peace and reconciliation to occur between God and humanity; and granting salvation to the human who receives it by faith.

[Diversified Uniformity] – 1) a term expressing the paradoxical idea that Joshuans are different and yet they are the same; and 2) a proviso within Joshuanism stating that aside from the Eight Immovables, the Joshuan can hold any theological or zoêological view and still be considered a Joshuan.

[The Eight Immovables] – 1) those fixed, essential elements of belief in Joshuanism; and 2) eight nonnegotiable stipulations that must be accepted in order to render one an authentic Joshuan (as opposed to a Christian, or something else altogether).

[The Extraction] – the collective group of believing Joshuans (or, all believers, Joshuan or otherwise) who have been extracted (called out, set apart) *from* the world, declared holy, and *sent back in* to the world to bring the message of Joshua *to* the world.

[The Five Elements] – 1) the private, personal aspect of Joshuanism; 2) a manifold selection of disciplines that the Joshuan practices in order to do their part in carrying out the Unfolding in their life.

[The Fusion] – the Joshuan expression for the marriage between faith and science; 2) the end result of this marriage; 3) the Joshuan belief that faith and science are telling the same story of the same God; and 4) Joshuanism's contention that the so-called "conflict" between faith and science is over and never need have existed in the first place.

[Godliness] – the achieved objective of becoming *like* God through: 1) the putting off of the *old* self; 2) being *transformed* through the *renewal of the mind*; and 3) putting on the *new* self, which conforms to God rather than to the ways of the world.

[The Great Barrier] – the idea that humanity's imperfection and sinfulness created a barrier between them and the only perfect, sinless God, thus cutting humans off from God and the life they so desperately crave.

[Helm] – one who leads a Table. He or she sits at the head, or helm, of the Table. In other words, the Table most likely meets in the Helm's house or apartment. The Helm's job is to steer the spiritual progression of a Table in the right direction. The Helm may give words of teaching, or merely facilitate discussions and prayer. A Helm should be a person of recognizable spiritual depth whose character and integrity engender them to a position of leadership.

[Illumination] – 1) the second of the Five Elements; 2) the Joshuan expression for ongoing, and consistent educative *study*; and 3) the act of methodically shedding light within through the disciplined attainment of *knowledge*.

[The Invited] – those to whom God's invitation for life and Absolute Deliverance has been given (everyone).

[Joshuan] – 1) a human who, by faith, has met God, now lives *in God*, and now has God living *in him or her*; 2) someone who has left their old life and old self, has been transformed, is *being* transformed, and is putting on a new self; 3) a person who resembles a Christian in many ways, but in other ways is a completely new conception; 4) a person who believes it is *through* the Son of God (*Joshua* to Joshuans; *Jesus* to Christians) that one is connected to the Son's Father; that is, God; 5) a person who is free (internally), alive (eternally), forgiven (completely), and absolutely delivered in a way that only those who have faith in the Son of God can be; 6) a person who behaves and operates based on what Joshua did and how he did it; and 7) someone who expresses all of these wonderful things through a life *reflective* of the one responsible for all of it: Joshua.

[*The Joshuan Pages*] – a Joshuan version of the *New Testament* in which certain Christian expressions are replaced with Joshuan ones, such as the name "Jesus" is being substituted with "Joshua," the title "Christ" is substituted with "Deliverer," among others.

[Joshuan Thought] – an attitude that presupposes we don't have all the information, a mindset that automatically assumes that as humans evolve so, too, does God's revelation of himself, i.e. that the more we know about God, the more God wants us to know. The more we *do* know, the more we *can* know, or, are then *able* to know.

[The Joshuan Way] – 1) the defining characteristic of what it means to be a Joshuan; 2) the reason a Joshuan *is* a Joshuan; and 3) the determination of the Joshuan to carry out, above all else, the two greatest commandments: to love God and to love humanity.

[Joshuanism] – 1) a *path beyond* Christianity, existing specifically for those people who want to go on living for God through faith in his Son, but who no longer find Christianity a satisfactory way of doing that; 2) a *way of life* that reflects a commitment to believe in Joshua, love Joshua, and live *like* Joshua; 3) the summation of Joshuan Thought, Joshuan theology, Joshuan practice, and Joshuan expression; and 4) a spirituality based on Joshua.

[The Liar] – Joshuanism's terminology for Satan, the Evil One, the Enemy, or whatever else believers may call this entity. The name "Liar" was chosen because Joshuanism maintains that whatever else this enemy of God does in the life of the believer, be it temptation or accusation, his first and most powerful weapon is *the lie*. After all, temptations and accusations are themselves just strategic lies. Moreover, Joshua himself calls Satan the "Father of Lies" (see *John* 8:44).

[Meditation] – 1) the third of the Five Elements; 2) a discipline practiced by the Joshuan which employs *silence, solitude,* and *stillness*; 3) the *quieting* of one's heart and mind in the presence of God (silent conversation); 4) the contemplation of spiritual matters and the reflection of scripture; and 5) the act of *observing the thinker* and entering into the Now.

[Mosaic Theology] – a belief that though Joshua offers the only way to *salvation*, other cultures, philosophies and religions have some interesting *insights* into God and life which should not be rejected at face value.

[Observation] – 1) the fourth of the Five Elements; 2) the Joshuan expression for developing an attentive, observant nature; 3) remaining watchful of how God works; and 4) documenting the Unfolding.

[Perception Separation] – an awareness that 1) God exists above and beyond our perceptions of him, or *separate* from our experiences with him; and 2) God is not limited to acting and performing in a manner that always concurs with what *we* perceive or know about him, or what *we* expect from him. God cannot violate himself, no; but he *can* violate what we know about him, because it's possible for what we know to be incorrect or faulty.

[Perpetually Incomplete Revelation] – the idea that since God is infinite, he can never be finitely known. In other words, God's revelation of himself to us could never be *complete*. Even if we accept that God has chosen to say no more, that is, to reveal nothing further of himself to humanity (Joshuanism *not* accept this), the window of sight we have regarding God is woefully incomplete. Joshuanism, however, maintains that God *does* want humans to see more of him, to know more of him, and to receive furthered revelations of him as they evolve in their capacities to do so—but even then, there will always be still more to learn, more to grasp, more to discover…perpetually unto infinity.

[Pilot] – one who leads the Helms of any given city. For instance, suppose there are three Joshuan Tables that meet in the city of Scranton. That means there are three Helms in that city. From among those three, one should be elected as the Pilot of the other two Helms. The Pilot's job is to pray with the other Helms and be a kind of spiritual mentor. The Pilot of any given city (themselves the Helm of a Table) meets with the Helms one on one, encouraging them, addressing any needs, and providing guidance. There can be more than one Pilot to a city, depending on how many Tables meet in a given city. Each Pilot should mentor no more than three Helms.

[*post/Christian*] – 1) a term meaning that which was/is Christian, but existing in a *furthered* state, or an *altered* state; 2) the manifestation of Christianity after having undergone a transformation; 3) the embodiment of a hybrid Christianity, which retains the main beliefs of Christianity, but which also proposes new *expressions* of those beliefs, suggests *new* beliefs, and asks new questions; 4) the *product* of a state of change within Christianity, or a term describing the process of that which is still in an *unfinished* state of change; and 5) a term referring to a new *time period*, similar to the word "postmodern," meaning that a new age is upon humanity, the *post/Christian* age, an age when believers are no longer a part of Christianity, but of *post/Christian*ity, or an age when believers are no longer that which was/is Christian, but are now characterized by that which would be considered *post/Christian*.

[*post/Christian* God] – 1) a term referring to a deliberate effort by believers to begin thinking of God in new or different ways; 2) the idea that it might be okay to begin asking new questions about God, re-evaluating previously held notions about God, and re-examining our theologies to determine whether or not our perception of God must change *as we do*; 3) an attitude of *openness* toward our thoughts about God; 4) a willingness to entertain the *possibility* that we might not and probably don't have all the information on God, nor could we, when we're brutally honest since that which is infinite cannot be fully, thoroughly, or finitely ascertained; and 5) a term referring to a commitment to seek God, a commitment to discovery, a commitment to the belief that if we seek we will find, and a commitment to a mindset that admits there is definitely still *more to learn*.

[Requisite Desire] – the idea that to be God is to *want* to be known. In other words, to be God is to nurture a requisite desire (or, a desire which cannot *not* be present) to be known. Joshuanism also maintains that this is why God created humans with the same requisite desire within them. That is, that to be human is to *want* to know God.

[The Respondent] – those who, by faith, have responded to that invitation (the believers).

[Scriptural Relegation] – the idea that 1) while scripture is sacred, useful, and transformative, it might not be infallible or inerrant; and 2) if it isn't infallible or inerrant, it is therefore subject to amendment *where necessary*.

[The Singular Fellowship] – the Joshuan expression for the Christian doctrine of the Trinity. The Singular Fellowship is the only infinite, eternal, divine entity (or God) in the Universe; existing, or coexisting, as three distinct yet unified forms in a perfect, unbroken, singular fellowship: the Father (God), the Son (Joshua), and the Soul of Godliness (aka the Holy Spirit in Christianity).

[The Soul of Godliness] – 1) the third person of the Singular Fellowship (who Christians call the Holy Spirit); 2) that aspect of God which resides within the believer, providing guidance, counsel, comfort, conviction, and discernment; and 3) that aspect of God responsible for the Unfolding in the life of the believer.

[Table] – 1) a home gathering of Joshuans, derived from the idea of breaking bread together at a table; and 2) a single unit of bonded Joshuans involved in each other's lives.

Joshuanism

[The Unfolding] – 1) the Joshuan expression for walking with God, growing in God, interacting with God, and developing spiritually; and 2) the pursuit of godliness, or the ongoing *unfolding* of godliness in the life of the Joshuan.

[Zen Joshuanism] – 1) a discipline within Joshuanism by which the Joshuan can use elements of Zen (such as meditation and the practice of the Now) to gain mental and emotional health in order to render them better equipped to fulfill Joshua's two greatest commandments; and 2) the addition of *enlightenment* as a goal alongside *salvation*.

[Zoêology] – 1) the study of the spiritual life imparted to the individual by God through faith in Joshua; and 2) the study of how that spiritual life relates to both the individual and to the collective group.

THE TEN TENETS OF JOSHUANISM

1. God exists, God is good, and God can be known
2. God has chosen to make himself known through *revelation*
3. This revelation is manifold, presented to humanity through three channels: a) through Joshua; b) through the scriptures; and c) through our ongoing experiences with God
4. God's revelation of himself to humanity is not complete (or finished) and never could be (Perpetually Incomplete Revelation)
5. God *wants* humanity to know him inasmuch as humanity is able to at any given time (Requisite Desire)
6. Despite this, humanity could not know God because of the Great Barrier
7. Because of his love for humanity, God *entered in* to humanity in the person of Joshua to dismantle the Great Barrier and succeeded in doing so
8. With the barrier thus dismantled, humanity and God are able to have fellowship; God can now be known
9. The individual human enters into this fellowship through authentic belief and faith in Joshua (the believer now *knows* God)

10. Once in this fellowship, the individual is now a partaker of God's irrevocable salvation, including all the benefits therein (Absolute Deliverance)

THE EIGHT IMMOVABLES OF JOSHUANISM

1. A belief in God;
2. A belief in the Singular Fellowship (The Father, The Son, and the Soul of Godliness);
3. A decision to view God's Son as Joshua rather than as Jesus;
4. Acceptance of the Ten Tenets of Joshuanism;
5. Acceptance of the Joshuan Creed;
6. A decision to gather together with other Joshuans in a definitively Joshuan way;
7. A decision to practice the Five Elements;
8. A decision to read primarily *The Joshuan Pages* version of the *New Testament*.

THE JOSHUAN CREED

We believe that God exists

We believe God exists as a Singular Fellowship of three separate yet equal parts: the Father, the Son, and the Soul of Godliness

We believe that God is eternal, unchanging, all-knowing, all-powerful, and ever-present

We believe that God created the Universe and initiated all matter, all life, all the physical laws, and all the processes found therein

We believe that God has no equal

We believe that God is good and kind, that he is loving and compassionate, and that he is love

We believe that God is fair and just, that he treats all his creation equally

We believe that God keeps his word, and is therefore trustworthy

Joshuanism

We believe that God is intimately concerned with the lives of each individual human.

We believe that God hears the words of those who pray to him.

We believe that all matter and all life is subject to God's authority and yet, in spite of this, God has granted free will to humanity.

We believe that God reveals himself to humanity, that this revelation is unfinished, and that as humanity evolves in its capacity to know more of this revelation, God enables humanity to know more.

We believe that God created humanity in his image.

We believe that humanity, thus created, is special.

We believe that humanity, though special, is inherently sinful.

We believe this inherent sinfulness produced the Great Barrier, which separated humanity from God, preventing humanity from knowing God.

We believe God, because of his love, sent his Son to be born as a human with the specific purpose of dismantling this barrier.

We believe the Son of God was thus born of Mary's womb.

We believe the Son of God was named Joshua (Jesus, in Greek).

We believe that Joshua was the promised Messiah, as foretold by the Old Testament prophets.

We believe that Joshua's message was primarily a message of love.

We believe that Joshua lived a perfect, sinless life.

We believe that Joshua was executed by crucifixion.

We believe that Joshua's sinless death paid the penalty for our inherent sinfulness.

We believe that Joshua's body was buried in sealed tomb.

We believe that after three days of death, Joshua rose from the dead, emerging triumphant from that tomb.

We believe that Joshua's death and subsequent resurrection succeeded in dismantling the Great Barrier.

We believe that through faith the Joshuan can enter into union with God, enjoying Absolute Deliverance.

We believe that Joshua now resides with God the Father.

We believe that Joshua will return someday, ushering the end of this world and the creation of a new world.

We believe Joshua has defeated all forces of evil in the spiritual realm.

We believe that the Soul of Godliness resides within the Joshuan, providing the Joshuan with guidance, counsel, comfort, conviction, and discernment.

We believe that the truth sets us free.

We believe in eternal life.

We believe that to love God and to love humanity are the two greatest commandments, and that these two commandments are the summation of all other commandments.

We believe that love therefore is the most important factor in the life and experience of the Joshuan, greater even than faith, hope, morality, and virtue.

We believe that God desires Joshuans to have a healthy mind, body, and spirit.

We believe we can accomplish anything through Joshua.

We subscribe to the Eight Immovables of Joshuanism.

We subscribe to the Ten Tenets of Joshuanism.

We observe the Five Elements (conversation, illumination, meditation, observation, and application), believing them to be necessary tools for spiritual growth.

We believe there need be no conflict between science and faith.

CLOSING PRAYER

God, I ask you to open the eyes and ears of all those who read this book. Lead them in your paths. Guide them in your truth. I pray you would steady them in their journey toward a greater knowledge of you. I pray also that you would steady me as I myself pursue a greater knowledge of you. More than anything, I ask that you would show all of us each day how we may be instruments of your love. Teach us how to love. Teach us how to allow others to love us. Grant us the ability to accomplish the two greatest commandments, which you said were more important than anything else.

I ask these things in the name of Joshua the Deliverer, the Son of God.

So be it.

Michael Vito Tosto

Other Books by MSI Press

A Believer-in-Waiting's First Encounters with God

Blest Atheist

El Poder de lo Transpersonal

Forget the Goal, the Journey Counts…71 Jobs Later

The Gospel of Damascus

Joshuanism

Losing My Voice and Finding Another

Mommy Posioned Our House Guest

Publishing for Smarties

Road to Damascus

The Rise & Fall of Muslim Civil Society

Syrian Folktales

The Marriage Whisperer

Understanding the People Around You: An Introduction to Socionics

When You're Shoved from the Right, Look to the Left: Metaphors of Islamic Humanism

Widow A Survival Guide for the First Year

Michael Vito Tosto

CPSIA information can be obtained at www.ICGtesting.com
Printed in the USA
LVOW08s1144140813

347817LV00002B/64/P